Roni Berger, PhD, CSW

Immigrant Women Tell Their Stories

Pre-publication
REVIEWS,
COMMENTARIES,
EVALUATIONS . . .

"*Immigrant Women Tell Their Stories* is a comprehensive and compelling text that could be used in practice, policy, human behavior, and research courses in BSW and MSW programs. Using contemporary qualitative research methodology, the author gives voice and meaning to the narratives of eighteen women who have emigrated to the United States, Israel, and Australia. These stories are preceded by a scholarly and thorough chapter that clearly presents the theoretical and empirical context for the narratives. The concluding chapters focus on the common themes and perspectives drawn from the women's stories and their implications for practice, policy, and program development.

In relating the women's experiences to professional service development and delivery, the text demonstrates core social work principles and appreciates the dignity, worth, resilience, strengths, and wisdom of those we serve. The book's narrative approach to knowledge-building will clearly resonate with and be valued by social work students and faculty."

Louise Skolnik, DSW
Deputy Commissioner,
Nassau County
Department of Social Service

"**R**oni Berger is not only a skilled interviewer, but brings to her work the added advantage of being, like her subjects, an immigrant woman with a foreign accent. As a result, she has been able to elicit personal, even painful, revelations from women struggling to make new lives in a new world."

Barbara Ribakove Gordon
Founder and Director,
North American Conference
on Ethiopian Jewry

More pre-publication
REVIEWS, COMMENTARIES, EVALUATIONS . . .

"**D**r. Berger fills a void in the literature about the challenges and opportunities of immigration by featuring the unique issues of women who have adjusted to relocation in a new culture. Resilience, adaptability, and dealing with social, emotional, and cultural losses are the salient themes explored through the unique and fascinating stories of nineteen women. Dr. Berger's focus on the positive aspects of each newcomer's experiences, rather than the traditional focus on pathology and problems, is an important contribution to professional practice. This perspective will be invaluable to those who work with immigrants and refugees."

Elbert Siegel, DSW
Professor of Social Work,
Southern Connecticut State University,
New Haven

"**A** welcome and important contribution to the growing literature on immigrant women, this book tells the stories of eighteen women who emigrated from different countries to the United States, Israel, and Australia. The narratives are skillfully and sensitively presented by the author, an immigrant herself, who also tells her personal story. The book offers excellent scientific perspectives and analyses of the collective experience of immigrant women. Often dependant on their husbands or fathers, immigrant women can be reluctant to speak of their experiences. This book makes their voices heard. The women are so different, yet alike—Sonia, who came to New York from war-torn Beirut; Rosa, who left the impoverished Philippines in search of a better life in Australia; Ana, who fled her disintegrating homeland, Russia, and came to Israel—all tell stories of migration, loss, confusion, struggle, and . . . growth. Indeed, one of the most unique contributions of this book is its focus on the empowering aspect of women's migration. Almost all the interviewees felt that they had grown and matured by their experiences as immigrants, and discovered inner strength and potentials they did not know existed. The reader has the privilege of sharing in this experience."

Julia Mirsky, PhD
Consultant on Immigration Issues;
Clinical Psychologist; Head,
Graduate Program in Social Work,
Ben-Gurion University, Israel

The Haworth Press®
New York • London • Oxford

Immigrant Women Tell Their Stories

THE HAWORTH PRESS
Titles of Related Interest

Immigrant Women
Tell Their Stories

Roni Berger, PhD, CSW

The Haworth Press®
New York • London • Oxford

The Haworth Press, Inc., 10 Alice Street, Binghamton, NY 13904–1580.

PUBLISHER'S NOTE
Identities and circumstances of individuals discussed in this book have been changed to protect confidentiality.

Cover design by Lora Wiggins.

Library of Congress Cataloging-in-Publication Data

Berger, Roni.
    Immigrant women tell their stories / Roni Berger.
        p. cm.
    Includes bibliographical references and index.
    ISBN 0-7890-1829-2 (hard : alk. paper)—ISBN 0-7890-1830-6 (soft : alk. paper)
    1. Women immigrants. 2. Emigration and immigration. 3. Emigration and immigration—
Psychological aspects. I. Title.

HQ1154.B4148 2004
305.4'092—dc21

2003009814

In loving memory of my mother Sarah Schwalb (Kutin),
an immigrant woman

The New Colossus

Not like the brazen giant of Greek fame,
With conquering limbs astride from land to land;
Here at our sea-washed, sunset gates shall stand
A mighty woman with a torch, whose flame
Is the imprisoned lightning, and her name
Mother of Exiles. From her beacon-hand
Glows world-wide welcome; her mild eyes command
The air-bridged harbor that twin cities frame.
"Keep ancient lands, your storied pomp!" cries she
With silent lips. "Give me your tired, your poor,
Your huddled masses yearning to breathe free,
The wretched refuse of your teeming shore.
Send these, the homeless, tempest-tost to me,
I lift my lamp beside the golden door!"

Emma Lazarus (1849-1887)

CONTENTS

ABOUT THE AUTHOR

Born and raised in Israel, **Roni Berger, PhD, CSW,** is Associate Professor of Social Work at Adelphi University. She also serves as a consultant to the Jewish Board of Family and Children's Services and as a freelance consultant to various organizations in addition to maintaining her private practice in New York. Her fields of expertise and research are families (specifically stepfamilies), immigrants, qualitative research, group work, and parent education. Dr. Berger is a diligent and versatile scholar, clinician, teacher, and writer. She has published two books, including *Stepfamilies: A Multi-Dimensional Perspective* (The Haworth Press), and over thirty-five articles and book chapters. Dr. Berger has presented extensively nationally and internationally and serves on editorial and advisory boards of professional journals and scientific/professional conferences in the United States, Israel, Canada, and Australia. Dr. Berger is a guest lecturer at colleges in Israel and Australia as well as at Smith College in Massachusetts. She is also a Research Associate with the Center for Comparative Studies on Immigration at the University of California, San Diego.

Following the World Trade Center disaster, Dr. Berger was involved in numerous activities designed to enhance coping with the trauma for survivors and witnesses, and trained students and workers to serve traumatized and re-traumatized populations.

Prior to her immigration to the United States in 1990, Dr. Berger worked in Israel in academia and in direct practice with individuals, families, and groups in the fields of health and mental health. She also held supervisory and administrative positions in diverse social, medical, and educational settings and served as a consultant to various organizations. In the United States, she served for five years as a supervisor in the Russian Adolescent Projects.

Foreword

Immigration by women has become a major reality for many women as well as a target of social policy. The news is filled with stories of sweatshop workers, home care attendants, mail order brides, foreign nannies, and traffic in sex and international prostitution. Women arrive in the United States or other countries to follow a spouse, better their personal economic situation, or to escape persecution.

For many reasons, and contrary to gender expectations and stereotypes, many women, especially from third world nations, migrate alone, frequently in response to the demand for low-wage female labor in the receiving country. Leaving home for employment in first world labor markets allows women immigrants from third world nations to send desperately needed money back home. But to accomplish this they must pay the price of long-term separation from their children, spouses, extended families, and communities. According to Rachel Parrenas, a feminist anthropologist, many immigrant women from the Third World become partial citizens in the receiving nation-state.[1] Not only are they separated from their families and homelands, but they often lack protection on the job, endure abuse, and live in a state of constant insecurity, especially the fear of deportation[2]

Popularly regarded as a matter of choice, the dynamics of immigration are considerably more complex. The personal decision to leave often reflects economic and geopolitical forces in both the sending and receiving nations. In many instances the "decision" to emigrate reflects consequences of the structural adjustment policies required of third world nations in exchange for loans from the World Bank and the International Monetary Fund. The indebted nation typically must divert national income to service the debt, which in turn limits both economic opportunities and public sector programs for its residents. First world nations are also pressed to initiate similar austerity measures (i.e., privatization, deregulation, and reduced social spending) in order to qualify for membership in the European Union.

Immigrant Women Tell Their Stories puts a human face on the lives of eighteen women who emigrated to the United States, Israel, and Australia from first or third world countries. The women departed from many different places: Albania, Brazil, Cuba, Ethiopia, France, India, Iran, Lebanon, Pakistan, the Philippines, and Russia. Few immigrated alone; even so, the women typically did not leave their home voluntarily. Most immigrated in response to decisions made by others, typically spouses, parents, or political leaders. Four of the women arrived as children, three met marital obligations, five participated in the decision to leave, and four made their own decision. Their stories reveal that a mix of social, economic, and political forces dictated their moves: the wish to avoid the ravages war, the need to escape religious persecution, the obligation to follow a spouse or to accompany parents, and the desire to pursue education or a career.

Berger applies a gender lens to the experience of these women immigrants. Seeking to redress the gender neutrality of traditional immigration studies, Berger, herself an immigrant to the United States, complicates the story by bringing the specific experiences of women into view. A social worker, she focuses on the stresses related to women's personal and cultural adjustments, especially experiences of loss, displacement, identity challenges, and mental health. Leaving home also exposed women (and male family members) to new gender norms while undercutting traditional family structures, gender-based roles, and the patriarchal authority arrangements that characterized their prior cultures.

The eighteen very different women talk about the risks and traumas they faced living through war, torture, displacement, refugee camps, separation, loss, and adjustment in a new nation. The women in this book are not among the most disadvantaged women immigrants. Yet they nonetheless faced numerous economic constraints, cultural dissonance, language problems, social barriers, prejudice, discrimination, and personal pain. Although many of the women experienced exploitation, marginalization, powerlessness, and more than one relocation, Berger's main point is that the women possessed considerable resilience and eventually most of them acculturated successfully.

Rather than focus on any one of the three receiving nations, Berger highlights the female experience. She reaches for what the female immigrants shared as women, without erasing important national or cultural differences. Berger carefully details how the immigrant women she met "negotiated strangeness" as they sought to carry out their prescribed wife and mother roles as well as the demands of employment in their new country. We learn how the women dealt with jobs and employers, but also how they managed their family lives. They had to learn about new foods, figure out how to calculate weights, measures, and currency, deal with schools, the health care system, and public assistance bureaucracies, all the while parenting children, soothing frustrated family members, and trying to maintain some degree of cultural continuity with their homeland.

The women reported both losses and gains, but also displayed considerable resilience despite the hardships of immigration and heavy responsibilities. Although they experienced poverty, unemployment, discrimination, and bureaucratic harassment, the women Berger interviewed placed the greatest emphasis on emotional, cultural, social, and psychological losses. The immigrant experience challenged their sense of identity, forced them to deal with the unfamiliar, left them fearful of making mistakes, caused them to ask for help from the wider society, created additional child rearing worries, and contributed to downward occupational mobility. Some of the women also reported a duality. Others felt misplaced without a sense of belonging anywhere.

The losses were offset by important gains. These gains included a wide range of financial, professional, educational, and social opportunities for themselves and their children. Women also reported personal growth such as greater appreciation of their own abilities, a new sense of freedom having escaped from the gender constraints of their traditional culture, and a broader perspective about the world at large. Some women translated the duality previously noted into a strength by drawing on two cultural resources.

Berger closes her book with a useful discussion on how the wider social service system might reduce its gender blindness and biases and more effectively enable immigrant women to gain greater power and control of their everyday life in the new country.

Mimi Abramovitz
Professor of Social Policy
Hunter College School
of Social Work, New York

NOTES

1. Parrenas, Rachel Salazar (2001). "Transgressing the Nation-State: The Partial Citizenship and Imagined (Global) Community of Migrant Filipina Domestic Workers," *Signs: Journal of Women in Culture and Society,* 26(4): 1129-1154.

2. Romero, Mary (2002). *Maid in the U.S.A.* New York: Routledge.

Preface: How and Why
This Book Was Born

I was sitting in front of my computer and summarizing research findings about launching firstborn sons to military service in Israeli families. Reading my own words, I felt lucky that emigrating from Israel to the United States spared me this stressful experience while exposing me to a wide range of other extremely stressful experiences. The idea suddenly struck me to take a thorough look at the experience of being an immigrant woman.

I am an immigrant woman. At the time that I started to write this book I had been living in the United States for ten years, after emigrating from Israel. I felt successful in my academic and professional career and happy in my social and family life when the idea for this book suddenly "popped" into my mind. In retrospect, however, this book had been accumulating within me for the previous decade, waiting to be ripe for writing and for me to feel strong and stable enough to write it.

This book tells the stories of eighteen women who immigrated to the United States, Israel, and Australia, as well as my own story of immigration. The women vary in age and cultural, ethnic, social, educational, and professional status. They represent a rainbow of family statuses and political opinions. They experienced relocation at various ages and have been in their new countries for diverse periods. They came from different places around the globe and speak different languages and dialects. Their English comes in different accents as well. Even those whose first language is English may use terms and spellings foreign to Americans. Annette Gallagher Weisman (2000) who emigrated from Ireland to England to the United States describes this experience: "I am always translating in my head from Irish English to English English and, finally, to American English" (p. 192). I myself learned English mostly from British teachers, and thus until my immigration, I spoke about a copybook rather than a notebook, in the evening I ate supper rather than dinner, and when I write "color" and "neighbor" I still feel guilty for omitting the "u."

The women who participated in this project relocated for various reasons. Some opted to come in search of better economic conditions, to follow a spouse, to pursue their own education, or to improve prospects for their children. Others were forced to leave by political, religious, or economic circumstances. Some spent years in preimmigration deliberations and preparations, while others had to make a decision overnight to flee without having a chance to say their good-byes. Some went back; others do not have the possibility or the wish. I interviewed women who, like myself, maintain dual citizenship and comfortably move between two worlds, as well as those who were stripped of their citizenship and remain symbolically with no national affiliation, since they no longer carry their original citizenship but were not yet granted citizenship in their new country.

In spite of their diversity, all of these women share the experience of being immigrants. This book tries to gain an understanding of the journeys they traveled and the experiences they lived in an effort both to gain new insights into what it means to immigrate as a woman and to open the discourse required so that effective strategies to work with and for immigrant women can be framed. I met with the immigrant women who agreed to participate in this project for long hours, recorded our conversations, and read and reread them trying to identify common threads.

It is significant that most, though not all, women wanted me to use their real names rather than pseudonyms, sending a clear message: "This is who I am, and I am comfortable with it, even proud, and wish to be recognized."

In this book immigrant women tell their stories, recount what the migration experience entails, and explain the challenges it poses to the individual. This information can teach us ways to help them cope successfully. A major goal of this book is to share what these women taught me about the migration experience. By sharing these experiences this book contributes to the emerging body of research on female migration.

Part I reviews the process and effects of immigration and the method of the research conducted for this book. Chapter 1 discusses the nature, developmental aspects, and effects of immigration with a special focus on immigrant women. Chapter 2 explains the qualitative research method and its use in this particular study.

Part II includes stories of women who immigrated to the United States, Israel, and Australia. It is organized into four chapters. Chapter 3 tells my own story as an immigrant woman. Chapter 4 narrates the stories of six immigrant women to the United States. Chapter 5 recounts the experience of six women who relocated to Israel, and Chapter 6 reports about the experience of six women who migrated to Australia or New Zealand.

Part III presents the results of the content analysis of the interviews, discusses and illustrates main themes in the narratives, and offers principles for development and delivery of services designed to address needs and issues of immigrant women on the basis of these findings. Chapter 7 summarizes main themes identified in the narratives. Chapter 8 discusses the implication of these themes for services. Finally, in the Epilogue, I share what I take from this journey to my personal and professional life.

Acknowledgments

Thanks to my husband Howard and my son Dan, who graciously tolerated my going far away to make this book happen, for their endless understanding and loving support. Thanks to the immigrant women who generously spent long hours with me sharing their experiences, feelings, and thoughts. Thanks to Adelphi University for granting me a sabbatical leave that made it possible to dedicate time and energy to this project. Thanks to my colleagues at Adelphi University School of Social Work who patiently listened to my endless monologues, accompanied me in my search for my path, and never tired of supporting and encouraging me. Thanks to my friends in Israel, the United States, and Australia who helped to recruit participants for this study. Thanks to my colleagues and friends at the Melbourne University School of Social Work who graciously helped me during my sabbatical leave with them. Thanks to Professor Jona M. Rosenfeld, of Jerusalem, who introduced me to the art of qualitative research and taught me the importance of listening to people's stories. Thanks to the people of the International House at Melbourne University who made me feel at home far away from home. Thanks to the devoted team at The Haworth Press for the helpful editing that made this a better and more readable book. And, above all, thanks to my parents, who immigrated to Israel as young people and worked hard all their lives to give me the opportunities they never had.

PART I:
UNDERSTANDING AND STUDYING WOMEN'S MIGRATION

Chapter 1

Immigration: The Process
and Its Aftermath

There is no greater sorrow on earth than the loss of one's native land.

Euripides (484-406 BC)

INTRODUCTION

Worldwide, there are over 100 million immigrants and over 13 million refugees, in addition to internal migration within individual countries (Potocky-Tripodi and Tripodi, 2002). The United States and other Western countries have witnessed in recent years an influx of immigrants (Hernandez and Charney, 1998). The foreign-born population in the United States has dramatically increased from 5.1 percent in 1970, to 6.6 percent in 1980, 10.4 percent in 1990, and 11.5 percent in 2002. More than 10 percent of Americans were born abroad, and an additional 10 percent of the population grew up with at least one foreign-born parent. This is particularly true for the states of California, Florida, New York, and Hawaii (Healy, 2002). This affects both the lives of the immigrants and their country of relocation. Consequently, there is growing concern among the public and among professionals about issues that relate to immigrants and ways to address these issues expeditiously.

Immigration is driven by geopolitical considerations in the culture of origin, labor needs of the culture of relocation, and familial, personal, and ideological reasons. Motivation to relocate includes seeking better economic, employment, social, and political conditions; improving children's opportunities for education; and escaping actual or potential persecution, war, natural disaster, and personal circumstances. Migration can be voluntary or forced and can grant people the status of legal immigrants, undocumented immigrants, refugees, and asylum seekers, each of which implies different legal and economic eligibilities and psychological and social consequences. For example, in the United States alone, between 1971 and 1995, approximately 17.1 million legal immigrants were admitted, most of them from Asia, Central and South America, and the former Soviet Union (Massey, 1995). Assuming that at least one-third of them were women (the rest are men and children) and estimating that a similar number of illegal immigrants entered the country, over 10 million women joined the nation in the aforementioned period.

Immigration can come in many constellations of the immigrating unit. For example, four types of migration patterns are typical to the United States: mothers first, chain migration, family migration, and multigeneration migration. Mothers-first migration has been typical for women from the Carribean Islands and Central and South America who migrate as domestic workers, leaving their children to be raised by relatives until they can be later reunited with them. Chain migration has been more popular among Mexican, Asian, and some Middle Eastern immigrants, in which one family member, often the man, comes to work and gradually brings his family to live with him. In this type of migration it has not been uncommon for women and children to learn that these men have established a second family during the years of living away from the original family. Immigrants from other countries also come in whole families, often multigenerational families, which is typical for immigrants from the former Soviet Union, for example. In Israel, a fifth version can be found, in which youngsters from Ethiopia or the former Soviet Union immigrate first and are placed in special programs, such as Naale, which is a Hebrew acronym for "adolescent immigrants without parents," to be followed by their families months or years later.

Irrespective of the type of immigration, it is a major disruption in a person's life, which may cause tremendous stress and potential trauma. In professional literature it has been recognized as a life crisis or traumatic experience (Garza-Guerrero, 1974; Glassman and Skolnik, 1984; Harper and Lantz, 1996; Ben-Sira, 1997). It shakes up physical, social, financial, legal, and emotional being and self-definition. The immigration experience is inevitably fraught with radical objective changes. These changes have been called culture loss (Furnham and Bochner, 1986; Stewart, 1986).

Immigration involves displacement and multiple losses. Some of the losses are symbolic. For example, an immigrant from Russia states, "Leningrad, the city in which I was born and raised and lived most of my life, is again St. Petersburg, so in a sense you can say that the place does not exist anymore." Many losses are tangible. One loses familiarity with landscapes, physical environment, climate, sights and smells, roads, knowing where to slow the car down and where to expect traffic, labels on products in the supermarket, currency, and measurement units for weights, distances, and temperatures. Irina, a recent immigrant from Siberia to Israel describes the feelings of strangeness.

> I came a little later than most of my friends and relatives, so I had some sense of what to expect, and yet it was very different. I saw pictures of Israel, but reality was unlike my imagination. The landscape was bizarre, the sights were strange, even the smell of apples was not the same. There [Siberia] you would go into the home and a fresh and sweet smell of the apples displayed on the table would hit you. Here they have a synthetic smell, like everything else.

A woman who left Cuba in her early twenties to return for a visit twenty-three years later writes, "The moment I stepped out of the hotel, I knew exactly where I was, what corners to turn, what buildings will be waiting for me on the next block, and which one of the buses going by would take me to which place in the city" (Espin, 1992, p. 14).

Immigrants lose significant relationships with friends, relatives, neighbors, classmates and teachers, and co-workers and bosses. Natural support systems either remain distanced in the country of origin or are not available because of their own struggle to acculturate, making immigration an experience of diminishing family contacts. Immigrants also lose an intimate understanding of cultural norms, social clues, acceptable behavior patterns, the ability to adequately perceive reality and the context for interpreting it, and an understanding of the way of life. One loses the comfort of shared memories, named by some "the sweet familiarity" (Donnelly, 2000, p. 50).

An immigrant from Greece to France described the experience: "In France I feel disconnected from myself; they [the Frenchmen] do not know about my childhood heroes. No coffee shop, no plaza remind me of myself when I was little. In France I have no past. French songs remind me nothing" (Alexakis, 2001, pp. 39-40).

Immigration often means a career change, frequently stepping down in the professional ladder, from a physician to a health care provider, engineer to technician, and teacher to child care worker, accepting nonprofessional jobs or remaining unemployed. Immigrants lose recognition of previous achievements, such as professional credentials, credit history, and driver's license, and must struggle to regain them. For example, Foner (2000), who studied female migrants to New York, found that many household workers she interviewed had been teachers and clerical workers in their homeland and experienced transition "from mistress to servant." Many health care aides in nursing homes had previously worked as nurses. Because their professional credentials were not recognized and their language proficiency was limited, they were forced to take jobs below their education and training.

Underemployment, professional disqualification, and unemployment are very frequent. My own experience, which is not uncommon, was of going from being somebody to being nobody to struggling to become somebody again. These losses may be exacerbated by xenophobia in the new environment.

Another major loss is that of language—the way of framing ideas, thinking about a belief system, mastering a means for making meaning, communication and self-expression, spelling and pronunciation of words, and knowledge of idioms and colloquialisms. Limited or absent literacy in the language of the new culture has been recognized as a key factor in determining the ability of immigrants to fulfill parental, professional, and social roles (Paul, 1999). Having command of the language of the new culture contributes to the prospect of securing employment. Thus Filipino women who come from an English-speaking background have been more successful than Korean immigrants in achieving emplyment (United Nations, 1995).

Immigration means emotional muteness, at least for some time, sometimes for life. A popular song by songwriter David Broza who emigrated from South America to Israel, where he writes and performs in Hebrew, is titled "I Dream in Spanish." It speaks of how deep one's language of origin is rooted in one's core. Many immigrants who are eloquent in the new language continue to calculate and to dream in their language of origin because their innermost feelings are in the mother tongue. Even for those who fluently speak the language of the country of relocation, much of the meaning they wish to convey is lost in translation.

Immigration often leads to a loss of safety because of shattered family equilibrium as a result of moving from a traditional gender-based role allocation and authority system to an environment with a different power structure (Balgopal, 2000). For example, moving from a "macho" culture to a culture in which women's status is more egalitarian challenges the familiar division of power and allocation of roles in the family, i.e., who makes which decisions and who controls the family budget.

All the aforementioned changes place the issues of identity at the core of the immigration experience. Moving from one culture to another tugs at the roots of one's identity. One of the women in this study describes it, "You leave pieces of yourself behind." Specifically challenged is one's ethnic identity, i.e., the way an individual perceives his or her place in and in relationship to ethnicity (Jasinskaja-Lahti and Liebkind, 1998). Ethnic identity is a complex and multifaceted concept that has two distinct aspects: one aspect refers to self-identification, i.e., the ethnic group one affiliates with; the second aspect reflects one's attitude toward and feeling about belonging to a given ethnic group (Liebkind, 1992). In the process of shaping their ethnic identity following relocation, immigrants face the need to choose between the options of mono- and bicultural ethnic identity (Szapocznik, Scopetta, and Kurtines, 1978). The monocultural identity can be either the culture of origin or the absorbing culture. The bicultural identity incorporates both cultures in some type of combination.

The process of developing one's new identity often involves revisiting one's original identity. Kamani (2000), an immigrant from India, comments, "Becoming 'American' is for me inextricably tied up with becoming fully aware of what it is to be 'Indian'; being born again as a self-aware Indian is what I equate with becoming 'American'"(p. 96).

Diverse efforts to deconstruct the acculturation experience have been developed. Higham (2001) observes diversity and assimilation as complementary processes suggesting "pluralistic integration," i.e., preserving traditions combined with assimilation and amalgamation, and shaping the host and the immigrant culture simultaneously. Berry (1986) identified four ways of coping with identity issues among immigrants:

1. *Assimilation*—relinquishing one's original cultural identity and moving to adopt that of the larger dominant society
2. *Integration*—combining components from the culture of origin and the absorbing culture
3. *Rejection*—self-imposed withdrawal from the dominant culture
4. *Deculturation*—striking out against the dominant culture accompanied by stress and alienation (a sense of "not here and not there")

Berger (1997) suggested a clinically based typology of patterns for coping with issues of ethnic identity among immigrant adolescents. Four types of patterns were identified: clingers, eradicators, vacillators, and integrators. *Clingers* adhere to their culture of origin and tend to live in national/ethnic enclaves in neighborhoods heavily populated by their compatriots that replicate the culture of origin within the new country. They consume books, movies, newspapers, and food from their original homeland, which they often visit if politically and financially possible, and passively avoid or actively refuse to acculturate to the new culture. Brighton Beach in Brooklyn, New York, Little Havana in Miami, Florida, and the Arabic community in Patterson, New Jersey, are inhabited by people who chose to replicate their culture of origin within the United States. Commerce and street signs are in Russian, Spanish, or Arabic, schools have bilingual programs, and people maintain much of their preimmigration lifestyle. Although many immigrants use such homogenous communities as a springboard, clingers tend to stay in them.

Eradicators reject and "erase" their culture of origin and totally adopt the norms of the new culture. They try to maximize their immersion in the new culture. The new country's style of dressing, eating, and living are adopted, and visits to the country of origin are minimal or nonexistent. Donnelley's (2000) description of herself gives a vivid picture of an eradicator. A British immigrant to California, she shares,

I bring so little of my old country to my new. I certainly do not run with the Brit-pack, and if occasionally I cook a British meal or rent a British video, it is to show curious friends how things are done in another country—my contribution, if you will, to the cultural melting pot—rather than to indulge any nostalgia or nationalism of my own. I cannot even fully remember by now how it felt to regard England as home. (p. 51)

Vacillators oscillate between the two cultures, sometimes tending more to the clinging pole and on other occasions (or periods) toward the eradicating end of the continuum. *Integrators* combine components of both cultures.

Portes and Rumbaut (2001) conceptualize three outcomes for children of immigrants in intergenerational terms: *dissonant* acculturation, in which children learn the language and ways of the receiving culture but their parents cling to the "old ways"; *consonant* acculturation, in which parents' and children's pace of moving from the "old" to the "new" is in sync; and *selective* acculturation, partial retention of the culture of origin combined with some adoption of the culture of relocation's norms and language.

Decisions regarding ethnic identity are affected by the immigrants' culture of origin, the dominant culture of resettlement, and the ethnic subculture (the diaspora) in the country of relocation. Facing the aforementioned financial constraints, language and social barriers, and prejudice and discrimination, immigrants attempt to maintain an ethnic continuity and to re-create familiarity with the host country (Hattar-Pollara and Meleis, 1995b; Wong, 1999). This process includes several phases that will be discussed in the next section.

DEVELOPMENTAL ASPECTS OF IMMIGRATION

Immigration is not a single event of being uprooted from the culture of origin and leaving behind the homeland to face the challenge of assimilation into a new culture. Rather, it is a lifelong, multifaceted and multilayered, complex, and never-ending experience. In this process, three phases have been identified: departure, transition, and resettlement (Sluzki, 1983; Drachman and Shen-Ryan, 1991). Unique stresses and tasks characterize each of these phases.

Departure (Preparatory) Phase

The departure phase is the period that precedes the actual reloca-tion. It may last for months and sometimes years, from the time the idea first occurs until the actual move. However, if immigration is forced by political, legal, or any other type of external pressure, in-cluding danger to one's life or personal or family emergency, this phase may be significantly shorter. Immigration is the result of a de-liberate decision to change one's life, especially for people who choose to relocate, unlike refugees who are forced to do so. This decision in-volves a conscious component of risk taking.

Two types of factors are involved in the decision to immigrate: the push factors and the pull factors (Berry et al., 1987). Push factors in-clude forces of expulsion that make one decide to go *away from* the culture of origin, such as persecution or economic, social, religious, and political ordeal. The pull factors are the forces that attract immi-grants *toward* the culture of relocation, such as economic opportuni-ties, liberal social and political realities, and personal freedom.

During the preimmigration period the prospective immigrant evalu-ates these risks, deliberates plans, and prepares for moving. These preparations have practical and emotional aspects. They include sep-aration from people, places, and possessions and making logistic ad-justments. Sorting out what will be moved to the new country and what is to be left behind involves a process of decision making, revis-iting memories associated with books, photographs, presents, and fa-vorite memorabilia. When immigration is potentially irreversible be-cause the prospects of returning are nonexistent, as is the case for most refugees, the pain may be enormous. Ambivalence, debating options, building expectations, and struggling with fears of the un-known are at the core of this phase (Berger, 2001).

Transition Phase

The actual relocation from the country of origin to the new country can last for weeks and months, if temporary stay in refugee camps or detention centers is involved, or may take only a few hours by plane. For those who travel by boat or those who have to spend time in tran-sition camps either on the way to or in the absorbing country, this means a prolonged period colored by uncertainty ("living out of suit-cases") and instability ("living in the great unknown"). Very often conditions in the temporary station are uncomfortable, leading immigrants to question the whole idea of relocation. For those who travel by plane directly from their homeland to their new land, the fast pace of moving from one place to another because of advanced methods of transportation has eliminated the opportunity of "time out," an interim period of adjustment, for the duration of the journey that immigrants had in previous eras. Today's immigrants may start the morning on a summery day in South Asia and finish it on a freezing New York evening. As familiar to most and evident in the experience of jet lag, the change is sharp, confusing, and disorienting. Some immigrants migrate in stages, relocating from their country of origin to an intermediate country before finally settling in the new country. For example, it is not unusual for families from Southeast Asia to live several years in Central America before continuing to the United States.

Resettlement

The process of adjustment to the new culture is long and complex. It usually lasts years and for many immigrants may last a lifetime. Two processes occur simultaneously, one with respect to the culture of origin and the other with respect to the absorbing culture (Birman and Tyler, 1994). Initially it involves finding a place to live and a source of income. Being absorbed in the all-consuming tasks of the struggle for survival often deprives immigrants the opportunity to reflect on the emotional meaning of their move and mourn their losses.

Gradually, as immigrants become more familiar with the new society, they become more aware of the permanence of the changes. They start to learn the new language, rules, and norms, to mourn their losses, and to struggle to re-create a sense of worth and mastery of life and to develop appropriate ways of functioning in the new reality. In addition, new losses emerge, mostly the bitter loss of a dream because of discrepancies between preimmigration expectations and the reality of life in the new country.

The process of acculturation to the new environment requires the immigrant to extend the boundaries of what one takes for granted and to incorporate into the personal world new and formerly strange aspects of life in the culture of relocation (Mittelberg, 1988). Berry (1986) identified and described three stages in this phase. The first is the stage of contact-encounter. In this stage the immigrant first meets the new culture and gets a preliminary sense of its differences and similarities, as well as financial constraints, language and social barriers, and prejudice and discrimination. Immigrants face bureaucracies whose rules they do not know in a language they do not understand. This phase often coincides with the initial efforts to establish a new life, find a place to live, and locate employment. This process exposes the newcomer to the dominant culture and paves the road for comparisons between the previous life and the new life. Being absorbed in the struggle to survive often deprives immigrants at this phase of the opportunity to be in touch with the emotional meaning of their move and to mourn their losses.

In the second stage of conflict, a dissonance between the two cultures evolves, which initiates a process of giving up and reshaping some original values and patterns and adopting some values and patterns of the new culture. Immigrants' willingness to go through this process varies, depending on their age, social environment, and personality. Typically, younger people, especially adolescents who wish to be like their peers, are faster to adopt new norms than their parents and other adults are. People who live in ethnic enclaves that encourage maintaining the culture of origin change less and at a slower pace than those who live and work or study in a culturally diverse environment.

In the final stage of adaptation, a wide array of ways to reduce the conflict develops. Immigrants learn the language of the new culture, including its colloquialism and norms. They learn to decode social clues. They mourn the losses that they suffered and experience the loss of their dreams about the new country as they face its reality. They come to grasp the permanence of the change in their lives, struggle to rehabilitate a sense of worth and mastery of life, develop ways of functioning in the new reality, and re-create familiarity with their environment within the context of the host country (Hattar-Pollara and Meleis, 1995a). They struggle to reinvent themselves and develop a new sense of identity. This is a lifelong and inevitable component of the immigrant's life.

To successfully develop a sense of ethnic identity, individuals need a social environment that provides them with support for their choice. The search for such an environment drives many immigrants, at least initially, to live in ethnic enclaves, which offer familiarity within an alien culture, and to seek employment, services, and social contacts with compatriots. Ethnic economy enclaves (also called an ethnic subeconomy), i.e., immigrant-owned firms that employ other immigrants, draw socioeconomic advantages from ethnic solidarity, social affiliation, and cultural loyalty to an ethnic group. Working in ethnic business and services (e.g., selling ethnic commodities such as food, clothes, books, and music of the immigrant's own culture of origin and providing services to their own community) often allows for easier work adjustment than in the context of the open market.

Some immigration analysts (e.g., Zimmerman and Fix, 1994) explain differences in adaptation of immigrants to their new environment as a function of immigration status. They claim that legal immigrants, undocumented immigrants, and refugees differ in their cultures of origin, social and economic characteristics, and starting point, and that legal immigrants adjust faster and better than undocumented immigrants because although both groups come voluntarily, the former typically have more education and more support than the latter. However, this statement does not take into consideration family dynamics and may be misleading regarding the immigration of women. For example, if the husband chooses to relocate and the woman conforms because of her subordinate status in many traditional cultures, she will be falsely considered as coming through choice.

The specific nature of the resettlement phase depends, among other factors, on the nature of the relationship that the immigrant maintains with the country of origin. Immigrants from some countries, such as the former Soviet Union, Cambodia, South Korea, Vietnam, and Cuba, took an irreversible step. They see the move to their new country as final and in many cases do not have the option of revisiting their homeland, although this situation has changed for some of theses groups (e.g., the former Soviet Union and Vietnam). Immigrants from other countries, especially from South and Central America, continue to have intense relationships with their country of origin and are a major power in their economy by pouring considerable portions of their income to support their families who remained behind (Thompson, 2002). Globalization, transportation, and communication systems that allow immigrants to maintain strong connections with the culture of origin, such as mutual visits, telephone, electronic mail, videotape, conference calls, and international commerce, changed many aspects of the immigration experience, suggesting new solutions and presenting new challenges. Immigrants now can maintain ongoing contact with the originating communities, participating in ceremonies and major decisions and being visited by people from their culture of origin (Foner, 2000).

EFFECTS OF IMMIGRATION

Culture loss is often accompanied by subjective reactions. These reactions have been referred to as culture shock (Bock, 1970; Furnham and Bochner, 1986; Stewart, 1986). Possible detrimental effects of immigration on individuals and families have been widely documented (Garza-Guerrero, 1974; Glassman and Skolnik, 1984; Harper and Lantz, 1996). Because emigration means uprooting and experiencing social, economic, and cultural insecurity, it creates an "existential vacuum," a disconfirmation of one's core assumptions about the world, a sense of personal annihilation, and possibly a sense of emptiness and meaninglessness in the life of the immigrant. Immigration often shatters traditional family structure and gender-based roles and authority (Balgopal, 2000). Consequently, it may have detrimental effects on individuals and families (Garza-Guerrero, 1974; Glassman and Skolnik, 1984; Harper and Lantz, 1996). These effects may include an existential crisis, helplessness, insecurity, social isolation, inadequacy, shaken sense of self, lowered self-esteem, confusion, disorientation, frustration, anger, loneliness, anomic depression, and familial instability and discord (Garza-Guerrero, 1974; Stewart, 1986; Drachman and Shen-Ryan, 1991; Hattar-Pollara and Meleis, 1995b; Berger, 1996; Harper and Lantz, 1996; Hulewat, 1996; Shin and Shin, 1999).

Immigration has been recognized as an etiological factor in mental health problems. It may create problems directly related to the relocation, escalate previous problems, and turn individual, marital, parental, and familial problems that were manageable prior to immigration into insurmountable obstacles to well-being and social functioning (Berger, 2001). Evidence in the literature indicates that different phases during the resettlement process are characterized by a higher level of mental health risk than others (Nguyen, 1984; Rumbaut, 1985), but the specific patterns of such changes are inconsistent. For example, it has been suggested that the initial phase after arrival is symptom free and marked by a subjective sense of well-being and euphoria—the phase of overcompensation—followed by increasing mental health difficulties, with a peak estimated to occur, depending on different researchers, six months to six years postimmigration (Nguyen, 1984; Rumbaut, 1985; Sluzki, 1983). Beiser, Turner, and Gansean (1989) and Flaherty and colleagues (1988) found postimmigration periods of demoralization that increase over time and reach a peak by the fourth or seventh year of residence in the new culture, while Scott and Scott (1989) proposed a gradual improvement of mental health over time.

However, traumatic events create not only the danger of emotional distress and functional decline but also the opportunity for personal growth (Tedeschi and Calhoun, 1995). In the past decade, a growing recognition has been developing that the aftermath of trauma has potential for both negative and positive changes in one's life (O'Leary, Alday, and Ickovics, 1998).

These effects vary. One factor that shapes them is the degree of difference and similarity between the culture of origin and the new culture. When immigrants come to a new country, an encounter between hosts and guests occurs. All such encounters involve the need to negotiate strangeness. When this encounter occurs in a cross-cultural interface, norms and values between the parties are incongruent. Consequently, events and behaviors may be interpreted in different ways and lead to friction, reciprocal stereotyping, and mutual misunderstandings, while similarity and congruence of the guest-host encounter may promote smooth communication (Mittelberg, 1988). Acculturation often requires walking in and out of cultural frameworks that are incompatible and coping with contradictions between the norms of the original culture and those of the new environment. Relocation to a very different social environment is more challenging than relocation within a similar cultural climate. For example, moving from a traditional society that emphasizes *being* (a focus on one's existence) and has a strong orientation to the past to a modern society with a focus on *doing* (an emphasis on one's actions) and an orientation toward the future is more complicated than moving between two Western cultures, although my own experience and those of participants in this study shows that the latter is also not easy.

People who emigrate from the former Soviet Union with its collectivist value system or from Japan with its family-focused values to the American culture, which glorifies individualism, find it harder to acculturate than people who migrate from Western Europe. In reflecting on her relocation as a child from Korea to the United States, Kim (2000) asserts,

> I became more aware of the beleaguering difficulties of having to live with two different sets of values and codes of conduct. Often what was "right" for one culture was "wrong" for the other, and what was accepted in one was rejected by the other. It was not possible to assimilate—to make similar—the two cultures, Korean and American, whose fundamental values and philosophies were opposite. (p. 117)

An additional determinant of the impact of immigration is the nature of the receivership and the status of the culture of origin in the absorbing society (Lalonde, Taylor, and Moghaddam, 1992; Brock-Utne, 1994). Portes and Rumbaut (2001) differentiate three levels of receivership: *governmental,* i.e., the nature of immigration policy; *societal,* i.e., by mainstream dominant society; and *communal,* i.e., by the immigrant's own ethnic compatriots.

Receivership policy of various groups ranges from *exclusion* to *passive acceptance* (i.e., a neutral position of granting entrance with no effort to facilitate adjustment) to *active encouragement.* Within this context, several approaches to immigrants' cultures of origin can be noted historically. The "melting pot" ideology demands processing together diverse cultures to allow the emergence of a new unified entity and erase differences. Michel Guillaume Jean de Crèvecoeur, a journalist who migrated from France to the United States in the eighteenth century and wrote under the pen name J. Hector St. John, observed,

> Here individuals of all nations are melted into a new race of men—the American. . . . The American ought to love this country much better the wherein either he or his father were born. The American is a new man who acts upon new principles; he must entertain new ideas and form new opinions. (de Crèvecoeur, 1782, p. 29)

In reality, immigrants were expected to "melt" into the (white, Judeo-Christian) mainstream and to maximize their assimilation into the absorbing culture, which was pressured to remake immigrants in its own image.

The melting pot ideology has been replaced by amalgamation and cultural diversity which represent approaches that allow diverse cultures to maintain their characteristics with mutual tolerance and respect for the "other" and cultural reciprocity that recognizes the mutual effects of the original and absorbing cultures on one another. Higham (2001) observes diversity and assimilation as complementary processes suggesting "pluralistic integration."

Although these ideals are currently advocated, immigrants from cultures that are looked down upon and marginalized still suffer more severe discrimination than do those who come from "higher-status" cultures. They also often experience segmented assimilation, i.e., assimilation into a specific social class, e.g., inner-city underclass, which is mostly nonwhite and where protection by the ethnic community is weak (Portes, 1998).

As Portes and Rumbaut (2001) note, although the offspring of white immigrants have the option to determine the degree of their assimilation, the situation is not so clear for children of today's immigrants who are predominantly nonwhite and who consequently face a different, often less welcoming and more discriminatory, receivership.

For example, those who relocate from poor Central American countries may experience more difficulties and be less accepted than those who come from industrialized, affluent European countries. Consequently, immigrants are experiencing a hierarchy of racism, a racist pecking order depending on the dominant culture's preferences. This hierarchy impacts and is reflected in differential levels of services, rights, and political and economic power.

The status of one's culture of origin within the context of the receiving culture's mainstream society is changing according to political global development. Thus, following the September 11, 2001, terrorist attacks on the World Trade Center and the Pentagon, Muslim immigrants in general and immigrants from Afghanistan in particular have experienced negative reactions toward their homeland and culture of origin.

Social acceptance of immigration within one's culture of origin also affects adjustment to the new culture. For instance, Israeli culture has traditionally discouraged emigration from the country, describing the concept with a term which in Hebrew means "going down." Emigrants have been labeled by derogatory concepts such as "fall out nonentities," coined by the late Prime Minister Yitzhak Rabin. Emigrants were seen as traitors and consequently felt guilt and shame. Although negative and judgmental attitudes toward Israelis who choose to live abroad have greatly changed, the negative connotations associated with it are very much alive in the collective memory, causing many Israeli emigrants not to give themselves permission to admit the permanency of their life outside Israel.

Culture shock reactions also differ by age, gender, level of education, and professional skills. Children adjust faster than their parents, women faster than men. Individuals may be at different places of the continuum of acculturation at different times, thus further broadening intergenerational and intergender gaps (Landau-Stanton, 1985; Berger, 2001).

Finally, personal and family history of coping with stresses and the existence of concurrent crises in one's life have an important role in shaping the reaction to immigration. For example, vulnerable populations such as adolescents and the elderly that are caught in a combined developmental and cultural transition experience a unique pile up of stresses (Stewart, 1986; Baptiste, 1993; Berger, 1997, 2001).

WOMEN AND IMMIGRATION

Women represent about half of the international migrant population, usually as "secondary migrants" following or joining other family members, typically their husbands (United Nations, 1995), and the majority of the world's 30 million refugees and displaced persons (Ferris, 1993). Although 100 years ago immigrant women were heavily outnumbered by male immigrants in the workforce, currently female immigrant workers outnumber males and are frequently the principal contributors to family incomes (Foner, 1999, 2000).

Immigrant women face the same issues that affect all immigrants but are also susceptible to additional risk factors because of their gender. Some of these factors have been described in a recent pamphlet:

> Women often comprise the neglected and forgotten face of migration. The experiences of war, torture and trauma, and the misery of refugee camps seriously affect women's health and well-being. However, these experiences are difficult to document. Women are often reluctant to speak about such horren-

dous crimes because of the pain of remembering and the fear of reprisal. (Royal Women's Hospital, 2001)

Immigrant women are among the most vulnerable to exploitation, abuse, and human rights violations (National Network on Immigrant and Refugee Rights, 2000). Because they are caught in an intersection of being immigrants, women, and often of minority status, immigrant women are vulnerable to triple discrimination and marginalization. The interface of gender, ethnic, and immigration discourses often causes immigrant women to find themselves affected simultaneously by racism, sexism, and class inequality. Research on the employment status of immigrants to Western societies consistently shows that immigrant women tend to work more than nonimmigrants (Weatherford, 1986; United Nations, 1995). However, they are less likely than men to obtain employment in their former occupation, at least in the short run, and are often forced to join the labor market in the lower levels of the occupational pyramid (Richmond, Kalbach, and Verma, 1981; Sabatello, 1979; Saunders, 1985). Consequently, immigrant women are the group receiving the lowest salaries (United Nations, 1995).

Between the years 1995 and 2000 it was documented that conditions for immigrant women in the world seriously deteriorated. They are engaged in domestic work, agricultural labor, and other low-wage jobs, and their rights have been seriously compromised and threatened. Illegal immigrant women are the most vulnerable and at the highest risk (K. Walsh, personal communication; National Network on Immigrant and Refugee Rights, 2000).

Two factors that shape the experience of immigrant women are the motivation and circumstances of their immigration. First, women often immigrate not because of their own will or decision but because of their husbands' desire to do so. Second, the majority of international immigrant women are admitted under the principle of family reunification. These factors create a situation of dependency for these women. McIntyre and Augusto (1999) identify in female immigrants a supercoping phase prior to immigration and a collapse phase after arrival to the new country because of a pervasive loss of sense of self and an inability to negotiate their identity in the new culture.

The inferior status of these women at work is aggravated by their subordinate status and double roles in the family (Remennick, 1999). They are thrown into the arena of the new society forcefully and immediately. They have to negotiate the school system on behalf of their children and cope with often unfriendly medical systems which observe an immunization regime that is very different from their country of origin. From the very first days in the new country they must shop in supermarkets that carry products different from those with which they are familiar, pack food in ways that are alien to them, and provide information about weights and content in a foreign language and unknown measurement units. How many packages of butter should one buy to make a cake that requires 200 grams? How do they pack raisins here? What is the American equivalent of 180° Celsius in the oven? Why is corporal punishment, a common and acceptable disciplinarian measure in the culture of origin, deemed illegal in the United States? Why does it put one at a risk for being charged with child abuse and having one's children placed in foster care?

In addition, the role of women as carriers of and those responsible for transmission of the cultural heritage of their homeland and educating the young generations about the beliefs, norms, and values of community life has been documented from early on. They "have the added task of ensuring that the family maintains some degree of continuity with the cultures, norms and values of the society of origin while at the same time embarking a process of adaptation to the host society" (United Nations, 1995, p. 8). Consequently, it has been claimed that women have been viewed as obstacles to their families' assimilation (Kasaba, 2000).

Grealy (2000) describes her preimmigration experience as a child in Ireland, watching foreign movies:

> What I was watching for was not the content of the shows and movies themselves, but the details, the background: the always wet streets, the phone boxes, the door handles, the tea pots, the road signs, the stone walls and hedges; the million details of daily life that are the true separators between cultures. (p. 80)

It is these million details that require immigrant women to quickly learn to navigate in the new culture.

An additional source of stress with special effects on women is presented by differences in gender-based expectations in the culture of relocation and the culture of origin. For women, international migration often means a shift in gender relations and gender stratification, moving from a culture of origin where roles are gender specific to cultures of relocation that are more egalitarian in role allocation (Knorr and Meier, 2000). Therefore, migration may have implications for changing women's status in society and inside the family (Lim, 1995). Women who emigrate from traditional modern societies face societal pressure to accommodate to more egalitarian roles often concurrent with familial pressure to adhere to traditional gender-based roles.

Kasaba (2000) asserts that the migration experience is especially disempowering for married women and mothers. In addition to their personal difficulties and responsibilities as mediators with the receiving society, immigrant women often serve as buffers and containers to frustrations of husbands and children who are torn between two cultures, thus experiencing indirect effects of immigration as well. Often they are also taking care of older relatives. Therefore, the burden may tilt disproportionately onto the shoulders of women who may be overloaded by the responsibility of performing too many roles and who have therefore been portrayed as being at risk for problems of adjustment (Damji Budhwani, 1999). It is not surprising that some studies suggest married women and mothers express less satisfaction with their life following migration than single immigrant women do (Freidenberg, Imperiale, and Skouton, 1988).

Mothering presents a special challenge to immigrant women. Often norms for parenting in the absorbing culture differ significantly from parenting norms in the culture of origin (Hattar-Pollara and Meleis, 1995a). For example, mothers from Russia, the Far East, and South America find it difficult to tolerate adolescents' demand for privacy and independence. They have expectations for obedience and respect of parental authority in such matters as observing curfew hours and dress codes that are strange to their children who are more exposed to and more affected by the liberal American norms. In their effort to fit in with their peers, children challenge their already vulnerable parents.

Women are often victims to pressures from both sides. On one hand, her children push her to permit them more freedom and tolerance; on the other hand, her husband demands that she practice a more strict parenting style. Fathers often blame the mothers for tolerating their children's "acting out," adding to the women's pressures in their effort to mother. The role reversal caused by dependence on children, who often acquire the language faster than their parents, as translators for negotiation with social institutions and as culture interpreters further shatters the already shaken authority structure and exacerbates the conflict.

Because of the double disadvantages in the workforce and at home, the shrinking of traditional support networks and the pile up of stresses described previously, immigrant women have been described as a population in high risk (Pittaway, 1991; Bernstein and Shuval, 1999; Remennick, 1999).

The aforementioned challenges for immigrant women are further exacerbated by immigration policy. The National Network on Immigrant and Refugee Rights (2000) published a report to assess progress on the platform for action set at the 1995 UN World Conference on Women held in Beijing, China, in which principles for promoting international standards for women's rights were established. It found that the particular challenges facing migrant women continue to be ignored.

In spite of all these unique aspects of female migration, recognizing the importance of gender in immigration is relatively new. Women as migrants were largely invisible in social sciences until the mid-1970s, and if mentioned at all, they were viewed as dependent on men (Knorr and Meier, 2000). The past two decades witnessed growing attention to sociological, psychological, and anthropological aspects of the female face of emigration and immigration (e.g., Simon and Brettell, 1986; Bilsborrow, 1994; Schwartz-Seller, 1994; Willis and Yeoh, 2000).

The focus of this book is the female migrant discourse. My goal is to give the voices of a diverse group of immigrant women an opportunity to be heard and to educate us about experiences of immigrant women across cultures. It is conceivable that women of different cultures of origin have different immigration experiences. Women who come from conservative, traditional, less industrial societies cannot compare their experiences to women who emigrate from industrialized, Westernized societies. Black women who emigrate from Africa have a different experience than Asian women who emigrate from Taiwan. However, anecdotal information and impressions that I collected through my interactions with immigrant women suggest that some common experiences transcend these differences and are unique to immigrant women in spite of their varied backgrounds. The book represents a systematic effort to analyze narratives of immigrant women in search of commonalities which go beyond specific demographic background, personal, familial and immigration status, and circumstances of immigration and which can teach us about their collective experience.

Chapter 2

Methodology: How the Research for This Book Was Done

This book tells the story of immigration of women as the women themselves experienced it. It reflects their subjective perception and interpretation of the reality rather than an "objective" picture by an "external" neutral observer. I was especially interested in comprehending the *experience* of immigration for women rather than a superficial description of behaviors and events. The focus is on the "inside story" of "how," "why," and "what does it mean" rather than a report of "what," "how much," and "how often."

A review of immigration literature indicates that most of the research to date was done from an "external," non-gender-specific, pathologizing viewpoint using linear models. "Much of what is commonly known about immigrants tends to be simplistic and monolithic. Immigrants are portrayed as having homogenous experiences. Only recently have some scholars begun to focus on subjective experiences of people who have made cultural transitions" (Bystydzienski and Resnik, 1994, p. 2).

TYPES OF IMMIGRATION RESEARCH

An External Perspective

Many existing accounts about immigration and immigrants were documented by researchers from the dominant absorbing culture (e.g., Schwartz-Seller, 1994). These studies tend to look at immigrants rather than looking at people who experience immigration. The former concept conveys the idea that being an immigrant is the totality of one's being and what one is; the latter views people who encounter a certain situation but acknowledges that the situation is not them—they are more than what they go through. As profound and long-lasting as the effects of the experience are, the person is still separate from and more than the experience. Those who struggle with the experience of immigration are often excluded and their voices are not heard. This is especially true for women who experience immigration.

Less attention has been paid to understanding the meaning and experience of those who go through the process of immigration, especially women who immigrate. Studies that document the experience of immigration by women are still limited in number and in focus. Immigration, like all human experiences, has both a universal dimension (i.e., our lives are shaped and constricted in some ways by socially determined agendas) and an individual dimension (i.e., our personal journey and discourse of life). Literature specific to women, including ethnographic studies and personal narratives that provide a phenomenological perspective, i.e., that extract the personal stories, are starting to evolve, and a number of dissertations recently documented narratives of immigrant women.

For example, Perez (2000) interviewed ten legal immigrant women from Spanish-speaking countries of South America who moved to the United States during young adulthood to pursue personal, educational, and occupational goals. She identified ten prominent themes: mourning the loss of the native cultural, social, and family environment; holding onto Latino cultural values; the role of language; refashioning relationships with friends and family left behind; the role of idealization and nostalgia; refashioning the self; psychological exile; increased social isolation in the new country; dislocation; and refashioning home. Wolfson (1999) analyzed migration stories of ten Irish women and identified a major theme of experiences of displacement associated with social constructions of gender and class in Irish society, which they sought to resolve through migration and repositioning themselves in the new context. Mallona (1999) discussed narratives of fourteen Central American immigrant women to identify the ways in which they make meaning of who they are in the context of U.S. society. The findings indicated that multiple contradictions erupted in many areas of the immigrant women's lives and constantly created new meanings.

However, these studies of the experiences of immigrant women tend to emphasize specific populations and look at the experience of women of a specific culture of origin (e.g., Korean, South American, Irish, Jamaican), leaving the question of commonalties of experiences for women with different immigration journeys to be explored. Furthermore, such oral histories often are presented but not analyzed for the collective experiences of their narrators.

Traditional analysis that views immigrant women from the outside both robs them of the opportunity to express their viewpoints and makes them passive subjects whose perceptions do not count. In the introduction to her recent book, Meri Nana-Ama Danquah, herself an immigrant from Ghana, shares her experience:

> Throughout my youth, I had seen and read books about immigration. None of them contained any information that even remotely seemed to relate to me. Where were the accounts of immigrant experience through the eyes of a black African-born woman? (Danquah, 2000, p. xv)

Non-Gender-Specific Research

Much of the research on the immigration process has lumped together all immigrants, muted gender-related differences, and viewed immigration as gender neutral. In referring to Australia, Hugo (1995) observes that the task of assessing the process of immigration and its effects on women

> has been hindered by the tendency of official sources of data to present information only for both sexes combined and by the failure of most immigration research in Australia to recognize that gender has a major significance in shaping the processes of immigration and settlement. (p. 217)

This observation is not unique to Australia and, with some exceptions, is mirrored in almost any source about migration of women in all parts of the world (e.g., United Nations, 1995).

One explanation for this was suggested by the United Nations' Experts Group, claiming that international migration has traditionally been viewed as a mechanism for redistribution of labor and that international migrants have been assumed to be mostly men. Migrant women were viewed as "dependents," and more attention was given to those "left behind" in the homeland. This invisibility of migrant women contributes to the lack of clarity about the role of gender in the process of immigration (Assar, 1999).

> Gender and immigration have seldom been studied in tandem, although the experiences and challenges faced by male and female immigrants are as different as they are in other life contexts. The countries of origin and resettlement may significantly differ in the extent and forms of patriarchy and in gender roles, adding a unique facet to women's experiences of acculturation. (Remennick, 1999, p. 163)

Although in recent years national and international organizations and advocacy groups have brought a great deal of attention to the issues of immigrant women, more literature exists about men and immigrants in general. Participation in research as informants offers women whose viewpoint is rarely heard an opportunity to voice their opinions and be acknowledged (Berger and Malkinson, 2000). Recently, some scholars have recognized that immigration of women has its own unique characteristics and issues which require study. In the mid-1980s serious research on women's migration started to develop (e.g., Kunek, 1993). However, most of the literature still focuses on men and on non-gender-specific approaches.

Pathologizing Lens

Much of the existing immigration research has been done from a deficit paradigm, emphasizing difficulties and pathologizing aspects of relocation from a problem-oriented frame of reference. Studies that are problem focused tend to neglect looking at resiliency, strengths, and positive outcomes, yielding an unbalanced, problem-saturated picture.

As described in Chapter 1, abundant empirical knowledge documents the negative effects of immigration on one's social, financial, and professional status and on individual and family psychological well-being and functioning (Garza-Guerrero, 1974; Glassman and Skolnik, 1984; Furnham and Bochner, 1986; Stewart, 1986; Drachman and Shen-Ryan, 1991; Hattar-Pollara and Meleis, 1995b; Berger, 1996; Harper and Lantz, 1996; Hulewat, 1996; Shin and Shin, 1999).

Although there is no doubt that immigration is a challenging experience which may have severe outcomes for individuals and families, anecdotal evidence suggests that it also has favorable aspects. However, very few reports document the positive effects of immigration.

Linear Models

Many of the models and conceptual frameworks used to understand the immigration experience have been criticized as linear and oversimplifying (e.g., Kasaba, 2000). Given the complex and multidimensional nature of the immigration process, models for conceptualizing and deconstructing it need to be sophisticated and comprehensive.

I wanted the voices of the immigrant women and their accounts of the experience to be heard. I wanted to know how women perceive being an immigrant, how they process their experience, and how they construct their reality to interpret and make meaning of it. Such knowledge about the intricacy of immigration for women is long overdue (Gabaccia, 1992). With a few exceptions (e.g., Guyot et al., 1978; Bystydzienski and Resnik, 1994; Danquah, 2000; Perez, 2000), reports on the experience of immigrant women from their perspective across cultures are limited. This book contributes to that emerging body of knowledge by documenting what individual women perceived, how they felt, and what the consequences were for them.

The kind of knowledge I was seeking is most effectively produced by qualitative research. This type of research has been known in the social sciences for many years, but in the past decade it has gained its place as a viable and popular alternative approach to research in social sciences, as numerous professional publications, conferences, and new software can attest. It is specifically helpful in exploring little-known fields, studying sensitive issues, and gaining understanding of complex multidimensional social phenomena. While traditional or positivistic research typically seeks to disprove or support an existing theory, qualitative research seeks to develop a new theory from individual cases and to develop "a subjective testimonial to other people's voices" (Ahearn, 1999, p. 15). To this end, an inductive approach is used. Therefore, qualitative research is often called discovery-focused research. To allow openness for new ideas to develop throughout the process, qualitative research does not require that the researcher name and defines a priori all the variables in the study. Rather, it leaves room for growth and emergence of new unanticipated directions. The assumptions and principles of qualitative research are briefly reviewed in the following section.

ASSUMPTIONS AND PRINCIPLES OF QUALITATIVE RESEARCH

There are diverse traditions in conducting qualitative research. They vary by the discipline in which they were developed (e.g., sociology, anthropology, education, nursing) and in their specific goal (e.g., descriptive, analysis), focus, and approach. However, all of them share common basic assumptions. Qualitative research assumes nonobjectivity and advocates contextualized knowledge and a multiperspective holistic approach. Qualitative research methods assume that there is no "objective" reality. Rather, "realities" depend on and reflect the view of the beholder and the specific circumstances. The same event can be perceived and interpreted differently by different people under different conditions. Because people construct their experience and make meaning of it and this meaning making guides their actions, to understand behavior it is important to know how people process and interpret their reality. Furthermore, objective reality cannot be achieved. A researcher will receive the respondent's version rather than the "true" story. Understanding the complex world of lived experience from the point of view of those who live it and seeing through their lens is the core of qualitative research. That is, the researcher studies how a person who goes through an experience perceives and interprets it and makes meaning of it (Schwandt, 1994).

Furthermore, because the perception and interpretation of events is shaped by the context in which they occur, this approach also advocates contextualized knowledge, namely, how particular individuals within particular sociopolitical circumstances and at a particular time and place view themselves and their experiences and what meaning they attribute to these experiences.

In the spirit of nonobjectivity, qualitative research recognizes that research is not a neutral and value-free process. We, the researchers, are people. We have biases, preferences, and worldviews. These thoughts, in combination with our cultural background, gender, racial, and social affiliation, and personal experience, impact the way we decide what to study how, when, and where, the questions we ask, the language we use, and the way we collect information and make sense of it. Therefore, awareness and recognition of the motivation, beliefs, and experiences that the researcher brings to the table are parts of the research process in qualitative research.

In the process of the research a new system is created. It includes the researcher and the respondent who develop a mutual relationship in which both are reciprocally changed and influenced by each other. The research process becomes a collaborative effort to understand the issue under study.

The importance of adopting a holistic and comprehensive perspective is an additional aspect that is emphasized in qualitative research. Many people believe that if we understand various aspects of a complex phenomenon, we can eventually put all the pieces together and get the "big picture." Qualitative researchers assume that the whole is more than the sum of its parts, and therefore combining the results of many partial researches might fail to capture the complexities of the full issue or situation.

Because of these characteristics, qualitative methodology has been recognized as powerful in eliciting the type of knowledge that I was seeking for this book. It offers the necessary flexibility, depth, and comprehensive perspective and allows the researcher to go beyond objective markers of migrant women's functioning and well-being (e.g., achievement at work, level of income) to capture the women's experiences and their meaning (Hamilton, 1994). This choice is in agreement with ideas of other immigration researchers. For example, Buijs (1993) rejects unilinear models for understanding the effects of immigration and emphasizes the importance of paying attention to "the complex and subtle shades of meaning and perceptions with which migrant women view the world" within the context of their culture of origin (p. 12). One attempt to do so has been completed by Danquah (2000), who invited two dozen immigrant women to write their stories of immigration. However, the contributors to Danquah's book are mostly educated and articulate women, including writers, journalists, educators, poets, and scientists. I was interested in casting a broader net to hear how women of different social strata construct, process, and make meaning of their experience as immigrants. Therefore, interviewing women who have gone through the experience and were willing to share it with me seemed to offer the best path.

INTERVIEWING IN QUALITATIVE RESEARCH

The interview is the favorite tool of the qualitative researcher. I interviewed eighteen women who emigrated to the United States, Israel, Australia, and New Zealand. The interviews were conducted in a technique called an open-ended interview. In this technique the interviewer has a general list of topics to be addressed in no particular order. This list is a springboard from which the interviewer and the informant take off on their journey. Interviews took place in various places—the interviewee's home, cafes, the interviewer's office—according to the preference of the women. They lasted between two and four hours in Hebrew, English, or mix of Spanish and English and many manual gestures.

All the women expressed willingness to share personal experiences and satisfaction that they were asked to express their opinions. I often heard comments in the spirit of "It is nice to for once be asked about my view rather than being told what I 'should' and am 'expected' to do, feel, think." I believe that my being an immigrant woman contributed to women's openness because my immigration status made me somewhat of an "ethnic insider" even for women from cultural, racial, and ethnic backgrounds different from my own. The women responded favorably to my having a heavy accent and having experienced the process of relocation and felt that this experience makes me better able to understand their own experiences.

The race, ethnicity, class, and gender of the interviewer and interviewee influence these interviews (Denzin and Lincoln, 2000). Personal issues that researchers bring with them affect the inner sieve through which we filter the world around us. This sieve is created and shaped through our journey in life and colors our understanding, feeling, thinking, and being. Hunt (1989) explains that the narrative of the interview "is partly biographical reflecting something about the researcher's personality as well as those of the subjects" (p. 41).

To prepare for interviewing, qualitative researchers are required to sensitize and familiarize themselves with the culture to be studied. This can be done by sharing it or immersing in it. I bring ample familiarity and sensitivity to the table in several ways. First, I am an immigrant woman myself. Furthermore, for many years I have counseled, taught, supervised, studied, and mentored immigrant women. Finally, in preparation for this study, I immersed myself in theoretical, empirical, and clinical knowledge about the topic and conducted dialogues with professionals and nonprofessionals who have familiarity with topics that pertain to the immigration of women. These included social workers who work with them, representatives of the Red Cross and other welfare organizations who serve this population, and many more.

Of course, such firsthand familiarity carried with it the risk of allowing my own experience of immigration to color the way in which I elicited and heard the stories of my interviewees. This risk is known as research bias, which results from selective observation, selective recording of information, and allowing one's personal views and perspectives to affect how data are collected and interpreted (Johnson, 1999).

This risk is part of the broader issue of the trustworthiness of the findings in qualitative research, i.e., assessment of the rigor of the results. Guba (1981) identifies and describes aspects of trustworthiness that should be met. They are (1) truth value, i.e., the degree of confidence in the findings, (2) applicability, i.e., the ability to generalize from the findings to larger populations, (3) consistency, i.e., the degree to which there is a dependable explanations for differences in findings, and (4) neutrality, i.e., freedom from bias. Krefting (1999) summarizes strategies to address these aspects of trustworthiness. Most of these strategies were used in the current study. The first strategy is called participants' feedback. This means that the researcher checks back with interviewees to seek their feedback to verify the accuracy of the researcher's perception and understanding. The second strategy is reflexivity, in which the researchers deliberately and actively engage themselves in critical self-study to identify potential predispositions. Data were collected during prolonged interactions under diverse circumstances from multiple sources. Finally, review by knowledgeable peers and debriefing with colleagues, my own credentials and experience in conducting qualitative research in general, and familiarity with the issues of immigration of women in particular also contribute to credibility.

Qualitative research is an "umbrella" concept that refers to various traditions. One of the major qualitative traditions is feminist inquiry. This tradition, which informed and guided me in the research I conducted for this book, is discussed in the next section.

UNDERSTANDING WOMEN'S PERSPECTIVES

Feminist inquiry is one of the qualitative approaches. Its basic assumption is that the world has been built by men for men. The restrictions on women because of the patriarchal world permeate all aspects of life. Women's life and behavior are affected, mostly in negative ways, by structural, financial, political, and economical rules and realities that are male dominated and male oriented. The oppression of women in our patriarchal world has affected not only the professional, family, and personal lives of women but also research regarding women's lives and experiences. Theoretical frameworks, research questions, and methodologies have traditionally been situated from a male-centered perspective, blurring and muting any perspectives unique to women and thus further enhancing the oppression of women in society (Olsen, 1994). Gender blindness, like color blindness regarding racial minorities, is one form of discrimination, by neglecting to recognize special aspects, issues, and needs of population groups other than white males. If one studies all immigrants together, pretending that gender does not matter and does not impact the immigration process and aftermath, unique issues of immigrant women go unrecognized.

This issue is not unique to the United States. The European Council on Refugees and Exiles posited that the difficulty of assessing the problems facing refugee and asylum-seeking women is increased by a lack of gender-differentiated data in European countries.

> The false assumption that all refugees, irrespective of their gender, face the same problems and will be treated equally can create the illusion of seeming equality. But this picture is misleading and discriminatory because it denies immigrant women the right and the opportunity to define their own issues [and consequently they] are unable to benefit equitably from current legal protection and social assistance measures. (European Council on Refugees and Exiles, 1997, p. 1)

Since the 1960s gender awareness has motivated feminist inquiries and development of research and practice agendas that reflect gender sensitivity. Feminist theoreticians, researchers, and clinicians began to critique theories and practices through a feminist lens and to search for ways to comprehend women's social realities and their practical translation into research methods to ensure racial and social diversity in the accounts of women's lives (Fonow and Cook, 1991). Women-focused and women-oriented perspectives have been developed, writers have advocated the creation of a realistic knowledge base and action principles, new interpretive frameworks for understanding women's lives have been constructed, and the importance of women's narratives has been emphasized (Van den Bergh and Cooper, 1986; Brooks, 1992; Jacoby Boxer, 1998; Hua, 2000). The main assertion of these approaches is that understanding the experience of women requires understanding their reality.

The feminist assertion that "women know differently," which posits special "women's ways of knowing" stemming from their ways of living in the world, reflects the feminist attempt to build on and validate women's own interpretations of experience (Jacoby Boxer, 1998).

From the beginning, feminists spoke in many voices. In spite of their diverse and sometimes conflicting views, all feminist approaches share the belief that it is important to understand the situation of women and circumstances that affect them as a basis for social change in these situations. Implicit in the feminist perspective are the principles of equality in rights, opportunities, and choices in all aspects of life, the assumption that women and their experiences have significance, and the assertion that subjective knowledge is important. The ground rules of feminist inquiry are consciousness-raising, equal opportunity for self-expression, and validation of each woman's experience.

In the spirit of this approach, it is of utmost importance to focus on special issues of immigrant women and to do so from the immigrant women's perspective. Although the recognition that issues of gender permeate all aspects of one's life is now much more evident, our world is still male dominated and true equality is nonexistent. Special attention to women's perspective is still unnoticed and is often addressed, if at all, in a marginal footnote comment—a minimal "lip service" section—or is limited exclusively to specific sections about domestic violence and sexual abuse. One result of this attitude is insufficient knowledge about the gendered nature of the immigration experience.

One way to promote better understanding of women's lives is by sharing experiences and, through sharing, learning the meaning of these experiences for their lives (Jacoby Boxer, 1998). Listening to women's narratives has been recognized as helpful in achieving this goal and promoting our understanding of the impact of the experience of uprootedness on psychological development (Espin, 1992; Sizoo, 1997). The feminist interview provides a vehicle for such sharing of experience. In a feminist interview, the interviewer and interviewee are "coequals who are carrying on a conversation about mutually relevant, often biographically critical issues" (Denzin and Lincoln, 2000, p. 634).

CONDUCTING THE INTERVIEWS

The strategy of the feminist interview was used to document narratives of women who emigrated from all parts of the world within the past decade and were willing to share with me their experiences, thoughts, and feelings, which reverberated with my own experience, making us cotravelers through the journey of immigration. Interviews lasted from two to four hours. I explained to each woman that I am interested in learning about the experience of immigration through a female lens and asked her to tell her own story. Some started immediately to talk and their stories "flooded," while others required a little more encouragement and probing. Some started in a chronically organized way, and others began from their current situation, flashing back in an associative manner. All the women seemed eager to share and happy to be asked to tell their story, and many of them expressed satisfaction for being invited to express their perspectives. During the interview I often checked with the interviewee my understanding of what she said to ensure that I reflect her experience and perspective accurately.

The content of the interviews was captured in extensive notes during and following each interview. Based on previous experience with in-depth interviews, I opted against taping the interviews because of trust, technical, and logistic considerations. Immediately after each interview I wrote it up in full. Women who were fluent in English and who expressed interest and willingness received the transcript of the interview for comments and revisions. Except for one young woman who asked me to omit a personal fact, all approved and expressed satisfaction with what they read.

THE SAMPLE

Eighteen women were interviewed for this book. They emigrated from Austria, Bosnia, Cuba, various parts of the former Soviet Union, Guatemala, India, Israel, Lebanon, Mexico, Pakistan, and the Philippines. They vary in age, educational, professional, and personal background, family status, and duration of living in the new culture, as well as in motivation for and pattern of migration. To be inclusive, I deliberately sought women of diverse backgrounds and experiences. Purposefully seeking such diversity of respondents is called maximum-variation sampling and is intended to obtain the best possible representation in terms of relevant factors to make the findings of the study widely applicable. The women were identified and located through diverse agencies that serve immigrants and refugees.

The women in this study settled in the United States, Israel, Australia, or New Zealand, all of which have been immigrant societies from their inception. However, the composition of immigrants changed with changes in laws and regulations. To contextualize their experiences, a brief review of immigration to these countries is presented in the next section. It is important to note that these four countries, like many other countries of resettlement, share a mixed message regarding immigration. On one hand, immigrants are welcome for ideological and economic reasons; however, a certain degree of demonizing immigrants as having negative effects on unemployment rates, welfare, and education is also present.

NATIONAL IMMIGRATION POLICIES

Immigration to the United States

The United States has always been a country of immigrants. Immigration accounts for at least one-quarter of the country's growth rate (Carlson, 1985; Reimers, 1989). The 2000 U.S. census indicated the largest immigrant population in United States history—more than 11 percent of the entire population (Singh and Siahpush, 2001). About 44 percent of the 30.5 million foreign-born Americans arrived in the 1990s (Schmitt, 2001). Most immigrants settle in large metropolitan area such as San Francisco, New York City, Chicago, Washington,

DC, Miami, and Los Angeles, with large concentrations in inner cities.

Both the composition of immigrants, from mostly European to mostly racially distinctive and from mostly men to mostly women, and the nature of immigration policy, from emphasizing assimilation to embracing multiculturalism, have changed throughout U.S. history. The higher reproduction patterns of immigrants and the attacks of September 11, 2001, reignited a heated debate regarding immigration laws and their enforcement.

Originally, most immigrants were Protestants who came from northern Europe seeking religious freedom. The roots of exclusionary immigration policy can be traced back to the seventeenth century, when the public charge doctrine was enacted to bar from entry people who could not provide for themselves and who relied on public assistance for their livelihood (Edwards, 2001). Since then it has been driven at different times by xenophobia (hatred of the "other"), nativism (the belief that the natives are superior to certain groups of immigrants), and restrictionism (concerns of negative effects of immigration patterns on society's cultural and social situation) (Schuck, 2001).

In the first half of the nineteenth century, wars and famine in Europe drove mostly impoverished Europeans to the United States. During the second half of the nineteenth century, European immigration expanded to include people from eastern and southern countries (Balgopal, 2000). Of the 32.5 million foreign-born Americans in 2000, over one-half came from Latin America and the Caribbean (Foner, Rumbaut, and Gold, 2000).

Migration from northern Europe slowed after 1890, and a new wave of immigrants from eastern and southern Europe begun. This wave included people who were attracted to economic possibilities offered by growing American manufacturing and Jews who fled the pogroms in czarist Russia. The rapid increase in immigrants led to the development of settlement houses, which were reform-oriented multi-service centers for poor immigrants.

Following an influx of non-European immigrants, exclusionary policies started to develop. Early discriminatory and restrictive legislation included the 1882 Chinese Exclusion Act, which marked the first time the United States restricted immigration on the basis of race or national origin. This measure was extended and tightened in 1892 and 1902, followed by a requirement for English proficiency, a literacy requirement in the beginning of the twentieth century, an Asiatic barred zone in 1917, and the 1924 Japanese Exclusion Act. In 1921 and 1924 nationally based quotas curtailed immigration and gave preference to northern European immigrants. Higham (2001), a historian who documented American anti-immigrant ideologies, movements, and policies, cites racist ideas and stereotypes embedded in the culture as justification of such discriminatory policies. Such exclusionary measures are still promoted by certain groups and organizations (Karger and Levine, 2000). Contemporary restrictive measures include Propositions 187 and 209 in California.

The decades of the 1940s through the 1960s saw the controversial Bracero program that allowed immigration of agricultural workers from Mexico to relocate to about twenty states to perform simple manual jobs for which no American workers could be found. A similar economic-driven political agenda informed the 1965 amendments to the Immigration and Nationality Act. These changes abolished the quota system that regulated the number of immigrants from each country, established a preference system based on skills and family unification, and allowed some refugees from dire political and economic circumstances.

Following this act, the nature and the volume of immigration to the United States considerably changed. Before 1965, many United States immigrants originated from Europe, primarily the United Kingdom, Germany, Italy, Greece, Portugal, Poland, and Ireland. In the past three decades, however, the size of the U.S. immigrant population has risen considerably, and most immigrants have come predominantly from Asian, Latin American, and Caribbean countries such as the Philippines, China, Taiwan, Korea, India, Vietnam, Mexico, Cuba, Colombia, El Salvador, the Dominican Republic, Haiti, Jamaica, Nigeria, Pakistan, Iran, and Trinidad and Tobago (Singh and Siahpush, 2001).

The 1965 Immigration Act had a specific impact on immigrant women. Because it opened the doors to unskilled and semiskilled labor, many women from the Caribbean, where male support to women and children is not institutionalized, immigrated to the United States leading to "feminization" of immigration patterns (Foner, 2000). Because many of these positions required living at the home of employers, many mothers immigrated alone and left their children to be raised by relatives in their extended kinship networks until the children could join their mothers later—thus creating the immigration pattern of "mothers first" (Francis, 2000).

During the past three decades, the pattern of immigration to the United States was mostly bimodal in terms of professional skills and educational level, with immigrants from Mexico and South and Central America concentrated at the low end and Asians and Jews from the former Soviet Union in the top end.

Because of the strict regulations for legally immigrating to the United States, many come as illegal immigrants, either by overstaying a legal visa or by entering the country with no visa at all. The immigration reform of 1986 granted undocumented immigrants who had been in the country for longer than five years the opportunity to seek legal residence, but the influx of illegal immigrants continues, especially from countries such as Mexico and Cuba.

The 1990s was the largest decade of immigration in the history of the United States, with over 10 million immigrants (Sachs, 2001). During the late 1990s, almost one million legal and 300,000 illegal immigrants arrived in America annually. These years also saw numerous changes in immigration laws and policy. The Immigration Act of 1990 expanded immigration levels by raising the annual limit for legal immigration to 700,000. In 1996 the Personal Responsibility and Work Opportunity Reconciliation Acts curtailed immigrants' eligibility for educational and social services and access to benefits, diminished legal and procedural rights of legal immigrants, toughened border enforcement, and expanded the classes of immigrants who can be deported without judicial review (Balgopal, 2000). Some of these restrictions were later mitigated. The 2000 Legal Immigration Family Equity Act made entry requirements more lenient for some specific immigrant groups (e.g., foreign-born adopted children, trafficking and crime victims, and severely disabled immigrants).

The terrorist attacks on the World Trade Center, the Pentagon, and in Pennsylvania on September 11, 2001, had a considerable impact on American immigration policy. Between 1996 and 2001 there were efforts to normalize the status of illegal immigrants, but the attacks stalled all such efforts and a wave of anti-immigrant feelings engulfed the country. Harsher interim rules regarding monitoring and addressing issues of immigrants were instituted, and an anti-immigrant atmosphere developed, including racial profiling and scapegoating. Voices blaming the United States' liberal immigration policy, suggesting that immigration laws and immigrants were a major social conduit of terrorism and demanding tighter measures to monitor the entrance of immigrants, have been heard in the media and the public (Glaberson, 2001). Immigration and Naturalization Services underwent major restructuring and reorganization, becoming the Bureau of Citizenship and Immigration Services within the U.S. Department of Homeland Security in March 2003.

Currently, most immigrant women are admitted under the provision of family reunification, continuing a tradition by which women have had more difficulty gaining entry to the United States than men based on racial nativism and the idea that higher fertility rates of immigrant women compared to nonimmigrants presents a threat to the receiving community (Kasaba, 2000). Immigrant women were treated as an addendum by the receiving society as well as by their own co-ethnic community (Seller, 1980).

In her review of the history of immigrant women to the United States, Weatherford (1986) asserts that with a few exceptions, e.g., domestic workers from the Carribean islands in the 1970s and 1980s, women most often were uneducated or illiterate. They faced more discrimination and scrutinizing than men did because they were believed to be less capable than men to support themselves. Typically, they came to reunite with their husbands after long years of staying behind in their homeland while the husband established himself in the United States—a situation that increased their status of dependency. Foreign-born women tended to marry more frequently and at younger ages than nonimmigrants. They also tended to work out of the house more and were major contributors to their families' income from their work in industry (garments, boxes) and domestic services.

Immigration to Israel

Since establishing its statehood in 1948, Israel absorbed about 3 million immigrants who make up more than half the Israeli population (Israel Record, 2001). Most of them came from the former Soviet Union, North Africa, Romania, Poland, Iraq, Iran, Turkey, Yemen, Ethiopia, Argentina, and Bulgaria.

Immigration to what is now the state of Israel started in the 1880s following pogroms in Eastern Europe. Jews from Poland and Russia relocated, driven by the dream to create a refuge for Jewish victims of oppression and persecution, which Jews in the Diaspora suffered in many of their host societies. After the Balfour Declaration of 1917, in which the British government expressed a commitment to creating a Jewish homeland in Palestine which was part of a British protectorate, Jewish immigration expanded rapidly. The 1930s saw heavy immigration from Germany and Poland of people who escaped the rising Nazi regime. In the late 1940s survivors of the Holocaust flocked to Israel, followed by immigrants from surrounding Arab countries in the early 1950s.

Eisenstadt (1954), one of the pioneer and prominent immigration researchers in Israel, differentiated between economy- and ideology-driven immigration, asserting that the former tend to maintain orientation to their culture of origin and preserve its values within the new environment, whereas the latter tend to negate ties to their culture of origin and seek to create a new identity.

The next wave of immigrants came from Eastern Europe in the 1970s following changing political conditions, and the late 1980s and 1990s witnessed the relocation of close to a million Jews from the former Soviet Union as the Iron Curtain was lifted and Eastern Europe collapsed. Most of the newcomers cited anti-Semitism, discrimination, and family reunification as motivating factors. Rescue operations in the 1990s brought over 50,000 Jews from the villages of Ethiopia, where they lived in mountain villages separated from mainstream Judaism for over 2,000 years and have maintained their traditions in the face of forced conversion, enslavement, prohibitions against emigration and land ownership, restrictions in their communal and religious activities, and other forms of persecution (Israel Record, 2001).

Immigration to Australia and New Zealand

Australia is an immigrant society. Except for the Aborigines who have been on the continent for over 60,000 years, all other Australians settled in their land within the past 220 years. Nearly one-quarter of the 18 million Australians were born overseas (Jupp, 2001). Immigration to what then was called New South Wales started with the establishment of a British penal colony in 1788, when convicts and soldiers settled on the continent, and for decades it remained dominated by men. A flow of free settlers followed since the early 1830s.

The face of immigration has changed dramatically during the years. In the early 1800s mostly British "free settlers" relocated to escape poverty and dire economic situations in their homeland. In the second half of the nineteenth century, immigrants from England, Ireland, Scotland, and China came in search of gold, and the potato famine in Ireland brought an influx of Irish immigrants.

When a federal government was established in Australia in 1901, its first act was passing a policy of "White Australia" to place restrictions on immigration and provide for the removal of prohibited immigrants from the commonwealth. During the second half of the twentieth century 5.7 million people from over 100 countries settled in Australia, greatly promoting its cultural diversity and challenging the policy of White Australia which dominated the beginning of the century (Mares, 2001).

Until World War II, most immigrants were of British and Irish descent. After the end of the war, a policy of "populate or perish" was adopted in an effort to strengthen Australia's economy. Passage permits and assistance programs were developed to help many displaced people from Europe who found their way to Australia mainly from Britain, Holland, Germany, and Italy (see http://www.immi.gov.au/facts/02Key.htm). In the 1970s wars and political unrest in different regions of Asia and the Middle East created an influx of immigrants from Cambodia, Vietnam, the Philippines, China, Pakistan, Sri Lanka, Bangladesh, Iraq, Iran, Turkey, Afghanistan, and, most recently, East Timor (Jupp, 2001).

Many of these people came by boats, creating the Australian version of "boat people" and igniting a heated public debate in the 1990s. The main issues in the debate are the effects of the number of onshore asylum seekers (people who overstay their visa or enter the country illegally and then seek asylum) on quotas of offshore refugees (who request refugee status prior to entering the country), voices against the "Asianization" of immigration, and the conditions in refugee detention camps (Mares, 2001). Many say that the selective and discriminatory tendency in accepting immigrants still exists (Laksiri and Kee, 1999). For example, during a visit of the Australian prime minister to Germany in July 2002, a manhunt for thirty-five immigrants who escaped the Woomera Detention Center in South Australia that was being conducted and the administration's tough policy regarding asylum seekers came under attack.

The most recent wave of immigrants comes from the Middle East. In August 2001, the Australian air force fought a boat stranded with 460 asylum seekers, mostly from Afghanistan, to keep them off the shores of Australia. Eventually an agreement was announced to settle them in New Zealand and the Pacific island of Nauru while the conservative Australian prime minister announced that the people would not step on Australian territory (CNN.com, 2001).

ANALYSIS OF THE INTERVIEWS

Each interview was transcribed and analyzed before proceeding to the next one. This practice offered several advantages. First, I could record fresh impressions immediately without allowing them to be diluted or "contaminated" by meeting another woman. Second, I learned from each interview additional ways of probing and more possible venues to explore, thus applying my learning and "growing" from one interview to the next.

The analysis focused on the content. There are many ways to analyze interviews. I opted to try to learn about the experience of the interviewees from *what* they told me rather than from *how* they told me. Therefore, I deliberately did not analyze such aspects of the interview as emotional expressions (laughter, tears, pitch, sighs), choice of words, pauses, sequences, and proximity of certain topics in women's narratives, which may indicate existing unconscious associations and streams of thought. I devoted full attention to understanding each woman's story about her experience.

In the analysis I searched to identify themes that came up in the interview and conducted research to enrich my knowledge about and understanding of relevant issues. For example, when I interviewed an immigrant from Ethiopia to Israel, I looked to educate myself about the history and dynamics of the odyssey of Ethiopian Jews. After interviewing a woman who came as a "mail-order bride," I researched information about this mode of exploitation. This knowledge has been incorporated into the discussion of the specific narratives and helps to contextualize the women's stories.

I also documented and explored my own reactions and their potential impact on the analysis. Finally, I related the experiences of the interviewee to those reported by women that I interviewed earlier. When analyzing each interview, I revisited all the previously analyzed interviews to determine if aspects that came up clearly in a certain interview were present or alluded to in previous interviews in a way that I neglected to identify. As a result, each interview was analyzed many times at different points along the road, and I was involved in a continuous process of self-critiquing (one may even say soul searching) to minimize and become mindful of possible effects of my own experiences and position on my understanding of participants' oral histories. Many of these thoughts, reflections, and comparisons are included in the narratives. I believe that this constant revisiting of all interviews contributes to my ability to gain an exhaustive picture of women's experiences and the construction of the meaning of these experiences which is shared with the reader.

LIMITATIONS

All methods of collecting and interpreting knowledge have limitations. The method used in this book is no exception. While it informs us about unique aspects of women's experience of immigration, it lumps together immigrant women of diverse ethnic, cultural, social, and political backgrounds and neglects to look at the particular experience of women from a specific context. Eliciting this kind of knowledge would require a different method—ethnographic research. Ethnography focuses on exploring in detail a particular social group or a culture from the viewpoint of people who inhabit that culture. For example, in the context of this book, this would have meant conducting a study of immigrant women from Taiwan, or from Cuba, and so forth. Such a method would, however, have failed to educate us about commonalties, i.e., gender-specific aspects of immigration that transcend ethnic or cultural backgrounds, which is the focus of this book.

Another limitation is related to the depth-breadth dilemma, which is typical to qualitative research. Opting to conduct in-depth, resource-consuming interviews limits the feasibility of collecting data from a large number of respondents and eventually limits diversity. Thus, for instance, some, but not all, of the many current immigration patterns to the United States are represented in the book. It includes interviews with women who immigrated on their own, with their family of origin, with their family of procreation, and as a part of chain migration, but none came in the context of mother-first migration.

In spite of these limitations and possibly others, I believe that narratives of women in this book open a window to understanding the life stories and experiences of immigrant women, illuminating their struggles and coping, and promoting our understanding of what it means to immigrate as a woman.

PART II:
STORIES OF IMMIGRANT WOMEN

Chapter 3

My Story: An Immigrant Daughter of an Immigrant Mother

My own story is placed first not for narcissistic reasons. Rather, it is to inform the reader about where I come from, about the lens through which I see, perceive, construct, and interpret the world. This is of utmost importance because who I am has a powerful impact on the way in which I heard what immigrant women told me.

A very famous Israeli poet, Shaul Tchernichovsky, who left Europe to create a home for the Jews in Israel, wrote "Man is but a reflection of the landscape of his homeland." My homeland's landscape, where I was born, raised, and lived most of my life, was in the golden dunes of the bright and sunny Mediterranean seashore, where I ran barefoot as a little girl. I carry these memories within me, and they outline the way in which I relate to people and experiences. I believe that it is important for the reader to be aware that the experiences of this little barefoot girl within me guide and affect how I see the world, judge events, and relate to people.

I am an immigrant daughter of an immigrant mother. When my mother was twenty, soon after Hitler won the elections in 1933, she emigrated from Poland to Palestine to work for her idealistic dream to build a homeland for the Jews. Fifty-seven years later I emigrated from Israel to the United States to remarry and build my new family in New York City. Of course, my nine-year-old son came with me.

Israel is an extremely Americanized society. The largest Israeli population that resides outside of the country lives in the United States. Import of scientific, professional, industrial, and cultural information and styles from the United States dominates Israel. Israelis consume American movies, music, clothes, food products, literature, television shows, housing, and lifestyles more than they adopt European norms and standards. Many Israelis express the affinity of Israelis to American culture by referring to Israel as the fifty-first state of the Union. One would assume that relocation should be less complicated for me. I was familiar with the culture, or so I thought; I spoke the language, and I had the educational and professional credentials. Little did I know. Differences were numerous and occasionally overwhelming.

Some differences were minor. For example, I still have to deliberately remind myself that summer is no guarantee against rain. In Israel one knows that between April and November there is absolutely no rain. In New York I gathered a nice collection of umbrellas because I failed to trust the forecast that predicted showers in July. In my experience this had simply been an impossible scenario. In a similar way, I was forced to buy several sweaters because I could not imagine that the sunny day, which I saw from my window, could become freezing. Different systems of measuring distances and temperatures also present a challenge. I still think in Celsius and kilometers and have a hard time figuring out how much is a pound. To bake in the United States using an Israeli cookbook becomes a real adventure. On the other hand, when I try to cook from an American cookbook, I often do not understand half of the concepts in the recipe.

Many differences between the two cultures are much more profound. I come from a society in which emphasis on the extended family and on long-term commitment is powerful. The mere idea of sending a seventeen-year-old away to college may send chills down the backs of parents. A common tradition is that "the kids" come for dinner on Friday or lunch on Saturday, even when the kids are in their twenties or thirties and have children of their own. This may sound surprising in light of the well-known fact that Israeli parents are obliged to send their children to military service at the age of eighteen. A lesser known fact is that on weekends and holidays the roads in Israel are packed with parents driving for hours to their soldiers' camps to feed them with homemade food.

The highly individualistic nature of American culture was for me very difficult to digest. Family is important to me. Nothing could have made me happier on my wedding than my stepson welcoming me as his stepmother and my son as his stepbrother. At the beginning when people asked me if my son came with me I was shocked. I could not imagine any alternate possibility. It plainly did not exist in my worldview.

When a neighbor said that her son went to school in California and I empathized that it must be difficult for her, she opened her eyes wide with surprise and said, "But I will see him soon; he will be back home for Thanksgiving." I quickly calculated in my head the number of weeks left until the end of November but bit my tongue not to say a word.

I also come from a society in which improvisation is the name of the game. It was not easy to get used to the level of abiding by policy, regulations, and rules that characterize life in America, sometimes to a degree of inflexibility that was very difficult for me to accept. One such example occurred a year after I emigrated. I took my son to Disneyland. We stood in the long line for lunch. I wanted the turkey with a salad and my son fancied the hamburger with french fries. Alas, the arrangement was that the burger came with a salad and the turkey with french fries. I asked the girl at the counter to switch the side orders. She first refused, and then upon my failing to understand the issue, she summoned the manager who explained to me in detail why my request was unreasonable and could not be respected. Frustrated, I asked for an extra paper plate, surrendered to the rule, and moved aside to do the switching myself. I did not know whether to laugh or cry.

Observing appropriate personal space may also be an issue for those who come from an open, warm, and embracing society like myself. In Israel everybody minds everybody's business. An Israeli colleague once tried to define her experience of the difference between the two cultures.

> In Israel, if I slipped in the street, everybody would be around me, give me water, give advice, call the ambulance; they would be all over me, choking me with caring. In New York, if the same thing happened, one or two people would make sure that I can get up, give me a hand, ask if I am all right and go on their way. Others, realizing that I am being helped would continue on their way and not stop to intervene. Some may mind their own business not wanting to get involved for fear of being sued.

Many immigrants have an oasis at home. Their struggle to acculturate exists as long as they are out in the world, but once they come home they slide back into familiar territory. For me the battle was twofold. I moved to a new cross-cultural marriage and a new country at the same time. I had to acculturate both outside and inside my family concurrently. Before I opened my mouth I had to remember to whom I would be speaking. With my husband I speak English. With my son I communicate in Hebrew.

I gave a lot of thought to the question of my son's education. Should he go to a bilingual English-Hebrew school? Will this not confuse him? Will this not delay his ability to learn English? Will he feel more empowered if he could do well at least in the Hebrew topics? I opted for a bilingual school. It is important to me to help keep my son's familiarity with the language and culture in which I grew up and which will remain mine forever.

Regarding the question of citizenship I was lucky. Israel is one of the few countries that has an agreement for the dual-citizenship option with the United States. Giving up my Israeli citizenship was not an option. There was no question that we would remain with two passports. Some people asked me why. There is no logical answer to this. Maybe it is not even logical, but Israel is part of who I am and giving up citizenship would be like giving up part of myself. I deeply empathized with immigrants from the former Soviet Union with whom I worked who were forced to give up their citizenship and return their passport to get permission to immigrate. I was grateful not to have to face this demand. We celebrate Israel's Independence Day and observe Israeli Memorial Day; we receive the weekend Israeli newspapers, and I keep up to date with current Israeli literature. Many of our friends are Israeli, and we often joke that we run a hotel at home for any Israeli who happens to be in town.

My son had to struggle with acquiring English while maintaining his Hebrew. He came to the United States without knowing the English alphabet and entered a fourth-grade classroom that demanded he study science, social studies, and so forth in a language about which he did not know the first thing. During the first year I spent my afternoons studying the fourth grade's material on the history of New York State. First I would read four pages and he would read one. Then I would read less and he would read more. It was a laborious and demanding uphill struggle. Occasionally I felt frustrated, often tired, but it never occurred to me to give up. In the second year I was a partner to the study of the fifth grade's book on the history of the United States. I did not master the material of the sixth grade because at that point my son knew enough English to do his work independently. Interestingly enough, when it was time to choose a high school different considerations kicked in. Cultural identity became secondary while educational and social considerations took priority. I guess that at this point our level of comfort with moving between our two cultures was enough to allow more freedom in decisions. Today my son's English is far better than mine and he does not have a foreign accent in either English or Hebrew.

The decision of where to live followed a similar pattern. After some exploration, we decided to live in a very large building in the Riverdale section of the Bronx. Overlooking the Hudson River, this huge building houses a large number of Israelis and a Hebrew school in its basement. The choice of the location reflected a compromise between our desire to live in the excitement of the city and the belief that initially a social environment in which Hebrew and being a foreigner not familiar with American ways was common would offer a smoother transition. Indeed, the place resembled a virtual kibbutz. Living an ocean away from our families, the small Israeli community developed into a "clan," sharing holidays, which are traditionally celebrated with extended family, and helping out with such matters as child care, missing ingredients in the midst of cooking, and after-school carpooling. In some ways, this took me back to the neighborhood in which I grew up, where we knew that if our parents were not home there were many doors on which we could knock to receive a warm welcome, help, and a hot meal. Years later, it was my son who urged us to move to the city.

In some ways the shift to my new culture was very easy. The hectic pace of life in Israel makes a typical New York day feel like a relaxed vacation. One example is the inviolable lunch hour. When I obtained my first consulting job, I was asked about my hours and responded that I would work from ten to six. "But you need to work eight hours," said the person who negotiated with me. I pointed out that ten to six are indeed eight hours. "But what about lunch hour?" When I indicated that I do not take a lunch hour, he looked at me as if I were a strange animal.

A workweek of five rather than six days is also a nice change. Growing up in a society in which one works Sunday through Thursday from eight to four and Friday until the afternoon, having a Saturday followed by another Saturday is a real treat.

New Yorkers may find it unbelievable, but even the city's taxi drivers are less aggressive than the average Israeli driver. If American traffic rules were applied in Israel, it would take about ten seconds for a traffic jam to occur. Everyone in Israel feels that he or she has the right of the road, everyone bypasses, and hardly anyone pays attention to regulations. In my annual visits to Israel, as soon as I land in the airport I have to turn the switch in my head from American driving to Israeli driving. My American husband tried driving in Israel but soon gave up. To drive in Israel one must be a native.

Some things were amazing and wonderful, such as the snow in winter. In Israel it never snows. Once every few years there are some flakes of snow on the high places such as Jerusalem and the mountains of Galilee. This is a good reason for half the country to stop functioning and for many to run to see the white wonder before it melts. When I saw the first snow in New York I was so excited. I put on my new woolen gloves and coat, which I had to purchase because there is no need for them in a country where the temperature hardly ever drops below the forties, and ran out to participate in the snowball wars. Initially I could not understand how one could even think in the cold, let alone function and work. However, the weather, like many other features of my new country, grew on me, and I came to love the whiteness of Christmas and New Year's Eve.

I also was impressed with the possibility to arrange so many things over the phone. This makes life so much simpler. In Israel you very often hear the statement, "This is not for the telephone." It was pleasantly surprising for me to find out how many things that I grew up to believe cannot be handled over the phone can indeed be resolved without actually waiting in line in inaccessible offices for long hours. There was also the convenience of always having public transportation and open shops and *The New York Times* daily. On Saturdays in Israel there are no trains or buses, no open shops, and no newspapers. This of course reflects the larger freedom that comes with the separation of church and state, which in Israel is inconceivable and which I cannot enjoy enough in my new country. I was fascinated by the awareness of Americans of their rights and their willingness to fight for them. I love the affordability of electrical appliances and seafood and the freedom to decide if one wants to eat kosher or not. In Israel all supermarkets are kosher, and nonkosher food is more expensive because the government does not subsidize it.

Immigration also means that one needs to establish existence in the new country not only socially, professionally, financially, and emotionally but also officially and legally. This means multiple interactions with governmental authorities, and these can be humiliating and frustrating. For example, the formal term that refers to immigrants who have been granted legal permission to stay and work in the United States is "alien," which carries less than positive connotations (the dictionary offers the following synonyms: bizarre, strange, foreign). A visit to the immigration office is often a full-day, unpleasant experience. It starts with an early morning wait outside for the building to open—men and women with babies and children, queuing in rain, snow, or under a burning sun hours before the office opens. Inside, one often encounters a suspicious attitude, pressure, long lines for the very few ladies' rooms (one of which was missing a door in two visits that were six months apart), and an examination for one's level of English, which is sometimes better than that of the examiner. Coping with the immigration authorities takes a strong sense of self-confidence, which immigrants often lack.

One step in the path to becoming a naturalized citizen is passing a qualifying test. First, my ability to read and write a couple of sentences in English was examined. Ironically, this happened a few weeks after I had published my first professional book in English. Prior to being asked to write what the tester dictated, we had conversed for a quarter of an hour and she knew that I had been teaching in a university and consulting with a social services agency in New York for the past eight years. It was certainly not her fault. The regulations required her to carefully follow the procedure. Still, I could not help smiling. It was surreal. An oral test about American history and government followed. Out of a pool of about a hundred questions, I was asked ten questions. How many amendments exist to the Constitution? Which of them constitute the Bill of Rights? Who are the governor of the state and the mayor of the city in which I live? How many members serve in the House of Representatives? At the end of the day, immigrants may have more knowledge about their new country than many native-born Americans, as colleagues whom I tested indicated to me.

A major difficulty in immigration for me was being away from my elderly parents. I was their only daughter, and when I left they were in their seventies. My son was their only grandson and they had a very close relationship with him and me. The decision to immigrate was not easy. It meant tearing a whole fabric of bonds. This left me with a heavy sense of responsibility, though not guilt. The result was that whenever anything happened with my parents I darted back to be there for them. This meant numerous twelve-hour trips for a brief stay, sometimes flying back and forth across the ocean after I addressed my obligations in the United States. Sometimes when I opened my eyes in the morning after a brief restless sleep, I was not sure if I was in Israel or the United States. Some saw it in terms of glamour: "Now you became part of the jet set, flying here and back nonstop." Others said, "You do not really live in either United States or Israel. You live in the air." Someone else framed it as "You actually are not a citizen of a country but a citizen of the globe." I could think only about how demanding and exhausting this way of life was and tried to make the best of it. I believe that immigrant women carry an especially heavy burden of responsibility for their spouses, children, and parents. Sometimes I wondered who was going to take some responsibility for me.

Immigration also offered me wonderful opportunities that probably would not have been available to me but for my relocation. It offered me an opportunity to review the path that my life had taken prior to immigration, reevaluate my options, and make major changes. In many ways it allowed me to live two lives in one. I met prominent leaders in my professional field, whom I would probably otherwise never have met. I thrived professionally, gained fluency in English, and traveled to places that would have been inaccessible to me because of my Israeli passport or because of financial constraints. Moving to the United States opened to me a whole new world of cultural and professional possibilities of which I was not even aware, let alone could have hoped to achieve. As unpatriotic as it is, I am happy that immigration saved my son from the mandatory military service required of all Israelis at the age of eighteen.

Immigration is inevitably a situation of duality, any way one phrases it. One can make it either an experience of being torn between the two parts of one's life or an experience of having the bargain of "two for one." I decided to celebrate my life as a story of multiplication rather than division.

Chapter 4

Immigrants to the United States

SONIA: FROM BEIRUT TO NEW YORK

Sonia is short and has dark hair and dark, burning eyes. She looks much younger than her age of forty-six and radiates a feeling of energy and activity—"I am young at heart." Her one-bedroom apartment is tastefully furnished with a mixture of American and Middle Eastern accessories that create a cozy and lively atmosphere.

Sonia is an accountant. She works for a large firm and is assigned to oversee and review the books of different companies in the metropolitan area. Her job requires constantly adjusting to new environments, building relationships with new people, and being assertive in a friendly way. She is well respected by her employers and is doing well professionally and financially.

Sonia goes back to her country of origin every year to visit her younger sister, whom she hopes to be able to bring to the United States one day. Both of her parents are dead, and her brother, who has recently remarried, lives in Washington state.

Sonia emigrated from Lebanon in 1983 because the ongoing war made life difficult: "I was a young woman in my early twenties. I did not want to spend endless days in bomb shelters. I wanted to have a life, so I decided to move to the United States." At that time she was a student at the American University in Beirut, so English did not present a problem for her. There was also a precedent in her family. Two older sisters of her father had already moved to the United States to study nursing and were thought of by the family as very successful, financially independent, professionally accomplished, and socially respectable. "So, since I was a young girl, I knew that there is an option, that that is something that a woman can do."

I interviewed Sonia in the midst of extreme tension between Israel and its neighboring Arab countries, four months after Israeli troops withdrew from southern Lebanon following eighteen years of Israeli control over a safety zone to protect the north of Israel from guerilla attacks supported by Syria. This interview was a special and exciting experience. In the Middle East we could not have met—we would have been enemies on different sides of the fence—but here, in New York, we sat peacefully in her apartment exchanging our thoughts and feelings about being an immigrant woman.

When war in Lebanon broke out, Sonia's school was closed. At the same time, her mother was very sick and was paralyzed. Sonia, who was home, took care of her mother until her death six months later. Soon after her mother died, Sonia decided to move to the United States to complete her education. Given that circumstances in Lebanon were unstable—her studies had been interrupted, she faced much uncertainty when life would return to normal, and she no longer had the moral obligation to take care of her mother—Sonia felt that "there was no reason for me not to go." I am intrigued by the way she chooses to phrase it. She did not say, "I had a reason to go" or "There was nothing there for me to stay for," but "I did not have a reason not to go." She is not speaking about positive motivation either to stay or to go. Rather, she emphasizes the absence of obstacles to going.

The implied element of seeking freedom became even stronger and clearer later in the interview when Sonia stated, "I appreciate the freedom to live as I find fit, without being concerned of being judged." For example, she does not accept the idea that marriage and having a family should be her ultimate goal. She feels accomplished in who she is and is willing to build a relationship only with a man with whom she really wishes to be with and share her life. She does not necessarily want to get married and instead contemplates the idea of cohabitation. This idea, which is so common in today's Western culture, would be condemned in the conservative culture of her country of origin. "I am not going to do things just because they [society, the norms] want me to," she said. "I abide by rules that make sense to me."

Thus, twenty-some-year-old Sonia followed in the footsteps of her aunts and her older brother. In the beginning she stayed with her aunt and her husband. According to Sonia, that helped because "I had support and she is a model of an immigrant woman who made it. This support was very important because initially I felt like a little ant. Everything is kind of scary."

One of the main difficulties was the lack of familiarity with American images, associations, and colloquialisms. "I knew most of the words, but I missed the associations and implications attached to them. I got the pieces but sometimes did not get the full picture." I can easily relate to the feeling expressed by Sonia. I am a university professor. I live my professional life in English. I teach, consult, and write in English. I have no problem communicating with students, colleagues, and clients, yet I am often frustrated by my inability to solve sophisticated crossword puzzles in English. Being a verbal person, I experience my lack of full mastery of the language and familiarity with its richness as a severe disability. It is very difficult to transmit this feeling of living with "tongue-cuffs" to others, especially if one speaks fluently. *Lost in Translation* is how Eva Hoffman (1989) titled her book. To me, this concept conveys the frustration experienced when one knows enough to know one misses subtleties and struggles for the accurate words.

Sonia also expressed difficulties related to differences in cultural clues: "I often did not understand why they laugh at certain points, what is conveyed behind the overt content, what is the punch line, and why it is funny." This description rings true for me as an interviewer. I remember sitting in a professional conference at which I was about to present a paper. The audience roared with laughter in response to something that the speaker said, while I remained serious. A colleague who sat next to me leaned over and, in an effort to offer friendly help, whispered in my ear, "You do not understand English?" Then, realizing that I was wearing a speaker's tag, she apologized. "Oh, I see that you are presenting, so you probably speak the language. Why are you not laughing?" I did not know how to explain without being rude that I could not see the humorous aspect of what was said.

Sonia quickly made friends and developed a rich network of relationships with other young people. She became especially close with one American roommate and spent a lot of her free time with this woman and her friends. "I was building my own little community, and these intense relationships with American young people taught me a lot about the culture, the way that people deal with each other. Even though I knew English, I did not know the slang, and some of the terms were not used in Lebanon. For example, I did not know what 'stereotypes' means." Sonia used this network of friends to promote her understanding of norms, social clues, and what is acceptable to share and what is considered inappropriate.

One issue that was particularly different in the new culture compared to Lebanon was the status of women and the relationships between genders. Women in Lebanon are legally equal but live under the pressure of many socially limiting norms and expectations. For example, following the death of a close relative, women are expected to wear black. Failure to do so initiates gossip and social criticism. When her mother died, Sonia refused to follow the custom. Soon she started to hear whispers. "Malicious gossip started to be spread that I did not respect the memory of my mother, even though it was well known that I cared for her day and night for the six months prior to her death." Yet Sonia insisted on her way, and soon she realized that a young neighbor, whose own mother had died a couple of months earlier, was inspired and also stopped wearing black. When she describes it, Sonia radiates with the feeling of victory, as small as it may be, over the patriarchal tradition of her homeland.

Women in Lebanon are considered second-class citizens, especially by the older generation. There are rich and powerful women in commerce and the financial world, but until recently women were rare in governmental and political positions. "When a rare woman achieves a position in the parliament or becomes a president of a bank, many people will denounce her as lesbian, or as not feminine," Sonia explained.

In Middle Eastern culture, women are not expected to work outside the home, which creates financial dependence on men. The message to women is "you do not have to work and you can be spoiled" and at the same time "I am making the money and put food on the table, so I have the power to tell you what to do." Sonia emphasizes how she appreciates the personal freedom that American society offers women as compared to the "controlled freedom" they experience in her homeland. She feels that although a glass ceiling for professional progress of women still exists in the West, this ceiling is much higher than the one in Arab countries.

After four years as a student, Sonia moved back to Lebanon and found a job. She could not stay in the United States because her student visa had expired. Going back to Lebanon was relatively easy, according to Sonia. "Not everybody that I knew left yet, I like the food, the climate, the country. It is still home. We Lebanese do not go away because we do not want to live in Lebanon anymore but because we have no choice due to the war. I would have definitely stayed in Lebanon. I had a good life there, but I had to leave. It was not a question of choice."

Although she enjoyed going back to her home country, upon her return she felt that she was torn between two worlds and experienced culture shock in each of them. She feels that she needs to readjust when she goes to Lebanon and also when she comes back to the United States. She is a Lebanese and an American, but not a typical Lebanese anymore, nor a typical American. "Now I enjoy going back, but I am not sure that I could live there, certainly not with a Lebanese person who never lived in the West. I am already a different woman." Sonia feels that her many years in the West make her not fit fully into either of the cultures, though she feels at home in both.

This feeling of duality is illustrated in her relationships with men. She explained that when she was young she did not like to date Lebanese men and preferred going out with Westerners. She finds Americans to be more open, more receptive of the fact that to err is human, and more comfortable about admitting mistakes, while Lebanese men have a tendency to "smother a woman." They carry the patriarchal attitude and values. This is especially true in Lebanon. For example, Sonia's family still owns a store in Beirut that is rented out. On one of the occasions that Sonia and her brother visited Lebanon, they met with the renter of the store to discuss business issues. The process required additional meetings that her brother could not attend. Because Sonia plays a main role in the fiscal decision making, she and her brother agreed that she would continue the negotiation and conveyed this arrangement to the other party. "Even though I am the accountant and I would be eventually the person who makes the final decision, the guy did not show up for the meeting. He would not perceive of a woman as a partner for negotiation. In Lebanon, because of the conservative Muslim tradition, as a woman, I would not be treated seriously in business. This guy would not come to meet me for a business meeting in the absence of my brother, the Man."

In conflict with the pleasure she finds in dating non-Lebanese men is the pull she feels toward those from her country of origin: "There is something pleasant about the fact that we come from the same place." This similarity in background is evident in all aspects of life from taste in food to preferences in recreation. Political, social, and moral interpretations of events, rituals, expectations, reactions, figures of speech, and metaphors—all are colored by one's culture of origin.

Her solution is to date Lebanese men who have lived in the Western world for some time. In a sense, she is looking for the male twin of herself, for someone who carries the legacy of her culture of origin yet has been exposed to American ideas and manners enough to have incorporated some of them into his thinking and attitudes. She smiled and said, "I guess that it is fair to say that I want the best of both worlds."

Identity and affiliation remain an issue, and Sonia believes that it becomes even more so as one gets older. For example, her brother moved to the United States as soon as he graduated from high school and has lived here for many years. He married an American at a very young age and they had a son. The couple worked hard trying to develop a restaurant, but the income was hardly enough. Soon the baby came, and raising it in the back room of the restaurant while both spouses worked long, intense hours added to the tensions. They soon divorced, and Sonia's brother remained single for many years, in spite of efforts by family members and friends to introduce him to women. Recently, he met a distant relative from Dubai and married her. They have a baby together and are expecting a second child soon. When I raised the question of culture in the divorce and remarriage, Sonia initially denied its effects. After some more thoughts she commented, "Maybe after all culture had something to do with it, and now that he is married to somebody familiar with his cultural heritage and comes from a similar background it helps things to work smoother."

She feels that at this stage in her life her culture of origin is more important and that it makes a difference to be able to share a similar culture with her partner, which cannot fully be shared with someone from a different culture of origin: "There are all these little things, which are seemingly not important. You suppress them throughout the years." She feels that one gets to a point in life when there is a nice feeling about not having to suppress these trivial details and being able to share them with one's partner: "Like we wish to eat tabbouleh [a Middle Eastern dish made of parsley, cracked wheat, onions, tomatoes, and olive oil], and we both know what it is and like it, while in the office, I eat a tuna fish sandwich with mayonnaise. In earlier years, if the guy did not know Middle Eastern food it did not matter, so we ate something else. Now, there is coziness of speaking the same language in many aspects of life. . . . When one gets older, one goes back to one's roots." So Sonia found herself in recent years dating first one and then another Lebanese man. She has known these men for years, but only in the last couple of years has she considered dating them.

I asked Sonia to tell me what helped her in the struggle to adjust: more than anything it was having friends, mostly American, some European. Of the Europeans, she said, "Their culture is somewhat closer to my own culture of origin." Thus, they could help bridge the cultural differences that she was facing. Living with Americans in close quarters and observing their ways, Sonia gradually learned to accept and feel comfortable with some of their norms and started to understand their cultural language. She especially appreciates the legitimacy of standing aggressively for her interests.

An additional source of help was her own experience of moving and coping with a changing social and cultural environment throughout her life. She recites a personal history in which instability is the most reliable component. Her father was orphaned at a very early age, and he and his siblings attended schools for orphans. Because they were ambitious and driven, they made their way into higher education. Two of his older sisters wanted to study nursing and moved to Jordan, convincing him to follow in their footsteps because they believed that in Jordan salaries and potential income would be higher. Her father moved to Amman, Jordan's capital, to study dentistry. Gradually he established his clientele there and married Sonia's mother. Sonia was born in Jordan, but soon the family moved to Lebanon, where she grew up.

When Sonia returned to her homeland after studying in the United States, she found a position with a company that distributed sewing machines for the region. Local customs make sewing machines very popular in Arab countries. The fashion industry is less developed than in the West. A sewing machine is one of the first presents a newly married woman gets because it is customary for women to make many of their own and their children's clothes. The political tension forced the company to move its headquarters from Beirut to Amman, and Sonia was one of the very few women who was willing to move with it. Later she was sent to Japan, and eventually the company moved to New York. Sonia had her green card by then as a result of her father's efforts, so she moved with the company, thus accomplishing a full circle.

All these relocations required Sonia to develop effective skills for adjusting to changing environments and circumstances. Her naturally pleasant attitude, easygoing style, and rebellious personality were helpful assets in meeting the challenges of constant wandering. "I always was a little different, a little kind of fighting for my freedom and independence. The immigration experience made me meet my own limits, stretched me to the extreme, and made me realize that I am much more powerful than I could have ever imagined. I would have never known that I have in me all these abilities and power had immigration not forced me to discover and apply them."

MARIA: I LEFT MY HEART IN HAVANA

Maria is in her early thirties. She illegally emigrated from Cuba in 1991. She lives in Queens, New York, in a barrio (neighborhood) that is heavily populated by immigrants from Central and South America. The family moved to its current location after having lived for two years in a mostly Irish and Italian neighborhood. Maria felt very isolated, lonely, and depressed in the previous location and put a great deal of pressure on her husband to relocate. "Here my people live and I can conduct my business in my own language, get the vegetables and seasoning that I like for cooking, and have friends who understand me and where I am coming from." The interview with her was conducted in a mixture of her limited English and my limited Spanish. The verbal conversation was complemented with pantomime and gestures.

Maria is married and has two sons. Her older son, a fourteen-year-old gifted violinist and honor student, was born in Cuba. Her younger son, whom she refers to as "my little one," is an active, demanding, mischievous nine-year-old who was born in the United States shortly after Maria's emigration. After his birth she had a tubal ligation to avoid additional pregnancies, explaining, "I wanted to give my children the very best, and with many children this is impossible." Her husband is a mechanic and she works off the books cleaning homes. She also occasionally works in the evenings and weekends in her original profession as a hairdresser to help the family make ends meet.

Maria's husband was the driving force behind their immigration. She herself resented the idea because she left behind a large extended family with whom she had warm and close relationships. This loss is very typical to Latino immigrants because of the emphasis on tight-knit extended families and commitment to familism in their culture of origin (Longres and Patterson, 2000). "But in our country a woman has no choice. She has to go after her husband." Maria represents what Hondagneu-Sotelo (1994) called "gendered migration decisions," i.e., decisions mostly made by men and obeyed by women. Similar to many men from South and Central America, Maria's husband came to the United States first, worked in two jobs, lived very modestly, sent some of his earnings to support the family, and saved to bring his wife and son to join him two years later.

Her husband has a work permit as a foreign visiting worker, and her younger son carries an American passport because he was born in the United States. However, Maria and her older son overstayed their tourist visa and cannot leave the country because of their undocumented status. Maria feels that "I am a prisoner in this country. I can stay as long as nobody calls the immigration and naturalization authority to report me and as long as I stay here. This may be very devastating. For example, recently my sister-in-law died in a road accident back in my country. My husband went for her funeral, but I could not go because if I left they might have put in my passport a note that I cannot come back. This broke my heart because I was very close with my sister-in-law. She was like my own sister, and here I could not go to pay her my last respect. In my culture this means a lot. Also, my little one is now spending the summer with his grandparents, but my older son cannot go there. I miss my son, but I cannot go visit him. It is like my family is split between those who have some freedom and those who don't. I am paying a bitter price for our family's immigration. My freedom is severely compromised, and I do not see any hope that this situation will ever change because the immigration authorities only get tougher and less understanding every year."

Maria misses her extended family but maintains strong relationships with them, mostly by sending them money on a regular basis. Twenty-three billion dollars are sent annually to Latin America and the Caribbean, making the flow of money a major source of income that tops all international development assistance and is increasing by an average of 11 percent per year (Thompson, 2002).

Maria feels that her efforts and sacrifices are justified in the hope to provide her children with a more secure future than they might have had in their homeland. "America offered my sons educational opportunities that my country could never have offered them. They have better prospects for a respectable job here. They will have opportunities to study and to have good jobs and a good salary. For me, this is why I came here. I feel good because I gave them the chance to succeed. Their success is my success." In spite of her inability to visit her homeland, Maria, like many immigrants from South and Central America, feels that the hardships are outweighed by the benefits that relocation can offer her children.

In contrast, however, Maria is furious about the way people from her culture of origin are looked at and treated in her new country. "The concepts 'Hispanic' and 'Latino' just make me so angry. It is true that we all speak Spanish and have some things in common, but this lumping all of us together into one sack as if we were potatoes is not right and [is] artificial. It is a word of the whites and not of my people." She feels angry at the generalizing and slandering of Cuban immigrants as "boat people." At the same time, she feels angry about the way that emigrants in Castro's Cuba are called *gusanos,* which translates as worms.

Maria feels that immigration split her family in two ways. On one hand, immigration cut her off from the majority of the extended family that remained in Cuba. "For years no telephone or mail contact was really possible, so we became two separate families. It is like somebody sawed my heart into two. One part remained in Cuba and one part here. I have my Cuban family and then I have my American family. I have many cousins, with whom not only don't I have contacts, I do not even know their names, what they look like, what they do. I did not even know that some members of my extended family existed. Theoretically, I could go by a cousin of mine in the street and not know who she is." Coming from the familistic Latin culture, Maria misses the sense of belonging to a large family.

On the other hand, her children are totally Americanized. They do not share her longing for Cuban landscapes, music, food, or culture. They become impatient when she reminiscences about her childhood in Havana and trips with her father to the seashore. They see themselves as Americans.

One aspect about which Maria feels a sharp difference between her culture of origin and American culture is gender relationships. She criticizes her husband for maintaining a macho attitude: "He is dominant and controlling. He still did not realize that we are here, in the United States of the year 2000. He still carries the culture of men and women like it was in my country." Comparing the male-female relationships she observes in homes in which she works to those in her own family, she cites a typical situation to illustrate the difference between the two worlds. "I come from work exhausted and stand in the kitchen to prepare dinner. My husband sits in front of the TV to watch the news. He is thirsty and calls for me. I dry my hands and come. He demands water. I go back to the kitchen and bring him water. He tastes it, mutters that the water is not cold enough, and sends me back to bring some more ice. Why can he not get up, go to the kitchen, and take the ice himself while I am busy in the kitchen? Yet I was brought up to respect my man's wishes and address his needs. Here I see that matters are different. Since I love him, I go along with it. The moment I enter the house, I shelf my American self and become the 'little obedient wife' that he wants me to be."

Maria sees herself first of all as Cuban and is ambivalent about the fact that her children are "too much assimilated. I was too successful and they became totally Americanized. They refuse to talk to me in Spanish; they do not even know Spanish that well anymore. Their language more or less remained like when they came here. They have the Spanish of young children and not of their age level. They even lost some of it. [Giggling] I think that the only reason they still have some of their Spanish is so that my husband and I would not be able to tell secrets in a language that they do not understand. All this gives me a lot of pain." At the same time, her sons follow their father's macho attitude. "My sons also demand the same services like their father, but I explain to them that a girl that grows up in America will not agree to do all these things for them. My oldest once asked me why I continue to provide all these services and allow his father to control me, but at the same time he expects me to serve him too."

Maria is jealous of the way a distant relative managed to maintain a much stronger Cuban identity in her own family. "She married a Cuban patriot. He insisted that the children have Cuban names, she cooks Cuban food, and her home is decorated in a Cuban style. When you enter that home, you leave New York and you are in Cuba. The children were always told, 'Here is Cuba.' They speak to their children in Spanish, insist that any note children leave them is in Spanish, and they do not respond if a child speaks to them in English. Their children are respectful and do not talk back to their parents. Expectations of chores for boys and girls are clear."

In recent years, windows for revisiting Cuba opened. Maria's husband rushed to revisit his homeland, while Maria cannot. "I wish I could go there, but I can't because of my status. However, even if I could, I am not sure that I would. I would have a lot of fear; there are forces that pull me back and those that hold me from wanting to go back. The crisis around Elian Gonzales's* case created in me a lot of mixed feelings. I probably would have eventually opted against going, but I am still not sure that this is the right decision. Going there would have made coming back here difficult. If things were good there I would wish to stay where my heart belongs. If things are bad, it would hurt me very much. So, no way is a good way; maybe it's better that I can't decide, it's not in my hands and I have no choice."

Maria describes language as the greatest hurdle. "Even though I speak English pretty well, I sometimes fail to understand what is being asked of me, and I quite often have the feeling that people lose patience with me. It may be quite uncomfortable, so sometimes I nod and pretend to understand the joke, but I really do not. Also, in arguments I feel an inferior position because it takes me longer to find the words that express what I have to say. Sometimes on my way home or later in the day, I find myself thinking, 'This is what I really wanted to say; I should have said so and so.' But, at the moment that things happen it is very difficult and I am at a loss. This is an awful feeling, like a lost sheep in unfamiliar surrounding."

Maria also feels handicapped in understanding the dominant culture and feels that she and her family miss opportunities because of her lack of familiarity with mainstream norms. For example, her older son is a gifted child. His teacher recommended him for qualifying exams for one of the two top schools in the city. This prestigious school offers excellent free education and is very competitive, and its graduates are traditionally admitted into the best colleges in the country. New York's brightest adolescents take preparatory courses and private lessons to get ready for the examination, which can be taken

---

*Elian Gonzales is the young boy who was saved at sea by fishermen in 1999, when an overloaded boat of Cuban refugees sank. His mother and stepfather drowned, but the boy survived by clinging to an inner tube floating off the coast of Florida. Following a heated public debate concerning whether to grant him asylum or return him to Cuba to his father's custody, the boy was returned to his father by the U.S. Supreme Court.

on only one date in each academic year. The high school entrance examination is a major agenda item in families of junior high students in New York for many months. The teacher was confident that Maria's son could achieve a score that would make him eligible for this special school, but Maria was not aware of the meaningful effect that participating in the test could have for her son's future and declined to reschedule a nonurgent medical appointment she made for the date of the exam. Only months later was she made aware of the significance of her decision. "Because I am not part of this society and do not know the rules, my son lost a golden opportunity. Nobody bothered to educate me about the meaning of the situation. In my country this would not have happened to me. I know all the unwritten rules. Here I am in a strange land and feel like it."

Three major factors help Maria in her struggle. The conviction that she is doing something good for her children's future has a central role. "I have it difficult, but they will have it easier. Hope that my compromises today promises my kids a brighter future is very powerful. After all, my sons are probably the most important thing in my life, and knowing that I contribute to their chances for success is very comforting for me and gives me the power to continue." Initially her children blamed her and she blamed herself. "You brought them there, so you ought to know, and yet you don't. You feel humiliated, guilty, and have a hard time coping with their complaints [of] 'so why did we come here?' I felt more than once like throwing my hands in the air in despair and going back." Gradually this despair decreased: "Now I and they are happy that I did not."

Having moved among neighbors with similar ethnic backgrounds also helps Maria in her daily struggle because it ameliorates her loneliness and homesickness. The fact that the family did not initially live in an ethnic enclave exacerbated her feelings of loneliness and alienation. Having initiated the family's relocation to a mostly Latino neighborhood helped Maria feel more at home in her new country. "I created for me my own village, my own local extended family where people speak my language, understand where I am coming from, and with whom I share and interact in ways that are familiar to me. People respect the same values as I do, think along the same lines, understand things in similar ways. It makes me feel a little bit at home. Like I have a bit of my homeland in Queens. Of course I would have preferred to live among my own people back home, but here I have like a little version of 'back home.' One of my neighbors here lived close to me in Cuba; people here know my family; this helps." Such mostly Latino neighborhoods are rich in natural support networks. Latino-owned businesses and services meet the needs of the community, as well as provide a venue for developing companionship, emotional support, and role models to help sustain Latino customs and traditions (Longres and Patterson, 2000).

Finally, the knowledge that she has no choice is a powerful force: "It is not like I have a choice. My circumstances do not leave me many options. What could I do? Go back and leave my husband and my little one? I must stay, so I struggle to make the best of it."

A famous medieval Jewish poet who resided in Spain wrote, "My heart is in the East [Israel] and I am at the end of the West [Spain]." Maria's version could be, "I am in the North, but my heart is in the South."

NADRA: THE "DESERT" GENERATION

Nadra came from India in 1999. In her early twenties, she moved to the United States with her family. Her father is a businessman and her mother a homemaker. "My mother was sixteen when she had me and we lived with my father's family, as the tradition is with many families in India, so that in early years it was practically my grandmother who raised me and my sister [a medical student, two years younger than Nadra]. Then, when we moved to a separate home, mother raised us single-handed. My father was always busy with his business, his friends, his mistresses; who knows what else. She is the one that always was there for us, yet he was the one who made, and to a great degree still makes, all the decisions for the family."

Nadra is a part-time student working toward a degree in business. She is also employed in her father's company. Her parents observe a very traditional lifestyle and demand the same of their two daughters. "It is inconceivable that I or my sister leave home to live on our own unless we get married. It would certainly have scandalized the family if I ever went to live with a boyfriend. My parents compromised quite a bit by understanding that we may not abide by arranged marriages, even though I know that my mother would still be very happy if I agreed to marry a young relative who would come from India to marry me here. This way she and my father could check his background, his family, his history."

Nadra did not choose to immigrate and was quite furious when it was imposed on her by her father. "When I was told that we were going to move to the United States, I was quite devastated. I loved the calm atmosphere in India; I had my friends, my things, my studies, and my life. I did not want to move, but I had no choice. My father decided that we move, so we had to move. Now that I know a little about the American ways, I realize that in many American families things could not happen this way. They might have had family discussions, ask all family members. I also can envision some of my friends refusing to do as their parents decide and standing on their own. Some might have not moved with the family. But with us things are different. My father is the head of the house. When he decided to move, my mother and us, the daughters, did not have much say. We had to go along. In my country it is so. My sister was quite happy, but my mother and me, we were not happy at all, but it did not matter."

In spite of her feelings, she soon found herself in a new country, with new habits, new ideas, and new friends. Yet she perceives herself as very much restrained by the traditional Indian ways. "I prefer to wear my hair cut Indian style, my dresses are mostly made by an Indian dressmaker who lives in my neighborhood, I eat mostly Indian food, we observe Indian rituals, and many of my friends are Indian. I know that this sounds stupid, but I have their [her parents] traditions in my blood. I also know that it will deeply hurt them if I do not keep many of their traditions. Recently my father started talking about inviting the son of his cousin, a single young man in his thirties, to explore the possibility of arranging a marriage between us. To my own surprise, I am not totally against the idea. After all, when I look around and see how frequent people who choose their own mate realize their mistake and divorce, causing pain to all involved, I think that maybe there is some logic to the idea that parents have a better judgment about their children's potential spouse. I know that this sounds so old-fashioned, but I guess that growing up the way I did clipped my wings."

She vows that when she gets married she will raise her children, especially her daughters, to have more autonomy than she has or believes that she will ever have. "You may say that I am the bridge, the desert generation that lost the chance to have it my way but I will do my best to raise my daughters to have more choices than I." Saddened and surprised to hear such surrender from a young woman, I asked if having so many years ahead of her to live in the United States does not offer her a chance to do things differently, if she wishes too. She shrugged and said, "I guess I have too much India in me." Perhaps even my question and the assumption that guides it about people having choices come from my Western mind-set, so different from Nadra's.

Nadra suspects that two factors have been crucial in shaping the way she is: immigrating in her late teens and immigrating with her family. Growing up in traditional, patriarchal Indian society, with its strict social stratification, she internalized the expectations of a woman to be docile, submissive, and obedient and to serve the needs of her husband, children, in-laws, and extended family. She describes feeling like someone who stands with two feet anchored in two separate lands, but the foot that stands in India is stronger than the one that stands in the United States: "I know enough to recognize the availability of other alternatives, I even appreciate them, but I feel that I personally can adopt them only to a limited degree."

Nadra believes that she would have been able to be Americanized to a greater degree had she come to the United States earlier in her life. To support her opinion she points to her younger sister who, unlike Nadra, went away to college. "My parents were very much against it. However, she convinced them that this is not really like going to live on her own and that she wants to get the best education that she can get. Education has always been a priority for my parents, and because she was accepted into a top medical school, they reluctantly gave in. They still expect her to come back home after she graduates, but I am not so sure she will. She spent her formative years here and learned many of the local ways. She has a way of doing her own thing and making my parents somehow live with it."

Immigrating with her family rather than on her own also held Nadra back from adopting American norms. "I was raised to respect my parents, and I know that they would not have approved of much of what American girls my age are doing." She feels caught in a bind that is largely created by herself rather than by any external pressure. She feels that she has "too much India in me" and could not in good conscience give herself permission to become more Americanized, because she knows that this would hurt and upset her parents. The story of Lee (2000), who documented her own struggle of being too

Korean for America and too American for Korea, lends support to Nadra's observation.

Nadra reports that adjusting to the American norms about male-female relationships is especially difficult for her. "I have been educated to be polite and shy around men. The confident, self-assured, and independent way of girls with guys here leave me bewildered, as do the expectations of men that I share the expenses when we go out. I find the open conversations among girls about their sex life also something hard to cope with. To me these are such intimate and private topics, and I would not dream talking with others about what and how I do with whom, not that I do much because I am quite old-fashioned in these matters."

A couple of hours into the interview, Nadra, who thus far had explained in detail how much of India she carries in her, sighed deeply and said, "The problem is that at this point I became a misfit in India also. Now I am a foreigner in both cultures, I feel [I am] the eternal 'other,' the one that does not belong." Having learned some of the ways of the new country yet carrying the heritage of the old one, receiving mixed signals from her parents who expect her to acculturate and adapt to American norms yet remain an appropriate Indian young woman has confused and often frustrated Nadra: "You want to know what is my story of immigration? I can summarize it in one sentence: To work I wear business suits and when I come home I change into a sari, and I do not feel especially comfortable in any."

In her confusion, Nadra found immersing herself in her studies a major source of support, satisfaction, and refuge. It also offers her a route for acculturation; however, her confusion is also expressed in her career choices, as she opted to stay at home and to work for her father. She is an honor student: "I grew up in a home where excellence was an expectation and mediocrity was not an option." Now the pressure to excel is translated into performance in the family business. She explained, "It looks like I am independent and have achieved all that I probably would not have achieved in India, but to a great degree this is a false front. In many ways I live within the same old traditional world and rules, except it is packaged as a modern one. It is the new version of the old reality where women are to be seen and not to be heard and in many ways belong to the men in their life."

KLARA: A LIFELONG TALE OF RELOCATIONS

Klara is in her third migration from one country to another, but her life included additional major relocations. When she was a toddler, she moved from Europe to Israel with her parents. Soon after the family resettled in the new country, her father died. Her mother remarried and her stepfather insisted that Klara be placed in an orphanage, to be moved to a residential setting when she turned six. "Most of us were immigrants. Our families survived the Holocaust, and we had to deal at the same time with the past, with being the 'outcast' vis-à-vis Israeli-born *sabras* [this concept, which is the name of a cactus fruit, is used to describe the 'thorny' and tough Israeli-born person]."

In 1986, Klara moved with her husband and four children to New York, where she adopted yet another baby. Her thirty-year-old daughter lives with her husband, who emigrated to Israel from the Netherlands, and her own two children in Israel. Recently the whole family moved back to Israel. The interview with Klara was conducted in Hebrew in New York when she came for a brief visit, about a month after she moved back to Israel.

"One does not understand what absorption really means until one experiences it firsthand. Only now, when I realize how everything is different and how I need to think about each step that I am used to take automatically, I start to understand what the newcomers to Israel when I was growing up went through." Israel was engulfed by immigrant Holocaust survivors in the late 1940s and by immigrants of eastern and North African origin following its independence in the early 1950s. Housing was scarce and the economy was very bad. People were packed into tents and temporary residences for long periods of time, where they experienced unemployment, disease, extreme poverty, and often unreceptive and insulting attitudes from the Israeli-born and veteran population.

During all of these moves, the absence of familiarity with the world around her was very challenging. Furthermore, from relocation to relocation it did not become easier. One might think that a person who successfully coped with one experience of immigration might be better equipped and have acquired skills for dealing with the hardships of migration. According to Klara, this is not the case. "With each additional relocation, one brings more 'baggage,' in the form of more tangible possessions that require more complicated decisions [about] what goes into the suitcases and what is left behind, as well as more experiences. To move with children is more complicated in every sense than to move as an individual or a young couple."

The escalating difficulty reflects an emotional issue. Repeated relocations create an anxiety of shortage and deprivation that lead to insecurity. This feeling of insecurity may create an urge to always be equipped beyond the real need, to be prepared for all circumstances. "I come for a ten-day visit in America with two packed suitcases. This is ridiculous and illogical because there is no sense in traveling with the whole house. After all, if I travel light and realize that I forgot something, I can always buy it, but there is that deep feeling of an immigrant 'lest I will miss it.'" Klara believes that the experience of loss and void from meaningful possessions translates in the mind of immigrants into an ever-present hole, which they constantly strive to fill. A major aspect of immigration is the need to leave behind all that is dear and familiar—a home, friends, a family—and to move to a new place where one lives, at least initially, with financial, social, and emotional emptiness.

Lack of familiarity with rules and norms in the new society is very complicated and may create embarrassing situations. For example, Klara recounted a situation in which the family was invited to a social event shortly after having come to the United States. "I baked cookies, and they smelled really good. I packed them nicely in a box. When my children first tasted them, they contorted their face with disgust. It turned out that, not familiar with the packaging of different sorts of margarine, I baked the sweet cookies with salted margarine."

Klara believes that women experience the greatest challenge because they are called on to cope with their own immigration-related difficulties as well as their spouse's and children's difficulties: "It all falls on the wife/mother. When we came to the United States, I had to deal with my own adjustment and simultaneously facilitate the adjustment of four children, each in their own level of development with their own unique difficulties. I had to take all the burden on me to allow my husband the quiet he needed in order to focus on his quick adjustment to free him to focus on making a living for all of us."

Challenges for mothers seem to her to be especially demanding. "As a mother I felt very challenged and occasionally helpless. My eight-year-old daughter requested that I explain to her how to solve long-division exercises and I did not have a clue what she means."

The current relocation to Israel is even more demanding: "Now, upon our moving back to Israel, I am again busy with investing in facilitating everybody's adaptation. I relocate with a twenty-two-year-old who is totally unfamiliar with the youth culture there. He left a girlfriend here and needs to find himself professionally, socially, and personally. My twenty-three-year-old loves the country and wants to live there, but he left it as a very young child and now has to accommodate his plans and dreams to a new reality. My fifteen-year-old has no Israeli friends at the tender age when peers are of utmost importance, and even the baby had to be separated from his beloved and familiar nanny and get used to a new environment, a new language, a new climate, in short, a new everything."

Klara was the motivating power for the relocation of the family to Israel. She has a vested interest that everybody will feel good, so that they will stay in Israel and not go back to the comfort and familiarity of the United States. These feelings should be considered within the political circumstances in the Middle East at the time of family's relocation. The collapse of the peace talks and the Oslo Agreement, ongoing violence and threats of war, escalating economic distress, and military instability are less than optimal circumstances for reabsorption. The fact that three of Klara's sons are at the age of mandatory military service is a potential exacerbating factor for tension and anxiety. She sees herself as having the major responsibility for the welfare of all, and this is a draining and lonely experience.

An incident from her first weeks in New York demonstrates the level of loneliness of immigrant women. "One day I hit bottom. Things were not going well for all of us. We were all in a crisis. I broke down and said, 'Enough, I cannot take it any more. I have had it. I am going.' It was snowing, the day was dreary, and I was depressed. I went down to the car. It was a cheap old one, because we could not afford anything better. I never knew how to clear snow. I did not have the necessary instruments, since I come from a country where it never snows. Somebody stopped and helped me to clear the snow. After much effort I managed to ignite the car and started driving . . . and suddenly I realized that I do not have anywhere to go. In my homeland I could, under similar circumstances, stop at any of several dozens homes, knock unannounced on the door, and ask for coffee and sympathy. [Norms of visiting in Israel are much more flexible than in the United States. It is perfectly acceptable to 'drop in for a cup of coffee' just because one happens to be in the neighborhood without making prior arrangement, and children seldom arrange 'play dates,' which is a surprising, not to say shocking, concept for many immigrants.] Here, I was just stuck, disheartened, and in need of camaraderie as I was, with nowhere to go. I drove around for a while and crawled back home beaten and defeated with my tail between my legs. At that point I made up my mind that I am going to make it, no matter what. I knew that I did not have the courage to pack my belongings and go back home; therefore, I had no choice but to struggle. This knowledge of no alternatives and being caught with my back to the wall gave me power."

It seems that having hit bottom was a pivotal point for Klara. She believes that what gave her power was the realization of weakness, of having no real alternatives. The power of facing one's lowest ebb as a turning point is not unfamiliar in human experience. For example, one of the most basic ideas in twelve-step programs such as Alcoholics Anonymous is that addicted persons are not ready to quit their habit until they hit bottom. Only when they confront the understanding that they are caught in a dead-end downward spiral are they ready to make a change.

Klara's main motivation for going back to Israel was her wish to maintain close relationships among family members. Given that Israel is geographically smaller and a much more familistic society than the United States, relationships between adult children and their parents remain more close-knit. Family is important to Klara, and she believes that the move back to Israel will contribute to her ability to continue to see her three adult children and their families on a regular basis. "If we stay in New York, they will all scatter to different parts across the nation. One will be in Michigan, the other in California, and I will only see them on Thanksgiving and the high holidays." In Israel she visualizes that all will remain close. Family is important to her, and she does not want to sit alone with her husband on Friday night. Israel, in her opinion, allows more opportunities for keeping close. "On Friday evening we traditionally sat a table for Sabbath dinner. The older the children are and have their own families, the larger the table we sat."

She disapproves of the American norm of children attending college away from home. Her son, who lives in a separate apartment in the same building, has a girlfriend who lived with him for the past three years. Now that he has moved to Israel, she must find another place to live. The modest salary she makes as a student does not allow her to rent an apartment, and her parents are reluctant to let her come back home to live with them in their large apartment for more than a short time. Klara resents this style of parenting. She sees herself as "mother earth," who likes her offspring to have their independent lives, yet remain connected to the family. She rented apartments for her older sons in the same apartment building in which she is going to live in Israel so that they will feel comfortable to pay a visit, come for dinner, and still maintain their own lives.

Coming from the same culture, I can easily relate to what Klara says. Relationships and commitment between family members are indeed stronger in the Israeli culture. We all find diverse ways to maintain family closeness. For example, when I go away to conferences, I call home every day. When my elderly parents were in their eighties and I lived in the United States, every small occurrence immediately caused me to drop anything that I was doing, jump on the first plane, and make the twelve-hour trip from New York to Tel Aviv to handle what needed to be handled. When colleagues and friends thought that I went beyond the call of duty and were concerned about how all this was affecting my work and my life, I was appalled, because to me it was clear that I was not doing more than what one should do under such circumstances. My parents were devoted to me for so many years, and I should be devoted to them when they needed me. By the same token, when my son decided to go to college in the city and continue to live at home, my Israeli friends assumed that I must be happy while my American friends expressed their sympathy for me "having to put up with him at home." When we renovated the apartment to create a private space in a way that allowed him to continue to enjoy all the services of the house, reactions such as "but in this way he will never leave home" were totally alien to my way of thinking.

Klara recognizes the bright side of immigration. Having lived in the United States allowed her to develop broader perspectives of people, approaches, perceptions, interpretations, judgments, and reactions to people, events, and experiences. However, she believes that when immigrants get involved in the daily stream of events, they cannot appreciate enough the benefits of the relocation: "Only when I went back to Israel, I gained the necessary perspective to understand what America gave me."

TARA: I WILL SHOW THEM

Tara came from Albania in 1981, following her dream since age seven to become an actress. Now forty-five, she "feels like two hundred and five" and is single. Tara grew up in a conservative aristocratic family. Currently she works as an office director for her brothers, who are in the construction business, and is writing and publishing articles and short stories in both in English and Albanian.

She remembers herself as a rebel from an early age. She always wanted to be free to speak, to express her feelings, and to accomplish her goals. She resented the idea of getting married at sixteen, as the norm was. In traditional Albanian culture, girls and women were clearly second-class citizens. The birth of a boy was celebrated, while the birth of a girl was tolerated. From an early age girls were raised to be housewives and mothers.

When Tara was a toddler, her father died, leaving her and her brothers to be raised by their domineering, smart grandmother and their twenty-five-year-old weak-willed, widowed mother who was always dressed in black and depressed. Tara feels that she carries within her the spirit of the two women who raised her and oscillates between her strong self and her passive self.

Tara's adventures of relocation started as soon as she reached adolescence. At age fourteen she ran away from home and used money that she stole from her grandmother and the passport that she took from her mother's drawer to go from Albania to Turkey, where an American family took her in. She was found out and deported back to her hometown to be met with criticism and resentment. "The situation was unbearable. I was treated like I did not exist, people distanced themselves from me, and I said to myself that I am not going to allow them to break me; I will show all of them." This experience might have shaped the way in which Tara dealt years later with the hardships of immigration. "Showing them" became a motto in her life.

The memory of being treated as an outcast and being excluded is vivid in Tara's mind today. Exclusion is a typical experience of immigrants. Some of it is done intentionally and some out of negligence. I am no stranger to the experience of sitting in company and, in spite of my good command of English, not understanding the conversation because of culturally related associations, idioms, and colloquialisms. For example, I was auditing a doctoral class at Columbia University and somebody mentioned that he did not have his ruby slippers on. Having not grown up with the legacy of *The Wizard of Oz* and not being familiar with the American icons of Dorothy and the Scarecrow, I had no idea what he was saying. Such incidents are part of the daily fabric of immigrants' experiences.

Immigrants also are subjected to much joking at their expense because of ridiculous mistakes they make. In professional meetings I often use expressions translated literally from Hebrew that make my colleagues smile. For example, I stated that a committee I chaired had created "a skeleton for a program," which is figuratively used in Hebrew to describe the general structure of a plan. An amused colleague asked me if the committee found all the bones. Once I was trying to alert against using a certain concept and warned that this concept would be like "showing a red rug to a bull." What I meant of course was "a red flag." On another occasion, I told somebody that "I like to pick up on his mind," and yet another that I would be happy "to cover up" for her rather than "to cover her classes" when she had to go away.

Such incidents make immigrants constant learners who are always climbing uphill. It is not surprising, therefore, that Tara asserts that the slightest sign of being ignored, rejected, or excluded throws her back to the painful experiences of her youth. When she answers the phone and people do not talk or hang up, the experience of invisibility is forcefully reactivated. "Even though I know rationally that the person on the other end of the line might have made a mistake and dialed the wrong number, I take it personally: 'Here I go again rejected, unwanted.' Every time it is a slap in the face."

Tara remembers being interviewed for a position as an administrative assistant to a famous and prestigious professor at an Ivy League university who specializes in understanding the experience of being uprooted from one's homeland. "I came all dressed up and excited to meet the person who is the embodiment of a successful immigrant. Just the idea of working close to such an icon filled me with pride and a sense of importance." A few days later his plans changed and Tara was not hired. Most painful and hurtful to her was the fact that he did not call to offer an explanation or an apology. "It was as if I am again that nobody, human dust that can be easily ignored and dismissed."

Upon her immigration she struggled with poverty, unemployment, medical issues, injuries, discrimination, and bureaucracy. "I worked in child care and elderly care. I served as a waitress from dawn to midnight. I served as a dog sitter. I was up and down in the world. I had servants and now I was a servant; I saw the world from both sides." Throughout these changes she never gave up on seeking opportunities to learn and develop her abilities—Hebrew, dancing, drawing. She soon became the first woman from her country to receive political asylum. She graduated college and completed a master's degree in liberal studies and performing arts from a prestigious university. Throughout this journey she always seized opportunities and worked to reinvent herself: "First you demolish, then you reconstruct." The demolishing phase took long years of pursuing education and assimilation. The process of reconstruction has been slow and difficult. Tara became involved in the Albanian community by helping with immigration papers, writing in Albanian newspapers, representing the Albanian community, participating in advocacy efforts that included a visit to the White House, and serving as vice president of a public interest group of Albanian women.

Six years after she immigrated, Tara brought her mother to the United States. Her mother hated everything about the United States—the food, the clothes, the culture. Criticizing the host culture is not uncommon among immigrants, while the homeland is often idealized and remembered with nostalgia. An immigrant social work intern from the former Soviet Union whom I supervised used to long for the smell of apples: "There, when you opened the door, the sweet fragrance of the fresh apples in a bowl on the table would make you drunk. Here the apples are like pieces of synthetic plastic." This nostalgic longing is more pervasive among immigrants who were forced to leave their homeland reluctantly than among those who opted to emigrate. Often opportunities to go back and visit help the immigrant develop a more realistic perception of both cultures. For Tara, however, her mother's reaction was perceived as an additional rejection.

What helps in coping with these experiences and their emotional toll? For Tara it was the need "to show them." She describes herself as having a drive for victory over the "evil forces." This has been a dominant force throughout her life. When she moved to Belgrade at a very young age, following in her father's footsteps and pursuing a career in pharmacy, it was a risky choice. As the war in the 1990s in the former

Yugoslavia proved, there has always been animosity between Albanians and Serbs. Albanians have been treated badly, ignored, and put down. For a young Albanian girl to go study in Belgrade was a provocative protest of daring to enter the lion's den. The same mechanism guided her struggle with immigration. She was determined "to prove them wrong." Who constituted the "them" varied. At times it could have been her mother, her Albanian compatriots, or American colleagues. Combative, determined, ignoring norms of personal space, involved in political and social activism, Tara challenged them all, tirelessly pushing forward.

The pattern of exposing herself to potentially hurtful situations and coping with them is typical of her. It brought her suffering as well as interesting adventures, but mostly it brought her a constant sense of walking on the edge and making it. Always incredibly determined, "I have an iron will and I am not a quitter," she struggled with an extremely stressful financial situation, a severe injury in an accident, and numerous medical issues to pursue her education and develop into a writer in English and Albanian. She relates her persistence to her constant search for love. "I grew up feeling unloved, but as a child I could not understand my mother and empathize with her difficulties. She lost her husband as a young woman, sunk into her depression, and could never fully mother me." Tara relates her mother's lack of mothering skills to her own circumstances. Her mother grew up as the orphan of a father who was exiled and a mother who died young of cancer. She eventually was wed in an arranged marriage to a man who did not love her and who died at the age of twenty-eight, leaving her to raise three young children on her own. Tara sees these circumstances of her own growing up as partly responsible for the long winding road she had to take until she could come to terms with who she is.

Now, at forty-five, after a hysterectomy and lifelong fights against injustice and discrimination of women in her culture of origin, she finally feels able to let go of the active "doing" part of herself, which she views as masculine, and to be in touch with her femininity. She can balance the strong, combative, struggling side of herself with the delicate, receptive side. "Now I am in contact with my tenderness, softness, emotionality. Now I can stand on two feet and write a book about the rebellious womb as my way to unify those two feet, the tough foot and the soft foot." Tara feels that she finally found her "true me." She feels that she got over the part of unfulfilled emotions in her family. "Being an immigrant, first you demolish and then you reconstruct. I got to the part of being reconstructed and being the full me."

Part of the reconciliation with herself is the wish to visit her homeland. "This impulse is always there, pushing me to retreat to my roots." Tara was the first in her family to leave these roots. She came to the United States with no command of English, no money, and no support. She has the wish to go back and show her country of origin that in spite of the cultural, political, social, and familial obstacles, she now has it all: a degree, status, strength, personal respect, and her place in the new world.

SARAH: THE QUIET FIGHTER

Sarah is thirty-five and looks much younger. She is modestly dressed, wears no makeup, and speaks softly, almost apologetically. The content of her speech, however, is assertive and determined, though expressed in docile gentle words and tone. She is married to a physician and has two sons who are eight and five years old. She lives in a nice, racially mixed, middle-class neighborhood and is studying for a PhD in clinical psychology. Sarah emigrated from Pakistan in 1991.

She runs a Pakistani house. In spite of her full-time school work and clinical internship, Sarah carries all the traditional roles of a homemaker. She cleans, does the laundry, shops, drops her children at school and picks them up, oversees their homework, attends parent-teacher meetings, and cooks. Cooking is one aspect of domestic responsibilities that has changed following Sarah's decision to return to school to pursue an advanced degree and professional education. "I could not be available to tend to my husband's needs. Previously I would cook two different fresh meals a day and we seldom ate out. Since I started school we do a lot of 'quick stuff.' That took some adjustment." A closer look at what Sarah defines as "quick stuff" reveals cultural gaps. She does not mean ordering in or using ready-to-microwave meals; rather, she refers to preparing barbecue and baking, which by any Western criterion would be considered cooking, instead of spending endless hours stewing traditional slow dishes. "One year, when I was really very busy, we even ordered sometimes Indian food from a nearby restaurant."

Her family and social environment did not support Sarah's return to school. Her conservative, traditional culture of origin has a clear and well-defined structure of strict gender-specific expectations. "As a woman, I am supposed to get married, have kids, and run my household." As she was growing up, the message was that the mission of a woman is to be a good wife and a good mother. Education was not considered important or desirable beyond high school or the necessary minimum for a "womanly" profession such as teaching. Listening to Sarah, one is thrown back to the time in American history when social norms pushed Betty Friedan to write *The Feminine Mystique* critiquing the limited opportunities allotted to women in the 1950s.

Sarah grew up in a traditional Pakistani family. She was orphaned at an early age. Her mother died when Sarah was thirteen. Her sisters and brother were all in their teen and preteen years. When her mother died, the extended family pressured Sarah's father to stop the girls' education. "In Pakistani tradition women are not expected to study a profession, just enough to be able to work and contribute to family income, if necessary." Sarah's father gave in to the pressures and refused to continue to support his daughters' education. However, the siblings were determined to help one another pursue their education. They developed a strong mutual support system, took on tutoring of younger children, and paved their way to government-supported affordable education. "I had no choice but to excel. I had to sacrifice my social life; I had no time for fun. My whole life was about learning and staying at the top. This was the key. I knew that I had to give up something to get something else, and it was clear to me what was more important in the long run." Sarah's persistence and dedication helped her attain high scholarly achievements. Excelling helped her regain the recognition and approval of the family that previously condemned and tried to sabotage her desire to learn. "This affirmed my determination and taught me a powerful lesson," she explained.

Meanwhile, her father remarried but then died seven years later, leaving the siblings to live together and continue to support one another. However, this sibling-based family could not adequately nurture its members. Marriage became the most practical and culturally acceptable way to proceed at that point.

According to the prevalent custom, Sarah participated in an arranged marriage. "Arranged marriage are based on reason and rational mutual evaluation of the families and especially the ability of the husband-to-be to support a family." In her case, the process was simple, since the families knew each other and belonged to the same community. Both families lived originally in Bombay, India. Indian society is highly stratified, and people tend to stay within their own caste. Sarah's mother was very community oriented and strongly believed in maintaining close and protected relationships with people from her own city. The family of Sarah's husband came from the same social circle and held similar values, making the match desirable for all involved, almost "self-evident."

Soon after her marriage Sarah moved with her husband to the United States. She was preceded by her sister who immigrated to New York in 1984 and her brother who relocated to the United States briefly prior to Sarah. In spite of the relocation, for several years she continued to live the Pakistani way and played the role defined for her by her culture of origin. "I knew that children were the priority culturally, so I had kids." However, the inner drive for personal development and acquiring more education continued to live in her. "I never gave up. At that point I could not leave my children and take on the responsibility for a full program in school, but I continued to prepare the basis for future learning. While I was home, raising my kids, I learned for my GRE, I learned to drive, and continued to prepare myself and set the ground." Her determination and eagerness for learning, pursuing more education, and reinventing herself as a professional never weakened or disappeared, it just went underground for a time to allow her to pay the culturally enforced dues.

At that time, in spite of the preparations for "breaking out," Sarah functioned very much within her culture of origin. "I was confined to my home. My friends were mostly the wives of my husband's friends." Though she does not spell it out, it sounds as if at that time Sarah lived for other people, according to their needs—her husband, her in-laws, her children, and the social norms of her culture of origin. Immigration presented her with typical difficulties. "Being an immigrant took me away from the familiar social structure. Such a structure is the compass that supports one to build one's life. Because immigration destroyed the delicate fabric of internal structure, I needed to look for an external structure." Immigration was, however, also an enabling force for Sarah. Being exposed to the norms of the absorbing culture encouraged her and served as an eye-opener. "I saw that things can be different than when I grew up and was encouraged all my life to believe." She found the external structure that she needed with her education and new friends.

After she established her new family, Sarah decided that it was time for her to pursue her own agenda. In Pakistan, prior to her marriage and immigration, she had participated in a two-year program for clinical psychology. When both her children were in school, Sarah went back to school for her doctoral degree. This was not easy. As she had done in her youth, she again had to pave her way contrary to her culture of origin. "If I did not have the real desire to go to school and advance my education, it would not have happened. My husband is a physician. We could have easily lived on his income and had enough. I could have been a housewife, like many of my friends. As a matter of fact, that would have been much more acceptable in my culture. No forces in the culture and in my environment encourage or urge me to pursue my education. I have to overcome the norms and expectations and pave my own way."

The only reason for a woman to work outside of the home in Pakistan would be to make money. "Women my age with degrees could immediately start working and contribute to the family income." Traditionally, the power of a woman within her marital relationship is affected by her earning: "The more you contribute, the more power you have." Sarah, however, opted for a route that makes her, at this point, spend money rather than make it. Consequently, her decision was met with many negative reactions. "I met with disapproval from all directions—family, friends, my husband, my in-laws, everybody, the whole social environment. Why should a homemaker and a mother whose husband makes a good income in a respectable profession all of a sudden go out of the home?" Her in-laws were very disapproving. "They are traditional; they did not understand why I need it. In their value system, a woman's place is at home." This attitude is not unusual. Women are traditionally supposed to get married, have children, and run a household. Education is not a priority. Sarah remembers with pain a girlfriend whose parents managed to convince her future in-laws to allow her to continue to study one more year to receive her diploma. However, as soon as the young woman took on family and domestic responsibilities, she had to drop out of school prior to graduation. Sarah's brother seemed to be the only exception to the chorus who spoke in unison against her studying. Having lived in the United States for several years and adopted some of its values, "He supported me and told me that he is proud of me."

Unlike her struggle for education during her youth in Pakistan, this time Sarah had the external norms of the absorbing culture as a source for help. Encouraged by the much more liberal American norms regarding women's education, she stood her ground. Eventually her husband concurred, not in the sense of "Great! Go for it!" but as in "Okay, if you really want it so much."

In her own quiet way, Sarah is as much a rebel as Tara, though their rebellions take very different routes. While Tara has a blunt and provocative in-your-face style, Sarah is introverted and gentle, almost invisible, yet very real and forceful. "I am patient by nature, even when there are stresses and certain conflicts." Yet as the saying goes, Sarah is the still water that runs deep. She is aware of the fact that what she has done is very unusual in terms of her culture: "I am going against the tide. I went back to school at thirty-one. In my culture, at this age, if a woman goes out of the home, she is expected to work and bring in money, not spend money."

Initially Sarah was amazed at the differences between the American way of thinking compared to the way of people from her culture of origin. She was well read and believed that she was well informed about the cultural differences regarding such issues as privacy, dependence-independence, and individuality-familism. She soon realized that reading is unlike living the different reality: "Direct experience is very different than knowing it theoretically in the book."

One difference that Sarah cites is the way experiences are perceived and judged, reflecting dissimilar expectations and norms. "For example, I would see a teacher as wonderful while my American classmates would complain about her. In my internship, I would naturally do as I was guided to do while my classmates would revolt and challenge. This caused me a lot of confusion, and I would ask myself 'What is going on? What is wrong with me? How come I do not see what they are seeing? Why is my perception distorted?'"

The feeling of being in a strange, unfamiliar land is a common experience for immigrants, even for those who have a good command of the language. It is not unusual to understand the words but not the music, the verbal content but not the cultural codes by which to process the meaning. For example, Americans tend to use adjectives that Europeans would interpret as inflated and exaggerated. What is perceived as indeed positive to the European sounds mediocre to the American, who would more often use concepts such as "outstanding," "terrific," and "exceptional." While in European English "good" is indeed positive, in American English "good" is actually "not bad." Translating information given from an American standpoint via non-American codes may lead to misjudgment of reality and of people.

For Sarah, this feeling of living in a culturally foreign land lasted for some time. "It took a while until I realized how misattuned I was to what is an acceptable level of expectations in the host culture. I was told that I am naive, I had doubts about my perception." Going to graduate school had a profound impact on Sarah's life. "It really changes you in many big ways. You open up to new possibilities, you take from the new culture and you want to change your own life."

Gradually Sarah learned the codes of her new culture. She feels that this changed her in a fundamental way: "I am not the same person anymore." Immigration to America gave her more opportunities and eventually more freedom. She understood that she is often expected to be independent rather than obedient. It is interesting to note that being independent because one is expected to be independent is another version of obedience. Sarah comments on this paradox, "The more freedom one has, the more responsibilities one carries, which eventually limits one's freedom."

Learning and adopting aspects of the American culture distanced Sarah to a certain degree from her culture of origin. "It made me a misfit in my culture. I do not dress, think, and act in the same way anymore; I perhaps do not even look the same any longer." The changes became very clear when she went back to visit her homeland. "The climate was different, the food was different, neither I nor my children could drink the milk there. Many things that make life convenient are not available there. I went there with very few expectations, and even those few were not fulfilled. This helped me moderate the nostalgia and feel more comfortable here. And all this was even before I started learning. I am sure that if I went now, I would have felt much more how significantly I have changed and get an even clearer perspective on what was and what is."

In her culture of origin, Sarah grew up to respect authority, though in her own way she has been quite a rebel. In the United States she gradually learned to challenge authority openly. She took what she learned in school home. "In my case, I became more assertive. I expect of my husband more involvement with the children. It also affected our personal relationships. I now expect of my husband things that I would not dare expect from him before, let alone express my expectations to him."

Financial matters in the family and patterns of decision making have also been affected by immigration. Sarah's husband still makes most financial decisions, so on the surface it looks as if roles are as they used to be. However, Sarah feels that on some deep level a significant metamorphosis occurred: "I am now aware that I can be more involved. Even though outwardly it looks like things are the same and I was not yet able to bring about the change, it really is not. Things are different, since the awareness of the alternative is present. For example, he may give me money for X but I prefer Y, then I may use it for my priorities, within limits, of course." This arrangement may seem extremely limited and unfair to the Western eye. In a country in which women rightfully protest being underrepresented in Congress, being able to change the channeling of domestic expenses hardly seems to be a victory. However, coming from a country where a large portion of the population—ultraorthodox Jews and orthodox Muslims—is very traditional and conservative, I can see the enormous progress that this state of affairs represents compared to her culture of origin. A recent memoir, *My Feudal Lord,* by the divorcée of a prominent Pakistani politician, provided insights into the vulnerable position of women in Muslim society and acceptable abusive norms of exploitation within marital relationships (Durrani, 1997). As the title suggests, the writer claims that Pakistani culture tolerates treatment of women as objects and inflicts upon them oppression, violence, and abuse. Within this cultural environment, Sarah's lifestyle is indeed a victory. Furthermore, some financial decisions regarding the family's expenses have been made to accommodate Sarah's choice to study. For example, buying a house has been delayed until after her graduation.

Although Sarah has adopted many norms from her host culture, she recognizes her ties to her culture of origin. "I am an immigrant, and as such I am aware of my past; I cannot just throw it away; after all, these are my roots and this is part of who I am." She also recognizes the difference between this past and her present life: "My future is going to be very different." She, like many immigrants, struggles to weave her past and present into a delicate fabric with a wide range of cultural hues. "In spite of all these changes, my husband and his parents are still my authority figures. I am more used than my American friends to a hierarchical structure. It gives you clarity and you know where your place is. It gives more certainty. In a democracy you have to find your own way, to invent yourself. I am aware that I will not always get my way, but I am learning how to get the best of both worlds."

Sarah carries dual citizenship. "The fact that I was not required to relinquish my identity was very meaningful to me and helped me combine the 'past-me' with the 'present-me.' One teacher asked me if I am more American or more Pakistani. I said that I am both. She pushed the issue further and asked where I would like to be buried when I die. When I said that I live in America and would be buried here, she concluded that I am more American." I can understand Sarah's discomfort facing this question. It reminds me of the unwise inquiry of a child "Who do you love better—Dad or Mom?" It is like asking someone "Do you like better your right arm or your left arm?" Love, loyalty, and belonging are not measurable by means of such linear and simplistic terms. They are much more complex. A person can love more than one country and belong to more than one culture in many rich and different ways. I loved living in Israel and I love living in New York. I fail to see why this should be an either/or question. "Where are you from?" is a difficult question for immigrants to answer. It immediately brings up questions of belonging, affiliation, and loyalty. Are they asking where I was born? Where I live? Where my accent comes from? It took me years to answer as I do now: "From Israel and from New York."

Immigration affected Sarah's life in additional ways. One is the distance from her siblings, especially her brother, who resides in another state, and her sister who remained in Pakistan. "In Pakistan we would keep closer family contacts; I miss it a lot." In Pakistani tradition, tight kin contacts are kept mostly around the parent-offspring relationship, which is a cornerstone in Pakistani culture. "The process of separation-individuation is very different. Children are expected to live with their parents until they establish their own family. For example, my male cousin did not get married until he was forty and continued to live with his family of origin. For us this is natural. For Americans, this is not normal."

The relationship with the family of origin is two sided. One is the commitment to parents as an overriding force that dominates family life and keeps siblings and their own families closely connected by their mutual obligation toward their parents. The other side is the function of family of origin as an ongoing source of support for married children, especially daughters. Traditionally, married young women visit their own families to be spoiled, "recharge batteries," and be nurtured, helping them to cope with demands by their often strict and demanding husbands and in-laws.

In Sarah's case, the premature death of her parents upset this delicate balance. "My case is somewhat unique because my mother died when I was so young. Once my parents passed away, the duty toward them that would have bound all of us together ceased to exist, and this caused my siblings and me to go our separate ways. The lack of a shared commitment contributed to the loosening of the contact." However, loosening of contacts in Pakistani terms differs from American terms. Pakistani culture is very familistic, while American culture is very individualistic and emphasizes personal accomplishment over family loyalty (Berger, 2000). Sarah sees her sister who lives in New York every weekend: "We take our children to a religious school on Sunday, spend holidays together, and so on." She misses seeing her brother and her other sister, with whom she was closest: "Geographical conditions changed the emotional balance."

The Pakistani social system is designed in a way that gives men power of control over women and the older generation domination over the younger. As a consequence, young women are subordinate to their husbands, parents, and in-laws. Women enter the household of their husband as dispossessed individuals, and young brides are often dominated by mothers-in-law more than by their husbands (Lamb, 1999). In the absence of her parents to obey and serve, Sara's full obligation is toward her in-laws. They still live in Pakistan but come to live with Sarah and her family for long periods. During these periods Sarah is expected to serve her in-laws, attend to their needs, and spoil them. "As far as my duties are concerned, it is like I have two additional children to take care of." Not only does her in-laws' stay with Sarah's family place additional burden on her already full plate, the visit brings with it additional criticism of her choices. "In their view, I am not a good mother and I am running away from my responsibilities."

What helped Sarah cope with all the difficulties? Sarah is a strong-willed person, who paved her own way from an early age. Immigration was yet another challenge to her ability to deal with stressful situations. In her words, "This struggle can make you very weak or very strong." She felt that to be true to herself she must accomplish her education, and this knowledge serves as a source of self-empowerment to withstand the pressures and the voices that have been speaking against it in her environment: "I felt that this is the only way that I could be myself." Sarah believes that if her parents were still alive, she might have given up. Education to her is nurturing, and missing being nurtured by her parents, she turns to learning as her source of support and rejuvenation.

Relationships with people, classmates, and friends helped her to find her way. As she opened herself to the new environment that spoke in difference voices, it became easier. The beginning is the hardest, but "once you are in it, you just keep going," she said. Now she is finishing her classes and internship and is preparing to work on her dissertation. However, she does not intend to stop there and plans to go on to complete postdoctoral education. "I am very determined regarding education," Sarah said. Her American friends are essential in this respect. She feels closer to them than to what she calls her "ethnic friends." "My American friends appreciate and support what I am doing, while my ethnic friends resent me for what I accomplished." She feels that now she found *her* friends: "I met five or six wonderful people with whom I am close. They help me to be my own self."

Chapter 5

Immigrants to Israel

GENEVIEVE: IMMIGRATION
AS A NEVER-ENDING PROCESS

Genevieve is a physician. She is married (her husband is also a physician) and has three children: two boys, ages fifteen and eleven, and a two-and-a-half-year-old girl, "Our Sabra." Genevieve is a petite charming woman who looks like the older sister of her children.

The interview took place in Hebrew with many manual gestures and some French concepts to explain words she does not know. We met in the family's nicely furnished apartment in an affluent town located in the center of Israel, which has a large population of immigrants of European and Anglo-Saxon (mostly South African) origin.

Genevieve emigrated with her family from France to Israel in 1998. For her, as is true for many immigrants from Western industrial countries, the motive was emotional and ideological rather than economic or political. Unlike many of the women interviewed for this book, Genevieve and her family did not seek refuge from oppression, danger, or poverty. Immigration worsened the family's economic conditions. "There we had a successful clinic and here we are struggling to survive. My husband still did not find a stable way of making a living, and my income is not sufficient to support a family." The market for physicians in Israel is oversaturated because the country has one of the highest physician/population ratios in the Western world, a situation which was further exacerbated by the immigration to Israel of more than 13,000 physicians from the former Soviet Union during the first half of the 1990s. Therefore, physician unemployment rates are high and their salaries are low (Bernstein and Shuval, 1999).

Prior to relocating to Israel, the family lived in Roquebrune-Cap-Martin, a wealthy seafront town in the French Riviera near Monaco. Both spouses were born, raised, and professionally educated in Paris, where they had successful careers. In 1994, they decided to relocate to live near the husband's mother and jointly develop a clinic that would focus on aesthetic medicine, including nutrition counseling and alternative treatments. The clinic was very successful, but the couple was not happy. "We felt that something was missing. We started to feel longing for our roots and gradually developed more and more awareness of our Jewishness. In Paris we were part of a diverse active social network, where we felt well integrated. We raised families together, spent time together, and enjoyed the good life. In the new place we were in a wealthy, competitive social environment. There were many Christians, many Lebanese. We started to feel different and occasionally rejected. We did not blend. We slowly started to observe the Sabbath and observe dietary rules of kosher food."

A pivotal point in the process of deciding to immigrate was the couple's participation in a seminar on Judaism in Cannes two years after their relocation from Paris to the Riviera. The initiative originated from her husband, and the couple spent a weekend together with a dozen other couples of diverse denominations that came from different parts of Nice to listen to a rabbi who was preaching about the importance for Jews to live in Israel. Genevieve was initially not fully aware of the nature of the seminar and mostly welcomed the opportunity to spend a calm weekend. This weekend became a meaningful spiritual experience and caused an emotional earthquake in the life of Genevieve and her husband. Upon their return, they found themselves increasingly struggling with basic issues of identity and their relationship with their Jewish heritage. The first weekend was followed with their getting deeper and deeper into learning about Israel, developing a stronger attachment to the Zionist cause, and greater involvement with the group of families who shared the process of reconnecting to their roots.

Originally Genevieve was devastated by the idea of a second relocation. She felt trapped. However, gradually, she became involved in the activity of the group. "A very special dynamic developed. Within our isolated worlds we found our brothers and sisters. We realized that our children are exposed to subtle yet very real rejection by their social environment, and the idea to immigrate started to take on shape and form. It was a slow yet consistent process."

Two years later, five of the families relocated to Israel. The rabbi accompanied them on their journey of adjustment. He prepared places for them in an ulpan (a special government-funded intensive program for learning Hebrew to which all newcomers are entitled) and helped with living arrangements and eligibility for federal assistance (every immigrant to Israel is entitled to an "absorption basket" containing time-limited subsidized housing, low-interest loans for housing, and time-limited tax exemption). The rest of the families, including Genevieve's family remained behind. "We were not ready. We still were not there, but that inner voice that said that 'in spite of the good life something is missing' did not disappear. Something felt not right, not whole. It was indefinable but very clear and loud. It felt like we have been carried with the flow of daily life for so long and here all of a sudden our eyes opened to the truth."

One day Genevieve realized that her husband had advertised their intention to sell the clinic without consulting her. Although she was initially furious, she approved of the family joining with five other families in preparation for relocation to Israel. "We were the last to join the group, but on June 25, 1997, we found ourselves on a plane."

The family was sent to an absorption center. "The following morning I opened my eyes, saw the small, crowded space, felt the heat, and asked myself 'what did I do?' I was in a shock. As if all of a sudden I found myself in the midst of a nightmare." For two weeks Genevieve refused to get out of bed, to open suitcases. "I wanted badly to go back, but there was nothing to go back to. It was extremely difficult. I was moving like a robot. I performed routine actions automatically, but I was not there. I was detached. Nothing felt real." Stress and trauma often precipitate episodes of depersonalization (Morrison, 1995). As discussed in Chapter 1, relocation is a potentially traumatic and stressful event, the consequences of which may involve derealization, depersonalization, and depression.

"Gradually I started to adjust to my new reality," Genevieve continued. "I studied hard because I realized that going back was not an option. We burned all the bridges and there was nothing to which I could go back. Our families could not understand what we did, and at some points neither did I, even though we were received here with warmth and friendship. However, realizing that we did it, I decided to try to finish the ulpan. I knew that having the language is *the* key to any possible adjustment." Genevieve worked hard to learn Hebrew and speaks it well, with a rich vocabulary. "My husband developed a blockage. He would not get it and does not speak Hebrew until today but he helped me in my studies. He prepared for me index cards with new words and encouraged me in every possible way. I studied for both of us."

Because they had savings from their work in France, the couple decided to allow themselves a year in which they focused on absorption and did not work. "We wanted to give ourselves an opportunity to learn to know the country and the people." Coping with bureaucracies was taxing and time consuming. "All the time we opened doors, [we] were disappointed and went on to open another door to be disappointed again and go on for the next door and so on. This is an exhausting process physically and emotionally. Sometimes we thought for a while that we found what we needed to realize later that we did not and we need to continue again in many other directions. This process is still going on today." Genevieve uses the following comparison to describe her experience of immigration: "It is like I am in front of a range of mountains. I have to climb up and go down all the time. Every single step is another mountain. Some of them seem insurmountable, and everything is a war, a struggle. We had the freedom and peace before we immigrated. Now it is an ongoing battle."

After the first year, the couple started looking for work since their resources started to shrink. The husband's lack of Hebrew proficiency and the saturated market presented a major obstacle to obtaining a position in medicine. He decided to turn his hobby of playing the stock exchange into his way of making a living. "He made an agreement with a bank that for six months he will work for them for free, and afterward they would assess his performance and negotiate a permanent arrangement. After the six months the bank did not want him. I meanwhile tried unsuccessfully to develop a private practice at home, concurrent with this effort I sent my resume to different health providers." Nearly all physicians in Israel are salaried employees of one of the four health maintenance organizations that provide medical care to the entire population or of the Ministry of Health which also provides preventive, curative, and rehabilitative services (Bernstein and Shuval, 1999). Language presented a major barrier. "I had two pages which I knew by heart, but if the interviewer asked me anything that was not anticipated and included in these two pages, I became lost. Whenever the interview went in any direction other than these pages, which became like the Bible, I did not understand and did not know what to say. I had the knowledge and the experience of over seven years in acupuncture, homeopathy, and related fields of expertise, but I did not have the words."

The economic situation started to become pressing. Genevieve's husband decided to go back to medicine. In the absence of an Israeli license, which he could not achieve because of his lack of Hebrew, he developed a regime of alternating between working ten days in emergency medical home visits in France and a similar time period at home. This arrangement lasted for two and a half years. It put tremendous stress on the life of the couple and the family. Meanwhile, Genevieve was struggling with a difficult pregnancy, helping her two sons to adjust, and commuting to a part-time position in a clinic in a city about half an hour away from her home. For fear of losing the opportunity to work, she did not report her pregnancy, which was not noticed until the final months. Genevieve gave birth to all her children by cesarian section. Because of a mistake in scheduling the date, she was forced to deliver the baby in the absence of her husband who was working in France his ten-day shift. "Circumstances were extremely stressful, but she is my present. The struggle was worth it for this 'made in Israel' little girl."

When her daughter was two months old, Genevieve started to work for the largest health provider in the country in a part-time position in her field of alternative medicine in Tel Aviv, which is about half an hour commute. The position gradually developed, and currently Genevieve works full-time. "I have a waiting list of two months," she said.

Her husband's injury in two road accidents while driving on his job as an emergency medical health provider further increased the family's stress. "We decided to stop with SOS (the ten-day shift job in France). Four months ago he went back to try to develop the stock-trading business." At the time of the interview the prospects were still unclear. "We are still, four years later, in the process of immigration and struggling to find our way."

Professional and financial hardships are not the only difficulties according to Genevieve. "People here are nice to us. This is the main reason for our decision to stay. However, it is very hard country. It is difficult to integrate socially. There are huge differences of mentality, and we often feel not understood. There is always that feeling that we are not in the same place. They [the Israelis] do not think like us. Their ways are totally different. They care for other things than we do. It is another world."

Genevieve believes that resettlement presents special challenges for immigrant women and especially for immigrant mothers. "They have to immediately participate in many things. They have no choice. They have to talk to the school, the teachers, the nurses and the physicians, the shopkeeper, and the servicemen. They do not have the luxury of waiting until they master the language. They have to start communicating early, with mistakes, with a limited vocabulary." The benefit is that women have no choice but to learn the language faster. "And language is the key to a successful acculturation," Genevieve emphasized again and again throughout the interview.

The adjustment of the children has been a major concern. The oldest son acclimated fast. "He liked it here from the very first day. He found himself in his new social environment and was happy." The younger son lived for a long time with his memories of France. He looked daily at the pictures of his friends in France and longed to be with them. "When he saw me crying, which I did a lot for quite a long time, he had even more difficulty to understand why we are here and do not go back."

Genevieve is convinced that the only solution to the situation is that "We need to change our mentality. A person who opts to migrate must be ready to become completely a new person." This message also resonated in the words of Natasha, who emigrated from Eastern Europe to Australia: "It is imperative for an immigrant to become as much of the new culture as possible." Genevieve's observation is that immigrants from Europe who relocate by choice because of idealistic reasons are more demanding and have a snobbish attitude compared to those persons whose relocation is guided by necessity and distress in their country of origin. "In the beginning immigrants from France came like stronger, more looking down because we chose to emigrate from the good life. Like we were better. And therefore, we expected to be understood and respected. I soon learned that this is not a reasonable expectation. We came here to their territory, and therefore we have to accommodate to them rather than expect them to accommodate to us. We need to understand them and not wait for them to understand us. We, the new immigrants, join the ride on the Israeli train, and we need to turn around and go in the direction that the train goes. We cannot expect the train to go in the direction that we want it to go."

Genevieve conceptualizes coping with the immigration experience as a process of metamorphosis. "To be an immigrant means to go out of who and what you always were and become somebody else. It is like looking in a mirror that elicits out of you the truth about your inner core, about who you really are deep inside. One's real nature is magnified in the process ten times larger."

Later in the interview, Genevieve qualified her statement about the totality of the change and talked about living in two worlds. "Inside we continue to live like we are used to with our mentality and our education. But outside, we need to learn to live with what is normative here." One example, which was echoed in the words of many immigrants to both Israel and the United States, is education. "Here children are disrespectful. They talk back to adults, the noise in classrooms is impossible. In France there is quiet and respect. We must work hard to understand that this is the way things are here and to try to accommodate."

With all the difficulties, Genevieve is convinced that they did the right thing. "My body was happy there [in France], but my soul was looking for something else. It did not feel at home. We remained in close contacts with the families with whom we emigrated, and we all struggle for making a living, but all of us say that we feel well because our soul found its place here."

A recent vacation in France reaffirmed Genevieve's conviction. "I spent ten days in France. I visited museums, saw theater, which I could understand, smelled familiar smells, saw familiar views, and was in my pond. My body felt good, but my soul did not. My soul feels intact here. It is not like I have finished immigrating. It is not easy to go from a successful physician of the rich in an upscale clinic to a poorly paid position that requires commuting to two different places [and] unemployment of my husband. I am still in the process and probably will be for a long time. I constantly open doors. The door is not closed, but my soul wishes to continue to open the doors here and that is the whole story."

PARASTU: A MINORITY WITHIN A MINORITY

Parastu is the Persian name of a delicate and sensitive migrating bird. It is used idiomatically to express concepts of wandering and nomads. This is the name that this slender, beautiful woman in her twenties chose for her story. With a cascade of dark hair and burning dark eyes, she indeed looks like an attractive swan. "My name has a special meaning in Persian. When I first came from Iran to Israel three years ago, people distorted my name and I decided that I wished to have a Hebrew name. I heard many names but did not like any. Eventually somebody offered me my current Hebrew name, Inbal. I liked its sound and its meaning, so I adopted it." Currently her family and close friends call her by her Persian name and all others by her Hebrew name. When she first meets people in school, at work, or socially, she introduces herself by her Hebrew name. "Only when I become close, I tell them to call me by my Persian name."

I asked her to describe the experience of living with two names. "This pretty much reflects my living in two worlds," she said, emphasizing that the beginning was very difficult. "I come from a society that expects women to be quiet, pious, modest, good, and obedient. I was like a boy even in Iran. I wanted to be free. When I became an adolescent, this became a real challenge. I did not wish to be the traditional Iranian woman. I wanted to be independent and unrestricted, to follow my heart." When she first came to Israel, Parastu was very conflicted: "Should I follow the path that my parents taught me? Should I go my own way?" She feels that during the past three years she succeeded in developing a duality that satisfies both sides of her: "I have the beauty of Parastu and the good of Inbal. However, none of them is 'pure' anymore. Parastu includes shades of Inbal, and Inbal has in its tones of Parastu."

Parastu feels that immigrating to Israel with its open society liberated her. "I always was independent, verbal, the 'smart' [one] of the family. I was my father's favorite because I excelled in school. When I reached adolescence it became really difficult with my mother and with my social environment. I could not do as I pleased. My sister, who is a year and a half my senior, is a true woman of Iran. She dresses as expected in a dark and proper way. She conveys chastity and [an] air of purity and appropriateness about her. I could not be like that. I started wearing long and modest attire at a relatively late age—around thirteen years of age. Until then I was like a boy. This caused a lot of conflict between my mother and me. After the revolution she became very conservative." In Iranian society, *sharm*, a word that combines "charm" and "shame," qualities that were considered to be key expectations, demanded that a woman be covered, unheard, and invisible (Lamb, 1999).

The 1979 revolution by Ayatollah Khomeini and his followers led to the enforcement of traditional Islamic codes of behavior for women. As the country became a theocracy, women were required to wear veils and the *hejab* (Islamic long, modest dress that covers the whole body); showing hair or wearing lipstick were punishable; and women were supervised by special patrols. Women were barred from learning certain subjects (e.g., management, engineering) and serving in certain roles (e.g., judges). Schools and public places became sex-segregated. Discriminatory marital laws were established, including polygamy, lack of custody rights for mothers, and temporary marriage *(siqeh)* that leaves women at the mercy of arbitrary decisions by their husband about the duration of the marriage and with no financial support or inheritance rights. Some women's rights have been restored since the death of Khomeini and the election of Mohammad Khatami as president in 1997, although discrimination against women still exists (Mayer, 1998). For a free spirit such as Parastu, living under such a regime was very challenging.

Parastu remembers that immigration had always been on the family's agenda. Her parents had wanted to relocate to the United States since she was a little girl, but her father's love for Iran caused him to constantly oscillate between the decision to leave and to stay. Eventually, after most of the family left, they emigrated.

Parastu comes from a multicultural family. Her grandfather married two wives. One of them was Muslim and one was Jewish. Her father is the son of the Jewish wife and her uncle is the son of the Muslim wife. Most people had believed that her father was also Muslim, but when his Jewish heritage was discovered, the family started to be scrutinized. Their telephone calls were under inspection. They became afraid. Her older brother left first with an uncle, and a younger brother joined them for a dangerous and illegal flight through Pakistan. Then one day her father came home with tickets. "My life was cut off all of a sudden. I did not have a chance to say goodbye to my close friend. I wrote her a letter and asked somebody to give it to her after we leave."

With hardly any preparation, Parastu landed in Israel. "Everything was so different—the climate, the language, the people. I did not know what everyone was talking about. It was like I moved to the moon. It took me two years to get myself together. I was scared. I hated not knowing Hebrew; I felt inferior and ashamed, I was afraid to speak. I also felt uncomfortable around men. Because I did not have much contact with my brothers, I did not know how to behave around men. I was concerned to be too seductive, to be misunderstood."

The first year was very difficult, and the family struggled with the dire consequences of immigration. "My father could not find a position. During the whole first year he was unemployed. He stayed at home, was depressed, slept a lot. He fell from an upscale place all the way down. Today he still works below his abilities and status in a hard physical job fixing air-condition systems."

Parastu reported in her fluent, accent-free Hebrew how she started to acclimate gradually. Language has been a very important aspect of her adjustment. "I still do not know Hebrew as well as I wish. At the same time I lost my Persian. Yesterday, when the director of my department at work spoke, I wished I could speak like him. I know that I have a very high, maybe exaggerated, level of expectation of myself," said the ambitious young woman. Unlike her sister, who allowed her fears to keep her at home, Parastu coped with her anxiety by daring to venture. "I dragged her with me to go to places. Together we attended a preparatory program in the university for future students who are not fluent in English. Originally I tried to be invisible, but in the second semester I started to show myself, not to hide anymore. I started speaking and even fall in love with a guy, though I did not let him know about this. It was between myself and me. It was part of my maturating and adaptation."

During this education program she lived in the university dormitories, thus meeting mostly international students and making few contacts with Israelis. "I like the atmosphere here more than in Iran. There I was an exception and stood out like a sore thumb. Here I found myself."

When the preparatory year ended, Parastu did not wish to go back to live at home because she was concerned that she would be stifled by her family's traditional Iranian ways. Yet she did so and gradually realized that her family had been changing too and has become more liberal and open, although they speak Persian at home, long for the shah, listen to Persian music, watch Persian movies, and eat Persian food. "I was surprised at how supportive my mother is in situations that I was concerned that she might be punitive. I guess that she has been also changing." Parastu took a year off from school to work and started to become familiar with Israelis at her workplace. She began to feel that she understands and knows her new environment.

Currently she is studying computing and management engineering. "I wanted to study something respectable, to be an engineer like my father. What I study now is what I was expected to and what I grew up expecting of myself. When I graduate next year I might explore other directions—maybe singing or a psychologist."

She is living with a Chinese boyfriend. "I went to look for work as a waitress, and a Persian friend whom I knew from the dormitories introduced me to him. Ever since I was a little girl, I was attracted to the Chinese culture. I have always been intrigued by its mystery and values as it was reflected in movies and books. Therefore, when I saw this nice and modest Chinese guy, I wanted to get to know him and his culture. Soon I was enchanted by his warmth and his love to me. I felt that he is very close culturally to where I come from, and we shared manners and cultural values. I soon felt a lot of respect, warmth, and love for him. During my first year in school I dated many guys—Israelis, French, Persian—but he is the first one with whom I lived."

However, Parastu has started to feel that she is ready to move on and that this relationship is over. "Searching for an apartment to share, I learned some unpleasant realities about my boyfriend. We have less and less in common. His Hebrew is weak, he is not educated, and not Jewish, and I gradually feel that I am not proud of him. Concurrently I became very fond of another guy. He had a girlfriend and I had a boyfriend, and neither of us was sure regarding the other's interest. This is the man about whom I have been dreaming for three years. I guess that living with my current boyfriend will help me to make the right decision."

Parastu believes that two major sources helped her in her struggle with the hardships of immigration. "First my character. I am an optimistic. I am determined to succeed. I expect of myself a lot and do not let my fears and anxieties stand in my way. I am fearful but go out and perform. I can 'die of fear' but go ahead. This has been me forever, since childhood." The second source of help came from friends. "I do not have many Israeli friends. One of my best friends is from Greece. I met her at the preparatory program in the university and we now work together. She helped me when I had bad times, she listened to me and advised me about my problems regarding my boyfriend. She is about to leave for Canada. I also have good relationships with several people who came from Russia. Only recently I started to socialize with Israelis. Their mentality did not appeal to me. I felt more comfortable with other immigrants, people who understand me because they share to a certain degree my experiences."

One aspect that differentiates Israelis from newcomers according to Parastu is their financial situation. "Immigration takes its financial toll. All the Israelis that I know have cars, work, a family. They are well settled and they fail to understand how difficult it is when one does not have these basics of a job and a home."

Although being an immigrant was difficult, being the only immigrant from Iran exacerbated the difficulty. Most Iranian Jews who immigrated to Israel did so in the early 1950s (Operation Coresh) and around the time of the 1979 revolution. In recent decades immigrants to Israel came mostly from the former Soviet Union and Ethiopia. Parastu was one of only a few new Iranian immigrants, which further augmented her sense of difference and loneliness. "However, I did not give up. I can manage, but I felt like a minority [Iranian] within a minority [immigrants]. Sometimes I am jealous. There are pubs for Russians, clubs for Russians—there is nothing like this for young people from Iran. I did not find my place in the Jewish school in Iran, and I am not one of the majority here, being an immigrant from Iran. I am a special species of a bird."

Parastu misses Iran badly. "There is more spirituality there. Here people must work, men and women, all the time. People want more and more material things, achievements. It is a constant race. In Iran when children come home, the mother is waiting for them, takes care of them, and prepares food for them. People expect less of themselves. People are very warm and very spiritual. Everything is more relaxed and calm. People are more giving. There is more respect to the elderly. Sometimes it is even exaggerated—people are too receptive and passive. For example, my mother suffers from her stepmother but would not dare complain. Israel is a more competitive society. People are more taking. People talk too much. There are less manners and people talk back."

The ordeal of immigration typically includes two different processes. One involves the hardships of the immigration experience and dealing with the losses, the other is becoming familiar with and adjusted to the new culture. "The most difficult part is to find myself again. At the beginning I lost myself. I did a lot but felt very passive.

My education limits my freedom to tell people what I do not like, to react. It took me a long time until I started to trust people."

At this point Parastu feels that she has adjusted to her new country. "I have a job, I am earning money, and this gives me a certain amount of power. I feel good. I have mastery of my life." In spite of this good feeling, she does not see herself living in Israel for the rest of her life. She is considering diverse options both in Europe and the United States because she feels more connected culturally to people of these countries and their mentality.

The topics of independence and mastery are of utmost importance for Parastu. "For me it is very important to be in control of my life and to know that I am in control. I am the most Israeli and the most educated of my siblings who include a sister who recently married and three brothers. They like me and are proud of me, yet they would have wanted me to maintain some of the traditional features."

Sometimes Parastu feels very confused. "I cannot be 100 percent Israeli, do not want to be Persian, yet I do not want to give up all of my Persian self. It is difficult to find the golden path, the middle. Sometimes I go all the way my way until I hit a wall, but this would not stop me from going on. I need to test things thoroughly even if I hurt myself in the process. I believe that this and my infinite ability to change are my strengths and I will be able to spread my wings and fly, wherever I am."

ANA: WOMEN ARE LIKE CATS—THROW THEM AND THEY JUMP BACK ON THEIR FEET

I came to interview Ana on a bright midsummer day when the temperature was 39°C (about 102°F) with 85 percent humidity. I walked into a room that looked as if it was transferred in its entirety from a Russian movie, as if the door to the other side of the mirror was open and I entered a place many miles away. I saw heavy, dark furniture and Russian-style ornaments, and a Russian-language movie was showing on the TV screen.

Ana is fifty. She is the widowed mother of two young sons, ages twenty-seven and twenty, both of whom live at home. "This is normal for us Russian. They do not leave until they get married," she said. Her husband died five years ago of cancer, several years after the family immigrated to Israel. "He hardly had an opportunity to live the fulfillment of the dream and died," Ana lamented.

Ana and her family live in an affluent town in the center of the country. "Financially this is not a simple place for immigrants to live. Everything is upscale and pricey, far above our abilities." The family originally lived elsewhere, but "I soon understood that if I was going to work long hours as I did to make ends meet, the street would have much more influence on the children and it was crucial to live in a good neighborhood to protect my kids' safety." Ana's observation relates to a forced-choice dilemma in which immigrant children are often placed. Their encounter with local lower-class populations, which occurs mostly in public schools that both groups attend, forces immigrant children to choose between maintaining their parents' ambitions for advanced education and professional accomplishments at the risk of being socially ostracized as "nerds," adopting the cultural outlook of their classmates at the risk of abandoning their parents' hope for upward mobility (Portes, 1998).

Ana came from Uzbekistan about ten years ago. "In my city there was a large Jewish community. Our family has been quite observant, and even though in the Communist era we had to do everything that related to Judaism in secret, we managed to observe many religious rituals and customs. We baked matzos in secret, performed circumcisions in secret, conducted Jewish wedding in secret, and so forth."

Ana used to be a piano teacher, as were her sister and sister-in-law, and is currently working as a bookkeeper. "Our life in Uzbekistan were quite comfortable, but here they [the Israelis] thought that we are 'sausages immigrants' [an idiom used to describe people who suffered from starvation and malnutrition in their country of origin]. We came mostly because we felt that Israel is our place." Similar to Genevieve, Ana's motivation was mostly ideological rather than escape from persecution.

The whole extended family of both Ana and her husband relocated to Israel. Ana's father and his wife (Ana's stepmother) live nearby, Ana's mother-in-law and sister-in-law and her family live near each other in the south of Israel, and many distant relatives live all over the country. "Our clan is all here. Many of them came before us, some after. We all are very much connected."

The extended family has served as a significant support system and cushioned the family's acclimatization, as often happens with immigrants relocating to a receiving society with a strong ethnic community of the immigrant's culture of origin (Portes and Rumbaut, 2001). Such support was of special importance five years ago when Ana's husband died of cancer. She spoke of her loss with a great deal of pain. "Finally we fulfilled our dream, but he did not live to enjoy it for a long time. In immigration I lost so much, and here I had to lose again. This was very, very difficult, still is in spite of the wonderful support I have been receiving from everybody—family, friends."

Ana and her family came with very limited expectations. "We knew that one cannot make a living here teaching music. Back there all children play a musical instrument, whether they want it or not. Not playing is not an option. Here children have much more to say, and many of them do not want to play. This meant that I had to look for other professional options. I was ready for it because we knew quite a lot about the situation here from people who relocated before us prior to our decision to immigrate. There were not many surprises." Initially she worked cleaning houses. "I cleaned three big houses every day and I watched an elderly lady during the nights." Soon her husband obtained a position in physical education. After he found his place and the economic stress lessened a little, Ana found a job in a large department shop selling jewelry while continuing to watch the elderly woman at night. "I knew nothing about the work of salespersons, but I was offered the job so I took it. It was easier than cleaning houses. I used my good interpersonal skills, made of each sale a big show, and it worked. I tried to use whatever I could bring to the table to perform my duty in the best possible way. I knew that since both my husband and I were willing to work hard, we shall manage. We will not go begging and not go onto the street. I learned the language faster than my husband and knew that we shall make things work."

A couple of months prior to the interview, Ana left her job because she became concerned about stable benefits, which the firm did not offer, following the death of her husband. She decided to learn a profession. Quite by accident she found herself in a course for bookkeeping. The time in the course was very challenging: "I studied for six hours and worked for six hours, and when I came home I attended to the needs of the house and the family and then I sat down to do my homework. I cried for the duration of the course. Numbers have never been my forte, and this seemed insurmountable." She completed the course quickly and extremely successfully. Then she found a company that was willing to let her work as an unpaid intern to have an opportunity to practice what she learned. The demanding schedule continued, combining the internship with her regular job. After four months she was offered a modest salary, and recently she was offered a full-time job with an accountant. "I cannot believe that this is me," she said.

One aspect of life in Israel that differs from her country of origin is the attitude toward education. "For us, education stands in the first place. In high school there children learn twenty-four subjects. Studies are more serious. Here, if you report to the social security that your child is a student, it is interpreted as an indication that your financial status is strong and you are not eligible for help." Ana believes that "the best investment is in education and schooling."

Related to this is a difference in children's attitudes. "They grow up here more cynical and more realistic. They have pragmatic attitudes, very goal oriented. All the soul food—romantics, sentimentality, nostalgia, art, and so forth—is remote from them." She observed the difference within her own family. Her older son, who immigrated as an adolescent "is not totally independent, more reserved, carries with him the apprehensions that were typical for Jews in Uzbekistan. He is more polite, would not take things without asking, more careful, and most of his friends are Russians." Her younger son, who immigrated when he was nine and has been mostly Israeli educated, is "totally a product of Israel. Independent, self-assured, standing tall emotionally. He belongs to a different mentality than his older brother. He is social, free, has friends of all origins. He does not feel the burden of the need to excel because one is a Jew." Ana recognizes this need in herself as much as in her older son: "When you come from there you feel that you must be the best. The best student, the best worker, the best immigrant. Being a troublemaker is dangerous, especially for a Jew. My older son and I brought with us the exile within us. My younger son who grew up here does not have this mentality."

Another aspect Ana discussed is work ethic. "People say that there is unemployment. I do not think so. If one wants to work and is willing to do hard work, there are opportunities." She recited anecdotes to prove her point. Ana is a very articulate storyteller who portrays people and incidents in a rich and colorful way. She said that the beginning was not easy: "I was a princess. I was not used to hard work.

When you leave your country, your home, your language, your profession, you may get lost. You lose all of how you are and what you accomplished."

Ana recalled what she defines as "the first hit" to her self-perception and pride. "We never asked for anything. We have always been self-sufficient and providing for others. Here we were forced initially to ask for help every month. I came to the Jewish Agency [the organization that provides help to new immigrants], and there was that Russian lady sitting, sipping her tea. She did not even offer me a cup of tea. I was deeply hurt, as if I was treated as nothing, as if I was not a person. I knew that I am not a taker. The first thing that we did once we found jobs was to return the 'absorption basket' [the financial help immigrants receive when they first arrive in Israel to pay for rent and basic living expenses]. This was not a comfortable place for me to be, and I wanted to be my old strong giver as soon as possible."

This incident was not isolated. There is a considerable amount of animosity and stigmatization in certain groups of Israeli society toward immigrants from the former Soviet Union. Immigrants were blamed for taking away jobs from Israelis, enjoying financial and housing help which Israelis are denied, and exploiting the system. Many Israelis perceive immigrant women from Russia as easy targets for exploitation. Because many came as single mothers and divorce was very common, the images of a Russian prostitute and "easy sex object" are very frequent. Also, in the 1980s immigrants from the Soviet Union were often extremely limited regarding the amount and nature of luggage they were permitted to take with them. Many brought fur coats as one way to bring valuables that they could carry. Many Israelis responded in a hostile manner to these immigrants' claims that they could not make a living, believing that the fur coats represented hidden wealth.

Ana recalled an occasion when she was looking for help with job hunting in a municipal job training service and declined to take a position offered to her because it was below her education and abilities. The worker exploded at her for being difficult and insisting on finding a stable position. "She told me to go back to do manual work. She scolded me for being demanding and ungrateful. She yelled at me that not everyone must work in municipal positions and that I should take what I am given. I was insulted not so much by not getting the position for which I applied but by the disrespectful attitude."

Ana also met many supportive people—"teachers in the ulpan, school personnel in my children's school, and a lot of help from everybody when my husband got sick and eventually died." A special source of support has been her husband's family. They maintain very close connections, though geographically they are spread all over the country. "We became so close that we forgot whose family it is. We are a good mix—some of us came from Russia, some married Israelis, and my sister-in-law is a kibbutz member." This diversified and extended family offered Ana financial, technical, and emotional help when her husband died: "Every weekend somebody would come to be with me."

Friends who immigrated earlier also helped. "When we first came they invited us to stay with them in their tiny apartment until we found a place to live. When we did find a place and the landlord required a year rent in advance, friends lent us the money." The same friends advised them to first learn the language rather than look for a job immediately because they strongly believed that gaining mastery of the language is the key to future success, even though it delays the possibility to start earning money earlier in the acculturation process. In retrospect, Ana recognizes the importance of this advice and is grateful to her friends. Ana's stories about support from family members, colleagues, and friends were numerous.

One incident of support she recounted with tears of excitement in her eyes. "My young son had his birthday a month after we arrived. The teacher called to request that my husband and I accompany the child to school on that day. When we came with some cookies for his classmates, we entered a classroom decorated with flowers, tables set with rich refreshments, and teachers, children, and the principal. They bombarded him with presents, sang, and performed. At the end they brought in a collective present—fancy bike, which at that point he could only dream of because of our stressful economic situation. I could not hold the feelings in me. We could not speak Hebrew. All we could do was say again and again one of the few words we knew 'thank you, thank you.' Now I would have given a whole speech. I will not forget this welcome as long as I live. Back there it would have never happened."

Ana believes that being a woman helped ease her adjustment. She observes that women cope with immigration stress better than men because they are more flexible, grow up to be more adaptive, and are willing to speak the new language even before they have full command of it. "In a storm women bend to straighten up later, men refuse to bend and break. Women are like cats—throw them and they jump back on their feet. I look around me and see several men who could not take it and committed suicide. They have a harder time finding themselves in the new environment and regaining their sense of self-esteem. There is a Russian saying that the man is the head of the family but the woman is the neck that controls the movement of the head. I knew that I should first support his efforts to acclimatize because I was sure that as hard as it is going to be, I would make it."

This observation is supported by scholars who study Russian-speaking women. For example, Remennick (1999) asserts that

> Women generally managed better than men under tense and unstable conditions of the daily micro-economy (in "hunting" for food and other supplies in constant shortage, for example). Additionally, women were often better oriented in the corridors of Soviet bureaucracy and took responsibility for most "social functions" (contacts with welfare, educational, housing, medical and other authorities). (pp. 166-167)

However, when her husband became sick Ana did break down and even attempted to commit suicide. "All I could see was a black hole ahead of me. I felt like I was a burden on my children, I started to be often sick. It took a while until I understood that I am important to all around me and I am the central axle of this family, so that I cannot afford to give up."

Ana also has what she defines as "a strong and positive character. I always see the half full part of the glass. Many of my friends complain about the weather, the people, the financial situation, but I am always positive. There is no other alternative. If one does not hold on to the positive, one may fall down, and I knew that I couldn't afford to not succeed. We all depended on me. I was a spoiled girl, like all Jewish girls. Then my husband pampered me. He treated me like I was an expensive piece of jewelry. After his death I felt that if I would not collect my powers and reorganize the family we would not make it."

Currently she feels that her efforts paid off. Her older son is about to graduate college; her youngest son serves in the army and has already saved money for his education. Recently, for her fiftieth birthday, both of them surprised her with a Russian-speaking tour to Italy with her best friend. "Even in Russian I do not have enough words to describe how I felt. I was standing there next to sculptures about which I have dreamt and learned and yearned to see all my life, and here I was living a dream. Since I was twelve I had the fantasy of standing by works of Raphael. I had many art books, I knew each fold in his stone clothes by heart, and here it was happening. I could stand as long as I wanted by a work by Raphael, take it in, and absorb it. I was doing things that Audrey Hepburn was doing in the movie *Roman Holiday*. It was like in a sentimental Russian novel, a surreal experience like I was in a movie. Now I know that everything is possible. If this happened anything can happen."

Ana feels certain that Israel is the right place for her to live. "Even though I often ask myself what I did wrong to deserve this, to lose my husband soon after immigration, I know that we made the correct decision. It is difficult, it has dire consequences, but it is home. Back there I had to do more than non-Jews to earn the same, I had to be best, to prove myself because I was a Jew. Here I am accepted for who I am. I do not have to worry that my son will not be accepted to the university because he is Jewish. I know that we shall not be deprived just because of our being Jews."

The family's decision to emigrate had been "cooking on a small fire" for a long time. They became determined to emigrate following the 1989 pogrom when 14,000 Uzbekistanis flooded the streets of the city, marched to the Jewish quarter, burned down houses, and destroyed the neighborhood. "We were hiding in the basement, hearing the noises, and had no clue to what was going on. In the morning, when we came out, we saw that the whole neighborhood was vandalized, though no one was killed. Then we decided to leave."

Ana realizes that not everything about her migration experience has been good, "but here it is easier for me to close my eyes." She feels that people relate to her, that she is recognized and acknowledged. With tears in her eyes Ana recounted in detail how the death of her husband was acknowledged throughout the town. His pictures were posted everywhere, a sporting event was arranged to commemorate him, and a trophy was named after him. "When he died everybody called to see if I need anything, to check on me. I needed nothing from anybody, but it was important to realize that I exist for people here. Back there none of this would have occurred. Here I am recognized as a person."

Throughout the interview Ana repeated, "Here is home. We are here forever, no matter what. I see also bad things and ways, which I do not like. But I turn a blind eye. Here I am more tolerant toward these things because this is home. I miss nothing. Even when times were very tough none of us contemplated leaving. This is where we belong. My mother-in-law says that she kisses the soil of this country every day. There none of my children could ever go on their own anywhere. It was never sure that they would come home safe. Here I never ask where they go and when they come back," Ana said, even though this interview was conducted in the midst of the Intifada, with terrorist attacks occurring and suicide bombs exploding on a daily basis in Israel. She continued, "Here it is the common fear of all. I do not have to fear because I am a Jew. I do not have to fear about their friends. When I meet somebody or my sons meet somebody, the first question that pops in my mind is not 'is this person a Jew?' I can focus on who the person is and let go of my Jewishness antenna. This is a big relief for someone who was always forced to be careful that way."

When asked to summarize her experience, Ana concluded, "Had all this not happened to me, I would not have been so strong. I would not have known that I have all these strengths in me."

MARE: A LONG-DISTANCE RUNNER

Mare, a dark-skinned Ethiopian woman in her late twenties, still thinks in Amharic in spite of her sixteen years in Israel. By her choice, we met on a Friday morning in a quiet corner of a cafe in the midst of a busy shopping mall. During the interview, she occasionally became absorbed in her thoughts. She said, "Sometimes when I wish to express an idea, I have the picture in my head, symbols and words are visualized in my mind in my language, and it takes a process of converting the thoughts and views in Amharic to phrases in Hebrew. I also dream in Amharic." At some points she stopped for long moments and then shared, "This question took me back to there and then. I see the pictures before my eyes." The pictures of which she speaks are unbelievable. For several hours I sat there, hardly uttering a word, listening to her story flowing, and what a story it is.

Mare was born and raised in a small village in Ethiopia. "We lived in small huts. People worked mostly in agriculture. I guess that in modern Western concepts we would be described as poor and primitive, but we had all that we needed. Everybody had a place to sleep and food to eat."

When she was eleven the family left Ethiopia to fulfill the dream of relocating to Israel. They started as part of almost 8,000 Jews who were rescued between November 18, 1984, and January 5, 1985, by a special, secret Israeli effort named Operation Moses (after the biblical rescue of the Israelites from Egypt by Moses). They made the harrowing trek to Sudan, where Israeli planes waited to airlift them to Israel. Many who could not stand the dire circumstances and the long, challenging trip died en route, leaving torn families and over 1,600 "orphans of circumstance" who were separated from their families, not knowing the fate of their parents, brothers, sisters, and loved ones.

Mare and her family wandered by foot for a month before they reached the Sudanese border. They could not stay in one place: "We walked during the night and rested during the day. We were attacked by bandits who stole whatever little belonging we had left. We, the children, were angry with our parents because whenever we were exhausted and refused to continue, they tricked us to believe that we are almost there. Our trust in our parents was broken. Older children were forced to become responsible for younger children. We were quieted not to cry and endanger the whole convoy. When we finally reached Sudan after a month of trekking, we were exhausted and desperate."

The rescue operation ended prematurely. Following a news leak, Arab nations pressured the Sudanese government to prevent any more Jews from using Sudan as a stepping-stone to Israel. Mare and her family were among those caught in Sudan. "All our hope was gone by then. Our parents still told us every day that 'tomorrow we shall be airlifted to Jerusalem.' But until that 'tomorrow' comes, we had to find a way to survive. It was very difficult. We had to hide that we were Jews because they were hostile toward Jews. We made up a story that we escaped to protect the young men from the mandatory recruitment to the Ethiopian army. The army would come to a village and load all young men on a truck, so we said that we ran away because of fear."

The wait in Sudan lasted a year. "This was a short year, but also a long year. A significant part of my memories is from the period in Sudan because we were sitting there and waiting for the dream of many years to get to the Holy Land of Jerusalem to come true, and the stay in Sudan delayed the fulfillment of a dream. It was like a cork in the stream of a fantasy. We grew up on the idea of going to the land of milk and honey, and here we were stuck in Sudan. No milk, no honey, no nothing. It was a big disappointment. Every day we were hoping—maybe today is the day; maybe today they will come to take us. We did not anticipate it to last a year. I had that fantasy that we come to Sudan and all the other Jews will be waiting for us and we shall all go to the land of our dreams. And we came there. Nobody was waiting for us. There were many hostile Sudanese and Arabs around us. We experienced a lot of animosity. And we had to sit and wait and did not know what tomorrow will bring."

The few local Jews who had been in Sudan for many years helped with negotiation and strategies for survival. Mare started to work to help feed the family. "I would help old women bring water from the well and clean to make some money to help my family. With this we bought from the Red Cross flour, oil, onion. However, we could not eat it. We were not used to the processed products like white flour, and we did not know how to cook it. I would then sell the flour that we were given and buy the familiar flour. The oil was not relevant for our diet, so I sold it in small portions in the market and got the products that we needed. My mother was pregnant, my father got very little money for his work, and since I was the oldest, I worked and helped feed the six members of our family."

The imposed stay in Sudan took its toll. Mare's family could not get used to Sudan and to the conditions in the camp. They suffered from the unfamiliar weather. "In Ethiopia most Jews lived in the north, where the climate was temperate and water was abundant. Each village had a stream and people were used to fresh water. In Sudan we suffered from the heat, all was dry and suffocating, there were no leaves on the trees, water was distributed in quota. People's health deteriorated, and many got sick."

An air of hopelessness replaced the previous excitement. "The situation greatly depressed us. The only thing that still held us was the hope that tomorrow we shall be taken to Jerusalem, which in our imagination was a city made of glittering gold. Yet Jerusalem gradually faded from the horizon and death appeared. Every day we buried ten to twenty people who died. Almost each family lost two, three, or more members. We saw friends, neighbors, children disappear. Every minimal headache caused people to fear dying. In the beginning we were hysterical and mourned loudly like our habit for each dead. The whole camp went out to bury the dead. Gradually, with so many deaths, we became apathetic. Death became a daily fact in our life. Hardly the immediate family participated in the funeral. People died lonely. All our cultural codes were compromised."

Mare's father could not single-handedly support the family. "I, as the eldest of the children, received the responsibility for my younger siblings. My mother used to say that when the Israelites left Egypt they also suffered. But I failed to understand, if we are indeed a chosen nation, why God deserted us and let us suffer so much." Hearing her, the words of Holocaust and concentration camp survivor and Nobel Prize winner Elie Wiesel (1960), who documented in his book *Night* the death of his family, his childhood, and his God, rang in my ears: "Where is my God? Where is He now?" (p. 61). Mare's mother did not give up her belief. "She is a strong woman. I come from a family with a legacy of strong women. My maternal grandmother who died a year before we left kept telling us, 'If I will not get there, you will.' And we did."

Because of the animosity from the locals, the family had to move from one temporary camp to another and to gradually progress toward the capital, where they were hoping to get a passport, then a visa to a third country, and from there travel on to Israel (visas to Israel were banned). "First we lived in tents, then we moved to straw unstable huts. Gangs of defectors called Salug controlled the roads and robbed people. Therefore, we had to pay them to be able to progress toward the capital."

Even within the camps life was not safe. "We had to organize guarding shifts to watch that families do not disappear. We had to pay the Salug to allow trucks with supplies bring food to camp. Whoever could left camp. The young and strong fled first, leaving behind the elderly and the weak. We could not leave. Initially we thought that we will send each child with someone, but this meant trusting strangers. This was too risky, because the dire circumstances turned people into animals. Everybody cared for himself and became indifferent to others, which is very much against our culture. Mutual help is a cornerstone of our culture, no one goes hungry, and everybody has a place to sleep. And in Sudan, when we most needed each other, everybody disappeared. You could trust nobody. Mutuality, the backbone and core of our community was broken." In a lecture delivered at the White House on April 12, 1999, Elie Wiesel stated

> To be indifferent is what makes the human being inhuman. Indifference, after all, is more dangerous than anger and hatred. Indifference is not a beginning, it is an end. And, therefore, indifference is always the friend of the enemy, for it benefits the aggressor. (Wiesel, 1999)

Mare's social environment became indifferent.

Mare's family, which increased with the birth of her brother, remained among the last in camp. They decided to leave together. They paid the Salug and left at night. Shortly after leaving the camp they were attacked by a rival gang of Salug and had to pay another bribe. In the process of reembarking, one of Mare's relatives was injured. The rest of the refugees were afraid that his cries of pain would endanger them. Therefore, they left the family, including the injured man, the young children, and a baby, alone in the middle of the road and promised to come back to help. The family waited to no avail and finally started to struggle back to the camp that they had left. The road was very difficult; they had to make their way through dark forests and overcome obstacles while trying to avoid being discovered.

When they finally reached the camp and settled and hospitalized the injured man, strangers invaded the empty camp and attacked them. Two weeks later they helped the injured relative escape from the hospital, and the family started again the journey to the capital, following two of Mare's younger sisters who had already gone with a childless aunt that pretended to be their mother. After much hardship, Israeli airplanes airlifted them on a Friday night. "They took us secretly, in covered trucks. It was dark and scary. All of a sudden we saw the airplane and all that was before, all the suffering was erased at once. It was that feeling of 'here we are going to Jerusalem.' It was worth every step of the road."

The plane stopped in Europe. Mare was not sure exactly where but remembers the snow. Then they continued to Israel. They were welcomed by a government official who greeted them with the help of a translator. "People started to cry, fall on the soil and kiss it. I was in a state of shock. I held the door of the airplane remembering all the people that I lost and did not believe that I am here. We thought that we were in Jerusalem. We were taken to a hotel in Ashdod [a town about an hour from Jerusalem]. I was amazed that everybody was white. I expected everybody to be dark like I am and like all Ethiopian people are. The buildings were tall. Because I never saw such tall buildings before, I was afraid that people would fall out of the windows. We did not really believe that we are there. People only wanted to pray."

Government officials soon started to fill out forms for the newcomers. "They asked our names and unilaterally decided on Hebrew names for us. They registered me as Miriam. We did not even know that they gave us new names. They told us to undress and gave us new clothes. They treated us like we were dirt. This is something that I find hard to forgive. They made women who never went to the doctor to undress in front of strangers. Privacy and dignity were compromised. Everything was strange and unfamiliar. We saw stairs and we did not know how you go down. We were scared that we should remain hanging there. They brought us to a dining room. All we could eat was bread and cheese. The rest of the food we did not recognize. We thought the jam is honey."

The first few weeks were extremely difficult. "Some people withdrew and did not speak or react. Others celebrated. Some were sent to hospitals. Emotions were mixed. On one hand happiness that we have made it. On the other hand deep sorrow that loved ones did not have the good fortune."

Gradually adults were placed in classes to learn the language. Reactions to the experience varied. "Some of them were very excited to study. Others never held a pencil before and had a hard time. Some were not in a mood to concentrate after their entire ordeal. Anger and hostility started to build around attendance issues. Israelis misunderstood our background and perceived us as lazy and irresponsible. This is a major distortion. Ethiopians are very hardworking. People would go out to the fields at sunrise and labor until sunset. It was extremely hard for people who were used to be outside under the blazing sun all day long to be closed in a air-conditioned room for the whole day. They were frozen and could not stand it. The locals could not perceive how one suffers from what are seemingly improved conditions. They were furious and saw us as ungrateful because they housed us in a hotel, fed and taught us for free, and we did not appreciate it. Friction started to develop."

Children were also placed in schools. "Initially everything was new and strange—the environment, the language, the people. I felt that people were looking at me like at an alien, a museum piece. We wanted to study so badly that we would stay in classes even during the breaks. The Ethiopian children were placed in a separate class for accelerated learning of Hebrew, and we had limited encounters with the other students. We were not well received. Children called us names, made fun of us, and touched us to see if the color of our skin can be removed.

"A couple of months later somebody decided to send us to boarding schools. In retrospect nothing was done in a logical or appropriate way, but at that point we were too fragile and confused to even realize that this was the case. Nothing was logical at the beginning, but we naively received whatever was done to us as a given. We did not rebel. We were too scared and too confused to ask questions at that point. Only a couple of years later, when we started to understand what was going on, the big anger came. I suddenly realize that when they say Miriam they mean me. We had to learn to respond to the new names, which were given to us arbitrarily. It did not feel real. Like it was not I, even though I learned to respond to it."

The separation from their parents was very difficult. "Suddenly we had to sleep without our families. This was totally strange to our tradition of tight family connections and familism. The school tried to integrate newcomers with born Israelis, but they refused to room with us, and we could not get the concept of sharing a room with nonfamily. We called our parents every day."

Exclusion of Ethiopian Jews by the religious establishment exacerbated the difficulties. "We were sent to a religious boarding school. However, our Jewishness was doubted. This was a terrible blow. We, who longed for our Holy Land, went through all this suffering, struggled with dangers, all of a sudden were excluded. We felt hurt, and it started to cause disintegration within our own community also."

An additional blow came from realizing that they were misled. "To us Jerusalem was a powerful concept, which was identical with Israel and the subject of our dreams and longing. On a trip to Jerusalem and a visit to the Western Wall, we realized that contrary to what we believed, we were not in Jerusalem the whole time. Only then we started to understand that Israel is divided into towns, cities, and villages like in Ethiopia, and we started to wonder where we were until then."

Mare reports having many dissociative experiences. "I was sitting in class, but my thoughts were back there. I could not grasp how it was possible that I am sitting here when just a month ago I was in great danger with everybody around me dying. The change was so abrupt that I could not cope with it. When the teacher noticed that I am in another world and called me, I started shivering and crying. I just could not get it."

It took some time before Mare adjusted. "A year later, I started to understand the evil that has been done to us. We expected to gradually be integrated in regular classes, but this did not happen. We were considered too slow and with limited potential, so under the excuse of protecting us we were robbed of the possibility to try to get on a track that leads to success. They maintained the separation and kept us on the low level. A special program was opened for Ethiopian girls to train us to become seamstresses and child care workers. They did not believe that we could do more than that. I wanted to study seriously but had to fight to get the opportunity to perform at the level of my ability. We were thirsty to study, demanded more hours. We were victims of a limited and insensitive perception of us."

Finally Mare won the battle. She and a few other girls were placed in a regular class but were at a severe disadvantage vis-à-vis their classmates. Most of the girls soon gave up, but Mare persisted. "I refused to surrender. I had no support and was told 'we told you that it would be too hard for you.' I would not listen. I was determined to make it. I fought minute by minute, hour by hour, day by day. And look at me now—a graduate student." Mare studies education and specializes in developing educational programs. "I have the ambition to become a principal and build an innovative school." Listening to her, one cannot but believe that she will.

Meanwhile, Mare's family relocated to an apartment in an absorption center near Jerusalem and, for the first time since their arrival, regained some privacy and independence. "They finally were able to do their own shopping of ingredients that they are used to and their own cooking. They could host guests, which is very important in our culture, and make decisions about their way of life."

After her graduation from high school, Mare spent two years in National Service. This is a popular alternative to mandatory military service for religious women. She worked with immigrants from Ethiopia who were rescued in Operation Solomon, which followed Operation Moses, on May 24, 1991, when in nonstop activity for thirty-six hours, 14,324 Ethiopian Jews were airlifted to resettle in Israel. "There I taught Hebrew in the mornings, worked with adolescents, and mediated between the educational staff and the adult newcomers in the evenings."

Currently Mare lives on her own and works with youth in distress in addition to her studies. "My experiences with immigrants from the other side of the fence as a helper gives me an opportunity to revisit my own experience, gain insight, and heal some of my emotional wounds from the time of the relocation. I learned that to be an immigrant is a daily struggle to find my own place within a competitive society, to find a way to be 'in,' maintain my place in the race; all the time I am on the run to catch up, not to stay behind. I need to keep up, integrate progress academically, socially, and at work. I need to help my family also not to lose the race. They have a lot of expectations of me. They see me as the one who knows. This puts a lot of responsibility on me just like when I was a child. They believe that I can do anything, which is not the reality. It makes it hard to live up to these expectations. I always run, but I do not always get there. I need to prove to people with whom I work that an immigrant can be as successful as they are. It takes a lot of hard work of an immigrant to get to places where nonimmigrants get easily and effortlessly. Society is hard. If you are not like them, a stranger, you are not accepted, you work twice as hard. This may sometimes create a conflict between remaining true to myself or to compromise in order to achieve."

Mare feels that she is facing a triple challenge because of being a woman, an immigrant, and an Ethiopian. "It is easier for men than for women, for natives than for immigrants, and for immigrants of other origins than for Ethiopians."

In spite of all these hardships, Mare thrived. "I had that power, which came from the support of my parents who wish to fulfill their dreams through me and my siblings. Since their circumstances did not allow them to study, they support us to achieve it all and they believe in us. Like I went in the Sudanese desert up and down hills without giving up, I go up and down hills in the desert of reality without giving up. I have no illusions. I understand how life is, and I am ready to face it and conquer. If I do not try, I do not know my limits. So I try, and if it does not work one way, I try another way. But I do not quit! We Ethiopians are shy, introvert, and quiet. To cope with the competitive, aggressive Israeli norms, we need to develop a thicker skin and different skills of coping, and I will. Moving here opened opportunities. I am exposed to the wide world, to educational alternatives, a different worldview. I have been building my own way to process and react to the world. I have been building myself out of the hardships and came out stronger. My younger siblings are already totally Israeli, and this creates a conflict with my parents, but my strength is having in me both Ethiopia and Israel. I am the bridge."

SVETLANA: ALWAYS MINING THE GOOD

Svetlana, fifty-three, is a cashier in a supermarket and her husband is a music teacher in a local high school who supplements his income by playing the accordion at weddings and social events. Both of them work below their level of education. In the Ukraine Svetlana was a sanitation consultant in a hospital, a profession that does not exist in Israel, and her husband was a professional musician. They live with their seventeen-year-old son and a 105-year-old aunt in a tiny fourth floor walk-up apartment, in a run-down neighborhood on the outskirts of a large city.

In spite of her eleven years in Israel, she writes Hebrew in Cyrillic letters. Unlike most immigrants from the former Soviet Union who left family and friends to relocate, Svetlana, her husband, and son were the last to join parts of their extended family who had emigrated to Israel in the mid-1970s. Reluctant to leave her sick parents who refused to relocate, Svetlana and her family stayed behind when her in-laws, their children with their own families, and many other relatives and friends left the Ukraine to resettle in Israel, the United States, and Germany. Despite pleas from members of the family living in Western Europe and the United States to join them, Svetlana's husband insisted on emigrating to Israel.

They came to Israel three months before the Gulf War and enrolled in an intensive subsidized Hebrew program. The war caused the program to end unexpectedly and abruptly, and the couple, who lost the opportunity to gradually acclimate and acquire the language, as well as the scholarship that provided for their living, were forced to look for jobs. This was not an easy task in a country suffering from a slow economy, missile attacks, and threats of biological bombings. The fact that both were in their forties and did not have professional education in needed fields made the situation more difficult. They labored long hours in any type of work they could find, including cleaning houses and offices and working as aides in a nursing home. "I was very spoiled," Svetlana said. "Never before did I do any physical work, I did not understand what I was told, and people got furious with me. I used to cry because my son asked for many things that I could not afford to give him. He used to say that when we would be rich, I would buy him all he wanted."

Her main concerns are very typical of most Israeli parents and revolve around her son's safety when threats of terror are constant and his forthcoming recruitment to the army. "He has a cell phone and I constantly call him. He was five when we came, and he is totally Israeli. It is hard to handle him. He believes that he knows everything better, talks back. I talk to him Russian, try to have him keep some Russian traditions, but he declines to maintain connections with our culture of origin. He refuses to speak Russian and communicates in Hebrew even with his Russian friends. He is 100 percent Israeli. He has friends of all cultures of origin—Israeli-born, Ethiopian, Russians. I know that when he is drafted next year, I will not sleep one night in peace, but this is reality. We are scared of the daily bombers and explosions. We watch both Russian and Hebrew television because the Russians change the facts and distort them to match the Palestinian interest because they get money from Arab countries."

Svetlana never went back to visit her homeland and does not wish to. Her husband did. "He just came back. Everything there is in terrible shape. The Ukraine used to be a prosperous country, now there is nothing there. No food, no money. He gave a friend $20. For us it is not much and for them it is a monthly salary. It breaks my heart to hear what it is like there now. I never thought that it could deteriorate that much. I would have loved to meet my friends, but there are so many other places in the world to see. I am willing to go there for three to four days maybe. I am not even sure about that. I prefer to go to other places, see things. We go abroad at least every other year."

She described her relocation as a challenging experience in a matter-of-fact and accepting tone. "Every immigration is difficult, and ours was no exception. We received a lot of morale help. My extended family was very supportive, including some that we never met before, just knew about them; for example, a second cousin whose parents came from Poland. I only heard about him, we never were in any contact, and yet, when we came, they all embraced us. We became so close in a way that I never imagined possible. We are one big family with excellent relationships with our relatives. There we were alone. Here we have this big warm clan. We went from loneliness to a family. We deliberated for a long time whether to emigrate. Once we made up our mind, we put everything aside. We knew that it would be difficult. We came prepared to cope with hardships. This readiness made whatever happened less difficult than we expected and imagined. We came with a realistic perception that because both of us were in our forties and did not have the language we would have to compromise. We said to ourselves that what was there was there. It ended. You need to forget and start all over again. We never look back and feel sorry for what we lost. Whatever we have we have. Relocation is never easy. We traveled in the Netherlands with a group of Russians who immigrated to Germany. Their experience there is similar to our experience here. People do not get jobs in their profession, the local 'Mafia' does not like strangers."

Svetlana oscillates between her report of hard times and mourning losses—"There I worked for twenty years in the same office, I had job security"—and her struggle to be happy with what she has now: "So I work in a less prestigious and less paying job, but we have to eat; there is less security and more tension, but we have friends, now I got tenure, so this is good."

Her tendency to minimize difficulties is significant. For example, she described her husband's acculturation, which started in an unexpected way. When they had just arrived, the ulpan, the intensive Hebrew program, organized a concert and he participated. A woman who attended the concert asked him to teach her son to play the accordion. He soon started to teach her three children, and the two families became very close. By word of mouth his name became known, and because of his ability to engage children, he became a popular instructor. The road to a position in a school was short. "There he worked individually with motivated children in a special music school; here he teaches playing the keyboard to fifteen or twenty children who do not wish to learn. He comes home exhausted, but it does not matter. He has a job in his field."

Svetlana expressed anger with newcomers who complain: "Newcomers now are different. We were kind of pioneers. We came first and were anxious, obedient, and naive. People now come with money and with demands. They think that they know everything. They want everything. Many of them are 'New Russians.' [This is a derogatory concept that refers to people who made large amounts of money in the post-Communist era in the former Soviet Union, not always decently and legally. They are perceived as uncivilized and dishonest.] People who just came and all they have to say is to criticize. I feel sometimes like telling them that if they are not happy, they should go back to where they came from. People have nostalgia, they remember the good and forget the bad. I was happy here from day one. My husband had to visit back in Ukraine and bring it to a closure before he could feel fully belonging here."

Svetlana's family is one of the few European families left in a neighborhood populated by immigrants from Ethiopia. "The 'whites' are escaping. When we first came there were many Russians around. At the beginning the Ethiopian were very nice and quiet. Now they became 'Israelis,' they are noisier. We have a different mentality, but we manage," she reflected on the Israeli version of ethnic segregation and tension.

Svetlana feels that immigration changed her in many ways. "For example, it made me lazier. Back in Ukraine, I always made everything myself. I baked and cooked. Here I became spoiled. I learned not to work hard and buy much more ready stuff." This reminds me of one of my first visits to a New York supermarket, when a customer who stood next to me in line gazed at the yeast and flour that I bought and asked me with astonishment, "What on earth do you do with this?"

Svetlana, like many of the interviewees, believes that men have a harder time adjusting than women. "Jewish men in Ukraine differ from non-Jews. They are more civilized, never do physical work, and were mostly musicians, engineers, physicians. Here, everything changed. They have to do physical labor, many of them below their education, and they take it harder than women, who are more flexible. There men were stronger; here they broke more."

Unpleasant experiences have not been uncommon. "There were situations in the nursing home where people refused that I take care of them because I was Russian. Sometimes I was insulted, one supervisor constantly pestered me, 'these Russians,' and I was discriminated against because of my origin. Never mind, I do not wish to talk about it, this is over. It is a thing of the past."

Although she has some Israeli friends, most of her social contacts are with other Ukrainian immigrants. "I moved [from] Tchernovitz [her hometown] to Israel. The friends that we left there are mostly non-Jews, and we, the community of immigrants from the Ukraine here, help them a lot with money, etc. When my husband went to visit, he took boxes of stuff for them. He brought a videocassette that they recorded for me. I watch it and cry."

Their elderly aunt presents a unique and special burden for the family. "She cannot be left alone. We take shifts taking care of her and use the help of a caregiver several hours a day. Her first family was killed in the ghetto during World War II, and her second husband died long ago. We did not want to put her in a nursing home. In Russia everybody lives together till the end. Now I developed a different perspective and understand the benefits of a nursing home, because if she will be sick, I will not be able to stay home and take care of her, but now it's too late to move her again. For now we will just have to live with our decision."

Svetlana concluded, "In life one makes many decisions. We never know how things are going to develop. I prefer to stay with the bright side of my decisions and live by them rather than mourning what might have been. I feel blessed to have lived in two cultures and to speak two languages. I have developed an outsider's perspective on both cultures—rather than follow conventional routes I developed my own independent way through observation and comparison."

TERESINA: A SPRING OF OPTIMISM

Teresina is a beautiful, slim woman in her late twenties with huge doe eyes, dark, smooth skin, and a radiant smile. She was born the youngest of eleven children to a very poor family in a remote village in northwestern rural Brazil. Although she has been in Israel less than three years, her Hebrew is fluent with current colloquialisms and only a very slight accent. She works in child care but aspires to learn to become a beautician, "because I like to see the beauty in people and help them to express it."

Teresina is married to an Israeli who studies photography. They live in a tiny rented apartment on the outskirts of a large city, but for weekends go back to the southern kibbutz where her husband was born and raised and where his family still resides. "My life here is split like I am living two different lives. There is the Teresina of the week, the city girl, and there is the weekend young woman in the kibbutz, but I like them both."

It took a little longer and many more hesitations for Teresina to talk about the bigger split of her life: the poor farm girl from a large tribe-like extended family in a remote rural Brazilian rainforest village and a modern, ambitious young woman in a Westernized Middle Eastern city. This split was reflected in her preparations for a visit to her homeland for the first time since her immigration. This visit was planned for a few weeks after the interview. "This is going to be a very sad visit. My father died a month ago. He was close to eighty, and I did not have a chance to go see him before his death. My aunt died a couple of months earlier. Most of my girlfriends married and moved away. I changed so much; I am anxious. I do not know what to expect. I am packing suitcases with stuff. I feel so rich now. I want to bring them things, but at the same time I do not want to embarrass them. We were supposed to go there earlier, but I kept delaying it. I want to go, and yet at the same time I do not want to go. Now we finally go, and I do not know how it will be and what I will feel. It is like I had one life and now I have another life, and I am not sure how it would be for me to go back to the previous life and look at them through my new eyes of the new life, the new me. I am not even sure if everybody will even remember me, especially the little children. It is like my existence may have disappeared from my own family like footsteps in the sand."

Teresina and her husband met when he was on a traditional post-military-service backpacking trip in South America. It is mandatory for all Israelis, men and women, to serve in the army. In recent years, a ritual has developed in which young Israelis, upon completing their service work, save money, and spend several months in the Far East or in South America, combining traveling and working, before they go back to go to school and settle down. The norm is to travel to the most inaccessible, exotic places and for risky and challenging adventures. A unique youth culture has developed around this ritual.

Teresina's husband stopped his travels to work for a couple of months in irrigation on the ranch where Teresina's sister lives. He soon became involved in the local culture and met Teresina. As their relationship developed and he was getting ready to go back to Israel, he invited her to come with him. "Now I realize how lucky I am. I met several other Brazilian women who were naively trapped by misleading stories in similar circumstances, and when they arrived here, they realized that reality is much harsher. For example, one girl met an Israeli man that promised her the world, and when she came here, pregnant with his child, she realized that he is married with children. She cannot achieve legal status [it is extremely difficult for non-Jews to become permanent residents or citizens in Israel if they are not married to an Israeli], and she is totally at his mercy."

Teresina, who never before left her village, made her way to the large city of St. Paulo, a six-hour trip from her home, to board a plane for the first time in her life and fly over the ocean to a new life in an unknown country. This was the first time for her to see a large city or an airport. "When I look back, I really can hardly understand how I dared doing it, but I guess that I was just naive and unaware of all that I am aware now. I just went ahead, unthinking."

Economically, immigration totally changed Teresina's life. She feels like she made a quantum leap. "I now have things that I did not even know existed. My family was very poor, people were little educated, worked in simple jobs, and we had very limited resources. I now live in much better conditions and have much more stuff."

Socially, however, the change was very challenging. Social acculturation has been very difficult. "In my country everybody is friendly, warm, and relaxed. Here people are rushing, nervous, and busy. The pace of life is hectic and restless. People are immersed in their own business and therefore are not so social and friendly as in my culture. For example, we live in our current apartment for almost a year, and I do not know my neighbors. Everybody leaves home in the morning for their work or school and comes home late to their own corner. This could not have happened in Brazil. We would have met to spend time together, be social, dine, and talk. Here things are much less social, each to his own. Nobody has time for others."

Teresina also feels isolated from mainstream Israeli society and finds it hard to be accepted. "This is a close society. People know each other, from elementary school, high school, and the army. They have shared history and newcomers have no entry. They are polite, welcoming, but you, as a stranger, are kept at a distance, an outsider. The circle does not open to include you, even though people are nice. This is especially true in the kibbutz, where they have been together from cradle, set on potties together. For example, when we were sitting with company, which naturally was my husband's friends, they would start talking fast in Hebrew, which I could not understand, laugh at their private jokes, and I was neglected, left out. Nobody made an effort to include me, as if I am air, nonexistent. Or I would go to the communal dinning room and nobody would sit with me. Everybody would sit with their own friends, discuss their mutual issues, and I would be alone at my table. Gradually, I started to develop a relationship with the volunteers. My English is good, and I like their mentality more than the rough Israeli mentality." Volunteers in the kibbutz are non-Israelis, mostly non-Jews, who wish to have a taste of this communal way of life. They live in the kibbutz for several weeks or months and work mostly in agricultural and manual labor in exchange for room and board. More often than not they create their own community which is separate from the kibbutz social life.

Language presented a special challenge. "When I came, I knew practically no Hebrew. I did not go to study it in any organize way." This is quite unusual. Because Israel is an immigrant society, a variety of intensive, state-funded language and acculturation programs exist for new immigrants. However, these absorption packages mostly target Jewish immigrants and their families. Being non-Jewish, Teresina's situation was different. She acquired her Hebrew "of the air," which may explain her speaking in a less formal and more popular fashion. She timidly admited, "I have a talent for languages," but expressed frustration with not being as eloquent as she would like to be. "I do not read Hebrew, but I read English quite easily. One of my plans is to attend an ulpan and study Hebrew as one should. I like to be good at whatever I do. I know that I can do it, and since I live here and need to speak Hebrew, I wish to do it well."

A major help in coping with immigration came from her husband's family, which extended to Teresina a warm and welcoming reception. "My mother-in-law also came to Israel as a young immigrant from France thirty-some years ago. She knew how it feels and helped me a lot. She immediately accepted me as the daughter that she never had. When I came, I knew nothing. I was like a baby. She had to raise me. She got me clothes, because I hardly had anything. She gave me dolls. She parented me from scratch. She is a wonderful woman, and I am grateful to her. Thanks to her I could cope with missing my own family. They adopted me into their family with open arms. My sister-in-law, the wife of my husband's brother, is also an immigrant from England. In our family people understand immigration because many of us have the experience. All the women are immigrants, so I came into a family that knew how it is and it helps me a lot."

After several years of living in a temporary status, recently Teresina married. She had to go to Cyprus and marry in a civil court. Because in Israel marriage and divorce are under exclusive jurisdiction of the orthodox rabbinical court, which does not permit or recognize interfaith marriage, this neighboring island serves as a refuge for Israelis who wish to marry in a civil ceremony or who are prohibited from marriage by Jewish law. No one from her family of origin attended. Such a trip is almost unimaginable to the poor farmers of the remote region from which she comes. "They live in another world, like I did until I met my husband. As much as I tell them, they cannot even imagine the kind of world in which I live now. For them it cannot be real, like it was not for me for some time."

In spite of the absence of her parents and siblings from her wedding, she remembers the occasion happily. "All my husband's family that is now my family was there. They got me a beautiful dress and flowers, and my mother-in-law did for me everything so that I did not feel like my family was not there. If it was not for her, I do not know how I could have coped with all the hardships."

In addition to her new family, whom she cannot praise enough, Teresina finds much joy in her friends. Her main social network includes other Brazilian immigrants similar to herself. "I am performing in a Brazilian dance group. We rehearse almost every evening. My husband works during the day and studies in the evenings, but I am busy with the group, so I do not feel isolated or lonely. We perform in social events, weddings, etc. We rehearse together, go out to eat together, and they understand me. They are like a piece of Brazil in Israel. I love it, and it fills my life. It all started by accident. In the kibbutz I danced once and they loved it, so on every celebration they asked me to perform. I did it happily because I am grateful for their hospitality and I love it. Somebody from the group happened to attend one performance and invited me to join the group. I made friends with several of the women. We talk together, laugh together; so I established my own network."

An additional benefit of the group for Teresina is the opportunity to speak Portuguese. "Originally my husband and I spoke Portuguese because I did not know any Hebrew and he learned Portuguese when he was in Brazil. When we came here I learned Hebrew and he started to forget his Portuguese, so we gradually started to communicate in

Hebrew. This is not easy, because this is not my real language and I cannot express myself as well in Hebrew. However, when I have children I want to speak with them in my own language. I could not mother them properly in a language that is not natural to me. I hope that now when we go to visit my home and we will be in a Portuguese-speaking environment for a month, my husband will get used again to the language, and when we come back I intend to maintain our communication in Portuguese. I see it with my sister-in-law. She is British by origin and insisted to speak English with her daughters. Because they grow up in a Hebrew-speaking environment, they acquired Hebrew naturally and quickly, but English required an effort. Now the girls are bilingual and my sister-in-law can communicate with her own children with comfort. They also can talk to their maternal grandparents when they visit England. I learn a lot from her and her experience. She does not fight. She achieves it in soft manner, just makes it happen. I intend to follow her model because when I have children I want them to be able to communicate with my own family. To us, Brazilians, family is very important."

Teresina elegantly bypassed a more basic issue related to the status of her future children. According to the dominant Orthodox Judaism in Israel, unless she converts before they are born or they are converted, Teresina's children will not be recognized as Jews. When the issue was raised cautiously, she shrugged it away and expressed her optimistic view that the question would be resolved in time like other issues were: "I see the good and refuse to dwell on problems. We shall deal with it when it will be necessary." She even mentioned in a nonchalant manner, "Who knows if we even live here when they are born?" When this comment was probed, Teresina revealed that the couple is contemplating the possibility of resettling when her husband graduates. "We both like to go to other places. The world has so many wonderful places. I am not a worrier. I have my talents, and I take things as they come. I am confident that just like my current life, which I could not have anticipated when I was growing up, whatever comes my way I will cope with and benefit from it."

In spite of the hardships, Teresina sees herself as fortunate. "I got a life which is nothing like I would have imagined. I am lucky that I live here, that I have my husband and my new family. I know that I can develop, become a beautician, have a good life, do whatever I want to do. I am a lucky woman."

Chapter 6

Immigrants to Australia
and New Zealand

ROSA: AN ASIAN IN A WHITE COUNTRY

Rosa came to Australia from the Philippines in 1998 to escape economic deprivation. She had been working at a low-level clerical position for the department of agriculture when political changes caused those who worked for the previous government to lose their job security. A former co-worker who had immigrated to Australia offered to help find a mate (husband) for her there. Seeing no future in her homeland, she agreed. Some time later, her acquaintance introduced her to a Greek Cyprian man, who claimed to be forty-five and to own an ice cream parlor. After a year and a half of lengthy telephone conversations, he invited her to come to Melbourne, for a visit, and she accepted. "When you are in a situation of high poverty and crime, you are willing to risk life and emotional stability. I was living in a third world country, which everybody wants to escape to find a greener pasture. When I had an opportunity, I grabbed it.

"It was extremely difficult to receive a visa to get out of the Philippines. They pile enormous obstacles in the way of outgoing tourism, and it is next to impossible for single people to achieve a permission to travel abroad." Gradually it became clear that the only hope for Rosa to obtain a visa was to apply for a fiancée visa, which is issued for a limited time on the basis of a declaration by an Australian of the intent to marry a visitor. Rosa became what is degradingly labeled a "mail-order bride."

The mail-order bride industry is flourishing, as reflected by Web sites catering to "patriarchal white men." Some of these sites define themselves as specialized Philippine tours, describing women from this country as "Coming primarily from a lower socio-economic class and looking for a man to provide a secure 'nest' for them because of the poor economic and social conditions in their home countries." Practices vary regarding language, the number of times the address of the same woman is sold, and the attitude toward the women. However, the general perspective is of women as a commodity for sale. (For ethical reasons, addresses of Web pages from which those quotations originate are not cited here.)

Some claim that there is very little difference between these relationships and the growing trend of cyber-relationships and online matching and romances. However, the status of being a mail-order bride deprives women of self-definition and creates an unequal relationship between men and their immigrant wives (Simons, 1999). The process of obtaining the fiancée visa lasted more than two years. It required considerable documentation to establish a genuine intent to marry and the inability to do so in the immigrant's homeland. After several appeals, the visa was approved. Rosa became one of the thousands of Filipino women admitted to Australia as new wives or fiancées of male citizens. In a way, this follows the long Australian tradition of "marriage migration" practiced in the early years of European settlement, when migration of single women was encouraged to redress the gender imbalance (Hugo, 1995).

Rosa was happy beyond words: "He promised me the world. He committed to help me and my family. I believed that because I had mastery of the English language it would be relatively easy for me to acculturate, but the reality was very different. The first disappointment occurred in the airport. He looked much older than he had claimed; his place was neglected and filthy. Still, I knew that I do not have many options." Rosa was caught at a very unpleasant crossroad. If she decided to give up the precious visa and return to poverty and misery in her country of origin, she would have suffered personal humiliation and caused her family to lose face.

Rosa became a hostage. "During the first month I kept asking him when we shall get married. This was important to me for two reasons. First, I was already sleeping with him and my family knew about it. In my culture this means marriage, because a woman is supposed to save her virginity. These delays caused me major embarrassment. Also, having come on a fiancée visa, marriage was a prerequisite for a permanent resident status." Rosa kept asking about formalizing the relationship legally, but her husband-to-be kept postponing it with various manipulations and excuses. Finally, under significant pressure from Rosa and an ultimatum to leave, when her temporary visa was about to expire, the couple married at the civil registrar's office.

It soon became clear that Rosa had fallen victim to a very disturbed and brutal man. During her entire stay with her husband he kept her isolated and ignorant about her environment. He did not allow her to use the Melway (an elaborate street, site, and direction map, commonly used to give directions, explain locations, and find one's way around Australia's large cities), prohibited her interaction with customers in the ice cream parlor, in which he made her labor long hours, locked her up when he went on his business, and refused to allow her access to money. He insisted on accompanying her for personal shopping (e.g., items for personal hygiene) and required that she submit a receipt and the change in order to control every cent that she spent. "I was his prisoner," Rosa said.

Rosa was subjected to sexual, physical, and emotional abuse. "At home he demanded that I will walk around naked so he can watch me. This was very difficult for me both because it was humiliating and because I had difficulty to get acclimatized to the weather, which is much colder that what I am used to and there was no heat." When Rosa related this experience, I shivered in response to both the amount of disrespect shown to her as a human being and the memory of my first winters in New York, when it felt like all the layers of sweaters and coats in the world would not block the freezing, bitter cold.

Rosa had been used to praying every night. Her husband used to make fun of her in a cruel way, "You are again talking to your devil?" He kept an airgun next to their bed, allegedly to scare burglars away, "but I could not sleep calmly. I was afraid that he will shoot me in my sleep." He did not allow her to make phone calls, and when her family called her he was listening and recording them.

Becoming a victim of domestic violence and spousal abuse is a common experience for immigrant women. Relocating to a different culture requires reworking domestic relationships, specifically gender relations, and often creates tensions that frequently have implications for family violence, which are exacerbated by the absence of close kin to serve as a social curb (Holtzman, 2000). Specifically, domestic violence has been documented as one of the most serious problems facing Asian immigrant women and refugee women (Friedman, 1992;

Balgopal, 2000). A survey conducted by the Immigrant Women's Task Force of the Northern California Coalition for Immigrant Rights revealed that 34 percent of Latinas and 25 percent of Filipinas surveyed had experienced domestic violence either in their country of origin, in the United States, or both (see the Family Violence Prevention Fund, <http://endabuse.org/programs/immigrant/>). Furthermore, domestic violence and spousal abuse increase in the postmigration period.

The nonreporting of the high prevalence of battering suffered by immigrant women due to language barriers, social isolation, patriarchal culture of origin, and lack of familiarity with available services in the absorbing society have also been documented extensively (Jang, Marin, and Pendleton, 1997). The victim often does not know protection is available or how to seek it. Many immigrant victims do not speak English and are uninformed about criminal and immigration laws and systems in their new country. Some victims lead very isolated lives; if they are undocumented, they live secret lives in which they literally have no legal identity and few if any ties to social services, friends, or family. Abusers often compound their abuse by threatening to call immigration services and have the victim deported if she dares to complain about the abuse.

Many women immigrate from countries where domestic violence is considered a private matter, and talking with people outside their families about their experience of family violence is unacceptable (Iredale, 1995; Dasgupta and Warrier, 1996; Easteal, 1996). In many immigrant groups, the victim may be ostracized, making it difficult to survive (Tiede, 2001).

In a strange terrain, with no support system and no resources, Rosa felt trapped. She could not go back because she did not have the means or the knowledge, and in a way, her bridges back home had been burned: "In my community, it would have been a big shame, and I would have been condemned. In my culture, a woman stays in a marriage, no matter what. Everybody knew that I was already living and sleeping with him, and going back would have been a disaster." Recognizing the difficult situation of immigrant women who are victims of domestic violence and depend on their abuser for their legal status, such women should be protected while they are waiting for their permanent residency. For example, in Australia a provision was introduced in 1996 to enable eligible applicants be granted permanent residence when the relationship which forms the basis of the claim has ended due to domestic violence. However, women are often not aware of their rights.

Rosa decided to stay with this man, whom she did not like and felt deceived by, and try to make it work. "I used to get up at four o'clock in the morning to clean the place. I scrubbed the floor. We Asians are very clean, even when we are poor. I was ready to sacrifice myself." Rosa's decision to stay with her abuser is not uncommon among women who have been socialized in patriarchial cultures. Many immigrant women feel forced to stay in abusive relationships because of poor language skills, inadequate training, visa problems, lack of support, and lack of financial security (Balgopal, 2000).

The first opportunity for possible escape came from a Malaysian female customer in the ice cream parlor, who happened to come in when Rosa's husband was busy. Rosa confided in her, and the woman connected her with a Filipino social worker from a service for immigrant women. This referral was her salvation. "I was not sure where I could go. I did not know whom to ask. In my culture you do not ask such questions. It makes you look bad." Only to a female compatriot did Rosa dare tell her agony. "Had this immigration worker not been from my own country, I would not have told her what was going on in my life." Her husband soon caught her talking to "a stranger" and brutally attacked her. She managed to run away to another Filipino woman that she knew from the neighborhood who called the police for help. The police became part of the abusive experience when they refused to intervene in what they defined as a domestic matter. Finally, Rosa found her way to a shelter for victims of domestic violence (called in Australia a women's refuge house).

However, in the refuge Rosa felt that living with other traumatized women exacerbated rather than helped her cope with her own trauma. A Filipino immigration worker helped her move to a shelter for immigrants. "I was lucky that I met a Filipino worker. I would not have shared my experience and distress with a white Australian woman. I can even hardly understand what they say albeit my English is not bad, let alone talk about such intimate and painful topics." English is Rosa's second language next to her original Tegalo. "It is much easier to talk with someone of your own culture. You can't relate properly and express yourself properly to somebody from another culture, even if you know that they have your best interest."

Rosa's ordeal continued as she tried to settle her legal status in her new country. "I met a lot of racism. In court I could not afford the fee of a lawyer, so I received the services of a lawyer on duty. He was not ready, did not know my case, and in court I was not understood and not listened to. I was very intimidated when I saw my husband with a proper lawyer while I was treated as a piece of nothing." She sought an order of protection and failed to get it and was ashamed to contact her family for help. Rosa felt she was at a dead end. Feeling that all doors had been slammed in her face, Rosa felt despair and contemplated taking her own life.

The social worker in the refuge submitted Rosa's application for citizenship even though it was missing necessary documents. Luckily, this occurred in the midst of a policy change and in spite of her husband's protests; Rosa was the first beneficiary of a legal change that decreased formal demands in cases such as hers.

With her legal status in place, Rosa moved in with her sister, who lives with an Italian man, and found employment, first cleaning offices and later clerical work in an insurance company, processing claims of injured workers. She started to participate in a support group. "I started to feel as if I am a real person again. I give back to the community." She also managed to get a divorce from her husband. In the process she found out that he was seventy-two years old rather than in his forties, as he first pretended.

Rosa still suffers from the trauma. She has nightmares, suffers from dissociative reactions, is afraid to develop relationships with men, and cries often. "I remained handicapped, vulnerable, sensitive. I felt and still feel that I live in somebody else's reality. I have to filter everything through my lens. The way people think here is very different than the way people think in my country, and I 'translate' from here to there all the time." She also struggles with residual financial problems from her ordeal and sends money to support her family.

In spite of these difficulties, Rosa feels much more at home in her new environment. She has decided to make her home in the host country. What helped her survive? Rosa believes that her knowledge of the language was a key to her ability to cope with the very challenging circumstances she faced. Even though she felt that her rights have been compromised because of being a woman, an immigrant, and a non-white, her ability to always express herself and to understand what is said to her and about her mitigated the feeling of being at a loss. "I encountered racism everywhere—in governmental offices, in the court. I was a poor woman from Asia trying to fight a white man. The government's attitude toward immigrants is always harsher and less understanding. Immigrants from Asia are treated like we are a danger invading the country, and the minister of immigration affairs wants us to go back where we came from. These people have no heart and no compassion for those who are not like them. But my knowledge of the language and gradual growing understanding of how they think helped me cope with them."

Her strong belief in God and spiritual support from the church gave her the power to fight her battles. "We Filipinos, when we are in trouble, go to the priest to confess. At my weakest points, when I felt low and drowning, saying the rosary, praying, attending masses, talking to the priest, and meeting with other people who share my belief gave me the power to struggle with my hardships." A study of female Muslim Somali immigrants to Australia found that turning to their religion and a strict adherence to culture served as a source of support that sustains them and enables them to cope, providing a "known in an unknown land" (Paul, 1999).

Having come across a social worker of a similar origin was also very helpful, according to Rosa. "Here was a person who knew where I come from, how things have been for me there, and she did not judge or condemn me. She could sympathize with my situation, hear me, and help me. Had it been somebody with the best will of another culture, it would not have been the same."

Rosa's family gave her complete support, once she found the courage to share with them what she has been going through. "They kept telling me that I am welcome to come back home. They said to me 'we are not rich, but if it is too difficult for you, we shall share whatever we have. The important thing is that we are all together. This is what counts.' Their reaction gave me the power to endure my difficulties. I knew that I have a back, that I am not alone."

Rosa summarized her immigration experience, saying, "I came out of the ordeal stronger. People tell me I am a survivor. I guess I am, even though I do not always feel so. Sometimes I feel weak and vulnerable. But overall, it gave me more confidence in my abilities to successfully cope with devastating situations."

NATASHA: IN AUSTRALIA, BECOME AN AUSTRALIAN

Natasha is a thin, meticulously dressed and groomed, articulate, Jewish woman in her early seventies, who emigrated to Australia fifty years ago but still remembers it clearly "as if it was yesterday." She was originally brought forcibly to Austria from her Russian homeland to work in an ammunition factory that served the German army. She refused to be repatriated after the war for fear of the terrible conditions in the postwar Soviet Union under the Communist regime. Claiming that she was Romanian rather than Russian in origin, she was placed in a transition camp, where she met her future husband. Together they moved to Munich, had two daughters, and decided to emigrate to Australia. "This was the best decision we could have made and the best thing we had ever done," she said. Seven years after moving to Australia they naturalized. "Australia is a very tolerant country and Australians are tolerant people. Sometimes visitors think that they are not smart," she vehemently defends her host culture, "but this is a big mistake because they are so relaxed and so laid back. They are very polite, gentle, hospitable."

As she spoke, I thought about the events that had been taking place in Australia during the week of the interview, leading to calls for judicial inquiries into the inhuman conditions of immigrants in Australia. For example, two days before the interview, a Pakistani refugee who sought asylum in Australia six years earlier and received citizenship on the past year's Australia Day (the equivalent to Independence Day in the United States) was fighting for his life. Having lost hope for his wife and children to join him, following a five-year battle to have his application for family reunification approved, the desperate man set himself on fire on the steps of Parliament House in Canberra and suffered fatal body burns. A couple of days earlier tear gas was used against protests by asylum seekers, who often risk their lives to flee persecution in their homeland only to be locked in prison-like refugee and immigrant detention centers, under inhumane conditions. I considered the immigration laws, which have become constantly harsher. I thought about the heated public debate regarding revelations of the horrible conditions and the cruel attitudes of Australian authorities toward so-called illegal immigrants, including strip searches of children, holding toddlers and their parents in isolation, and severe prison sentences for poor people who try to escape from dangers in their own homeland. I also remembered horror stories recounted by people who emigrated to Australia under circumstances similar to Natasha and around the same time, which I heard at a recent reunion I attended of "alumni" of Bonegilla, an immigrant and refugee transition camp near Albury, on the border of two of Australia's eastern regions: New South Wales and Victoria. Finally, I thought about Rosa's feeling about the Australian attitude toward immigrants.

Upon their immigration, Natasha's family lived in difficult conditions: "I had no language and no work. We lived in a small hut in the bush, which we built with our own hands. We were like the Australian pioneers of the 1950s, cutting down timber and building our own house." Natasha and her husband worked hard to carve a new life for themselves and their children. However, she recalls getting used to the new life as relatively painless, and when asked about hardships of immigration, she mostly denied any. "We were young, and young people get used to new places easily." Another explanation which she offered was, "We have lived in Germany five years prior to coming to Australia, so we got used to some differences." Finally, she related the absence of difficulties in acculturation to the fact that "this was paradise. We came to the land of plenty. In the transition camp we had a lot of wonderful food. Some people, especially from Poland, used to complain because we were often fed with sheep, which to them was poor people's dish, but we thought that it was excellent. To us it was as if we had an Easter feast every day."

Natasha soon started her intense effort to assimilate into Australian society. This in her mind is the only strategy that makes sense for immigrants. Throughout the interview, she emphasized in many ways that immigrants need to let go of their homeland, memories, compatriots, and nostalgia and become one with their new land's compatriots. Her words reminded me of the Biblical Ruth, one of the earliest documented women immigrants. Following the death of her husband, an immigrant from Judah to Moab, Ruth insists on joining her mother-in-law to relocate to her late husband's homeland: "For where you go, I will go. And where you stay, I will stay. Your people shall be my people, and your God my God" (Ruth 1:16).

A first step in assimilation was changing her name to Netta. "Natasha was not familiar to Australians, not a common and not an easy name for them to pronounce, so I became Netta." Only years later, when she was in an ice cream parlor and heard an Australian mother scolding her young daughter, "Natasha, I told you to stop it," she reclaimed her original name. "I said to myself that if now Australian recognize Natasha and give the name to little girls, I also can become Natasha."

Natasha is convinced that immigrants have the sole responsibility for their own success or failure: "If you work hard, you make it." The myth of the American dream that a poor child can become a successful businessperson/lawyer/physician/professor echoes in her picture of the world. Though she does not openly comment on it, I get a sense that Natasha would not approve of bilingual programs and similar measures designed to help immigrants adjust gradually. She has high demands for self-reliance and independence. Her motto is that to succeed, immigrants should use all their personal resources, work hard, and "make it" on their own. As soon as her youngest daughter went to school, Natasha looked for a job. Because her formal education was limited, she found work in a guesthouse, later to move to working in a hotel.

Like Genevieve, who emigrated from France to Israel, Natasha always thought that acquiring the language of the host culture is a key to success. "If you do not have the language, you do not have the people. If you do not learn the language first, you become isolated, your children need to translate for you, and this is humiliating." Her opinion about the importance of language in the acculturation and adjustment to a new society is supported by immigration research (Zapf, 1991). Based on their belief in the importance of language and true to her conviction that immigrants are responsible for their own path, Natasha and her husband took correspondence courses in English. "English became so much our language that soon we spoke only English; it became such a second nature that my husband and I even spoke English to each other."

Natasha is so dedicated to gaining mastery of English that following the recent death of her husband of heart failure, and in spite of the fact that she is struggling with cancer, she continues to learn creative writing, poetry, and public speaking in a special university program for the elderly. She reads only in English and makes a deliberate effort to be totally immersed in the local culture. "Being a foreigner by origin, I merged into the Australian society and I am one of them."

However, learning the language is only the first step. Natasha believes that adopting the customs of one's new environment is equally crucial for successful acculturation. "There is no need to maintain the customs of the country from which you came. It was OK there, but there is a sense in being terribly different from your surroundings. People stare at you. While in the beginning everything seems strange, the right thing is to observe how things are done in your new place and to merge in. Gradually you find that what seems strange in the start has a good reason for it."

At moments Natasha paused and yielded to a less decisive perspective: "Integration is useful. I will not cease to be a Russian girl," but promptly went back to her slogan, "but it is important to become as much of your new culture as you possibly can." In a similar way, when I probed her never-a-single-immigration-related-problem posture, she admitted, "Maybe in the start the girls were called German sausages at school." However, she dismissed it casually: "I don't think it was anything; they quickly became very popular. It hardly was and went away as soon as it came."

She quickly became fluent in English and very good at her work. "In the start it was very difficult," she said. "I would arrange three or four rooms and feel that I cannot do it any more, and yet I knew that a dozen additional rooms are waiting for me." However, it seems that she has a pattern of putting her whole energy and effort into whatever she is doing, quickly mastering necessary skills. From her self-description, it appears that Natasha has excellent skills of adaptation to new roles and new circumstances, and when she masters a skill, she becomes bored and looks for new challenges.

Natasha is very proud of how well she has been accepted by her new social environment, by which she means the dominant, white, mostly Christian society. "I was completely surrounded by native Australians," and by this she does not mean Aboriginal. Although some immigrants tend to seek communities of compatriots, Natasha's connection with other Russian immigrants was very limited. At one point she and her husband developed some relationship with a local Russian community, but this did not last, because she was very disappointed with them. Although she did not specify, it was implied that she discounts their "Russianness," clinging to their roots and not totally immersing in their new country, as she did: "At home we remained Australian." Natasha spoke with a tone of disapproval regarding people who tended to adhere to compatriots. She believes that people who relocate but fail to adopt their new country's language, norms, and way of life "make a big mistake." She discounted any nostalgia as nonsense: "It makes no sense to think that one country, one people, such as one's country of origin, is any better than any other place or people. This is chauvinism at its worst. When one leaves one country to live in another country, the new country should become one's homeland. It is no good to stick to your own. You should try to fit in."

Her great pride is that from early on she worked to become and was accepted as "one of them." She proudly recounted an incident when her co-workers were talking about newcomers. One of them noticed that she was around and hushed the others, "Not in front of Natasha," to which somebody else responded, "She is one of us." This was an important victory to Natasha. She believes that her mild and unassuming manner made it easy for her to be accepted, and she emphasized, "I never experienced any discrimination; everyone was nice to me. I was working very hard and they appreciated me.

"I never believed that immigrants should remain loyal to where they came from. If one relocates to a new place, one needs to do the best to fit into the new environment and become part of it. If one does not do it, why do they relocate in the first place? Immigrants with condescending and patronizing attitudes cannot make it. You have to modify your attitude, your belief system, and your life when you emigrate. If you come to Rome, you need to become a Roman."

SABIN: TO IMMIGRATE AS A LESBIAN

It is hard to say when Sabin emigrated from Austria to Australia, because her story of relocating evolved as she was living it. In 1988, then in her late twenties, Sabin left her native central European, history-rich country to take a yearlong trip to the South Pacific. Although she wanted her journey not to be predetermined in duration, it had to be somewhat defined, because her partner at the time had two young children who were living with their father. Their mother felt that she needed to give them some date for her return, and a year was long enough to meet Sabin's wish for freedom and her partner's need for a boundary. Sabin had dreamed about the trip for ten years, although she cannot exactly identify what drew her specifically to this part of the world.

After a brief stop in Tahiti, where Sabin felt very uncomfortable in light of the huge gap between the living conditions of the black and white populations, they went to New Zealand for four months. During this period Sabin met people and made friends. She also went through a complicated experience when the two women decided to end their romantic relationship but to continue traveling together.

It was Good Friday when they arrived in Sydney with very little cash in their pocket, hardly enough to pay for a train from the airport to the city, and no credit card machine was available in the airport. Having been so engulfed in their own issues, the two did not realize that banks, like shops and other businesses, would be closed. Somehow they managed to arrange for a place to stay for the weekend, but the memory of being totally at loss in a strange place with no person from whom to seek help embodies a feeling that is quite familiar to immigrants. I still vividly remember my panic when I needed some emergency help with child care and realized to my horror that I did not know anyone in the whole big "Big Apple" whom I could call for help. This was a painful wake-up call to my deeply felt loss of the socially embracing environment I had left behind.

Sabin and her partner soon realized how different life is in Australia compared to their homeland. "One can not imagine more difference than between Australia and Austria. The gap between the Austrian strict appropriateness, where I stuck out like a sore thumb, and the casual, relaxed Australian style was overwhelming. Everything was surrealistic. Coming to Australia had been my dream for ten years. However, it was a romantic dream. I did not really know what to expect. I felt like an alien who fall down to earth, not understanding the rules of the game, making all the possible mistakes, saying all the wrong things."

Not having a valid work permit made surviving a real challenge. Sabin found herself living in a neighborhood full of drugs, sex for sale, and violence. "I could not afford a train ride, and Sydney is a huge city. As a matter of fact, everything was gigantic." One week after I interviewed Sabin I went for a week in Australia's Outback. Only when one drives for hundreds of kilometers in a red and yellow desert, with an occasional family of emus crossing the road and a lone kangaroo hopping around, can one get the sense of how big this continent is.

Sabin stayed in Sydney about three or four months, the last of them on her own, as the other woman moved to Melbourne. At that point she contemplated the idea of going back to New Zealand. "Part of what I wanted in this trip was to meet people who do not know me and my history and who can get to know me from scratch and to accept me for who I was, as a total stranger. However, at that point I was already tired of the experience of having to start from zero every time, and I needed the comfort of familiarity. Since in New Zealand I already made some friends, the idea to go back to their warm lap was tempting." Before going to New Zealand, Sabin stayed some time in Melbourne, where she met an Australian woman with whom she soon developed a close relationship.

Upon her return to Australia from New Zealand, she knew that she needed to make a decision. "It was a long and difficult process. The decision to emigrate is emotionally consuming, because you really have to decide about your whole life. I was determined to get through. I am not even sure why. I knew that I could not live there [in Austria]. Austria makes you feel closeted, choked like in a straitjacket. People stare at anybody who does not perfectly fit in."

Many gay immigrants seek to be able to have a more openly gay lifestyle (Longres and Patterson, 2000). Sabin was one of them. She decided to apply for permanent residency in Australia. She felt that she could not, and to this day has not, apply for citizenship, because that would have meant giving up her Austrian citizenship. "I am not ready to cut the umbilical cord. I could not imagine going to my own country as a tourist with an Australian passport. And what if at some point in the future I wish to go back to Austria? Will I have to apply for citizenship in my country of origin? This is inconceivable to me."

Australia is one of the few countries that allows "a compassion visa," which grants spousal immigration rights for gay and lesbian people. Sabin's new partner agreed to support her application. "This put me in an emotional maze. I was totally dependent on her. I could not end the relationship if I wanted to." Her partner's lack of understanding and empathy to Sabin's distress exacerbated her agony.

Encounters with immigration authorities were very stressful. The process took four years, because during some periods processing of applications for permanent residency stopped. It was an exhausting, occasionally humiliating, and anxiety-provoking experience. A lot of documentation was necessary, and piles of paperwork had to be submitted more than once. Every single detail in the application had to be supported by documents and statements. "Sometimes I deliberated with myself for several days before I called the immigration authorities. What would the immigration officer request this time? What kind of response will I get? Will I be able to handle it?" The fact that her native Australian partner could not understand what she was going through and called her hysterical made the experience more lonely and difficult.

Sabin felt totally infantilized by her dependency on her partner and on the immigration authorities. "Your whole life is in the hands of other people who do not always mean well, and there is nothing that you can do about it. You are totally at the mercy of other people. They can decide to send you away and you have no control. You are helpless and powerless like a leaf in the wind. I was afraid that in the interview I will get mixed up, forget names and details. I used to rehearse the information. This was a very depressing experience."

As she spoke, I remembered the anxiety that engulfed me when my then nine-year-old son stated as his birth place a different city from what the documents showed, and the interviewing immigration officer started to attack me with many suspicious questions in a hostile voice which made me shake with horror in spite of the fact I knew that all the documentation had been carefully reviewed by a lawyer.

In addition to feeling deprived of her independence to shape her life as she pleased, Sabin experienced the process as infantilizing and frightening. "It feels like living under a magnifying glass with each step closely scrutinized by Big Brother. It casted a constant shadow over me. Can I afford to participate in a demonstration about environmental issues which are dear to my heart, or will any act which can be viewed as antigovernment be held against me? Can I sign a petition, or will this boomerang on me? Could I resign from a job which I resented? How will I live, since I was not eligible for unemployment benefits? You put your whole life on hold during the process, and you live in constant fear. You do not know the limits of your liberty and [this] may hurt you. You are paralyzed by the ambiguity, by not knowing the rules of the game. I felt stripped of my freedom to speak and was extremely insecure."

The experience took a toll on Sabin's emotional and physical life. "I was sick a lot, I was stressed, I cried, I was deeply hurt." She felt as if she stopped living. She felt trapped, hindered from pursuing her goals. "Once I participated in a photography course. Only halfway through the course I realized that it was for permanent residents only and I felt immediately at risk of retaliation."

In the immigration offices she witnessed even worse treatment of immigrants from Africa and Asia. This helped her view her own hardship within a broader context. "I had a fairly good understanding of English and was white. I could only imagine how difficult it must be for non-whites and non-English-speaking immigrants."

Finally the procedure was completed. Sabin became a permanent Australian resident. "I received a phone call from an immigration officer who told me, 'I am going to make you happy.' I felt such relief. I ran through the hallways of the agency where I was working and excitedly yelled, 'I got it! I got it!' People looked at me as if I lost my mind, but I did not care. A dark curtain of anxieties, stress, and impatience was lifted. I could breathe. I could concentrate on other things. I could get my life back. I remember thinking that now I will not have to prove anything to anybody. I could do as I please. I do not have to constantly worry about a financial security net."

However, Sabin still carries the effects of the experience. Whenever her reserves are low, she reacts with that familiar insecurity and must remind herself that if circumstances become very bad, she is eligible for social security benefits.

Sabin views the whole ordeal as a humbling growth experience. "I developed much more understanding of people and more ability to empathize. For example, I used to wonder how my two aunts who have emigrated to England and the United States (you see, immigration of women runs in my family) could have lived there for thirty years and not become a citizen and deprive themselves of the right to have their opinions shared and counted. Now I understand. One remains in many ways tied to one's country of origin, and the administrative act of changing citizenship is heavily loaded emotionally."

She also learned what support from friends meant for her. "My friends said that they would rally for me if my application is denied. They promised I could stay with them, if things did not work for me." She also learned to look at tradition through a different lens. "Back in Austria I experienced tradition as restrictive and customs as binding. It is conservative and oppressive. Being exposed to the place of tradition in the Aboriginal culture made me realize the vivid, living, and nourishing aspect of tradition. I came to appreciate the beauty of heritage."

Sabin went back to her country of origin three times during her dozen years in Australia. Her life in Australia provided her with a different perspective of her homeland. "Everything about the relationships between white man and Aborigines here could have been effectively transferred there—the shame, guilt—except here they deal with it while there they don't. You can still hear people referring to 'inappropriate' attitudes, 'Hitler would not have had approved of this.' This makes me very uncomfortable."

Sabin also learned about empathy and sensitivity. "When I was sharing how difficult the experience of immigration was for me, I often met judgmental attitudes. I did not come from a war zone or extreme political or financial distress. I did not have a 'justified reason.' Rather, I opted to emigrate. People implied that I did not have the right to complain because I always had the option to go back. As if when one is emotionally suffocated by the climate in one's country of origin it is less acceptable to emigrate than from a war-torn country. As if there is 'deserving' and 'nondeserving' in the immigration experience, and I was among the 'nondeserving.' I got the message that I do not have the right to complain. I learned from this lack of understanding not to judge people until you stand in their place. Not to assume that you know how it is to be there. Not to have the pretension to judge whose suffering is more difficult. I developed a lot of compassion. Immigration made me a more mature and better person."

MATIJIA: THE LEMONADE MAKER

Matijia, twice an immigrant in nine years, always finds the bright side of the picture, and when given a lemon in life, she finds a way to make it into a lemonade. She is a forty-six-year-old worker with an agency that provides services to immigrants and refugees in a large Australian city. She emigrated to Australia in 1996 with her husband and her then thirteen-year-old daughter and ten-year-old son. "It is difficult to say which is my first language. I was born in Bosnia to parents of Croatian origin. When I was growing up, the dominant language at home and in school was Serbo-Croatian. Today, with the growth of nationalism and separatism in my homeland, this could not have flown. One has to be and speak one or the other, but we grew up in a mixed society and spoke a mixed language."

Prior to coming to Australia, the family lived for four years in Croatia. When the war in Bosnia broke out, they escaped and became refugees in the neighboring state. Matijia defines this time as the worst period in her life. "We had no means for survival. We were scared and hopeless. In Bosnia, I was an educated woman with a decent salary, a good job, and a reasonable quality of life. Here, all of a sudden I had to stand in line to beg for a package of food from Charitas [a church-based charity organization]."

She recounted a situation which made her feel that she had hit bottom and became a pivotal point in her migration experience. "I was standing by a telephone booth to make a call. The telephone did not work. While I stood there contemplating what to do, a man standing next to me started to chat with me. We found out that I attended school together with his nephew. He started to ask me about myself, and he explained that I could not expect to get in my new environment a position as good as the one I once had. Gradually he made me feel more and more miserable. Eventually he offered me a job as a saleswoman in his shop and hinted that it would help if we had a personal meeting to settle the details, 'an attractive woman like you.' I felt humiliated, like I am having a bad dream. I felt that I just couldn't take it anymore. I must do something to change my situation. I cannot let something like this happen to me again. In his nasty way, this man did me a favor, because the encounter with him made me pull myself together and get out of the bad situation in which I was." His offer helped her realize that she was gradually sliding down a slippery slope. This realization gave her the strength to begin seriously looking for a position, which she quickly found as an interpreter for the Standing Committee of the United Nations High Commissioner for Refugees in Croatia.

Four years later, in light of the continuing unrest in the former Yugoslavia, they decided to follow her sister's family who had relocated to Australia fifteen months earlier. "My parents would not move, but we wanted to live as close to each other so that we can provide each other mutual support."

The move was not easy. "I went from struggling there to struggling here. During the last nine years all I did was struggle. This is a very tiring experience. There is no stability, no security, and that exhausts one's resources." However, she assesses the struggle in Australia as less difficult than her experience in Croatia because of a financial safety net provided by the absorbing culture, which was totally absent from her previous refugee experience. "If you can prove that you are looking for work and cannot find it, the government helps you, unlike in Croatia."

Initially, however, Matijia did not look for work because she felt overwhelmed with taking care of her family. "We had to take care of immediate survival needs such as a place to live, food to eat, clothes to wear . . . the very basic, and it all fell on me because having been an English teacher by education, my language skills were much better, and in our culture of origin these kind of arrangements are the woman's territory and responsibility."

Helping her children start their process of acclimatization presented a major challenge. "Understanding the educational system, the expectations, the mechanisms for decision making, the whole culture of schools and what is going on for your children, the academic plan; it was very difficult to figure out in the beginning, and it is one of the first big challenges for immigrant mothers. It takes a lot out of you. You want to make sure that your children get what they deserve, yet nobody tells you the norms, what is good and what is bad, whom to approach how, which channels one has, which options and how to make sense of them for the benefit of your kids. These are the important things that 'everybody knows'; that is, everybody that grew up in the system or has been here for a while. This is a roller coaster into which an immigrant mother is thrown in her first week in the new country."

Because the family lived in a neighborhood populated mostly by immigrants, Matijia's children did not feel exceptional in their refugee status. "There were many other refugee kids from all over the world, so they did not feel rejected or isolated as I have heard refugee kids in a more 'Australian' environment feel. They learned English with other non-English speakers. This made it easier for them, and when it is easy for the children it makes it easy for the mother."

In spite of this, her son experienced social difficulties. "He used to come home crying because he felt intimidated by other children about his appearance, his clothes. I tried to encourage him, but he kept saying that 'Australian kids do not like us.' Consequently, he preferred to choose other immigrant children for friends and stay away from Australian-born children. He has been struggling, and I have been struggling with him."

Soon staying at home was not enough for Matijia. She attended a yearlong postgraduate business course, but halfway through the course she decided that she should not delay looking for a permanent job. "I was in my forties and knew that my age would present an obstacle in job hunting, so I decided to delay it no further because it would become more difficult with the passage of time. The most difficult challenge was to start everything all over again from scratch."

Matijia applied for a job at two commercial places and at the agency for which she currently works. "I started doing volunteer work with this agency since my very first days in Australia. When we arrived, I was referred for professional assessment and guidance to the government job-finding service. When they heard about my experience in interpreting, they immediately suggested that I volunteer to work with refugees here. So I did. It was my natural field."

In spite of having volunteered for the organization, obtaining a paid job required a struggle. After two rejections, Matijia finally received a position. "I am a fighter, I do not give up easily. I tell myself that I am not a child, I am a mature woman who made a decision to relocate to give my children a better chance in life and a sense of security, and I have to take the consequences that accompany my decision, including professional difficulties." Matijia joined the 24 percent of foreign-born economically active women in Australia who are gradually gaining access to the higher end of the occupational scale, although they face greater obstacles than native-born women (United Nations, 1995).

Combining full-time work, full-time study, and full-time mothering and housekeeping was very challenging. A major hardship was presented by the constant feeling of lack of stability. "Everything is temporary. We lived in five places in the last five years. For the last ten years, each year we had to pack and move. Only recently we managed to buy a house. My first house in my whole life. Maybe now I found my Safe Haven [this is a concept used to describe the shelter offered to refugees]."

Matijia feels that people who do not share the experience fail to appreciate the difficulties. "If you look from outside, everything seems good—work, school, food, a place to live—but to live it is very, very difficult. The main challenge of immigrants is to stay normal." She is exhausted by the constant effort to stay alert. "I always need to check and double check myself if what I think and do is acceptable within the context of my new environment, and whether it is appropriate. I often feel uprooted, displaced, not fitting. I am afraid that I wear the wrong outfit, say the inappropriate sentence. I am not in my natural environment so things do not just come to me naturally. Everything, even the minutest step, requires an effort, consideration, and calculation. Even to speak English all day long is fatiguing. It is very, very hard when you have to function all the time in a strange territory."

She relates the hardships mostly to the difference between her culture of origin and the absorbing culture. "Moving from Bosnia to Croatia was less difficult in spite of the worse conditions there than here, because the Bosnian and Croatian cultures are similar. Here, in Australia, things are fundamentally different, and this makes acculturation much more difficult." She feels like an alien lost in strange territory and not familiar with the codes: "You lose your compass, your criteria for what should be done and how. All the time I am scared to make mistakes."

According to Matijia, immigrant women are often the ones who carry the heaviest load. "The main burden of the family's acculturation and adjustment to the new environment was on me, as it is on all immigrant women. We are like sponges that absorb the pain and hardships of children and husbands, and often in-laws and other relatives, as well as our own." Her husband did not provide much help. He usually expected her to do most of the necessary arrangements. "He pushed me to be the one to negotiate the educational system, the medical system, and the job market to find a job while he went to study English," she said. This story is not uncommon, and I heard it many times from immigrants from the former Soviet Union with whom I worked. Women are often put at the forefront of the battle for life in the new country. "I was afraid to ask questions, to look stupid and not know what 'everybody' knows. I felt embarrassed and awkward," Matijia said.

Matijia sometimes feels frustrated by her own children: "I do not always have answers to their questions, and this breaks my heart. I am not so happy with the way that I cope with my children's issues, because I am so exhausted as a result of having to handle all those issues and time goes by so fast." She feels that the many challenges placed on her by immigration deprived her of time that she would like to dedicate to her children. Being absorbed in addressing their practical needs takes away from her ability to devote more time to her interactions with them and dedicate to them.

Matijia indicated that a certain degree of estrangement and distance is an inevitable but heavy price in parent-child relationships caused by immigration. "Sometimes it saddens me that our children do not respect our achievements because our accent and English are inferior to theirs. They grow up in a culture which is different than ours. It is good for them to feel comfortable in their environment, but this creates [distance] between us. To the normal generation gap immigration adds a culture gap. Their taste is more Australian in many ways. Sometimes I feel that immigration causes us to lose them, they are sliding between my fingers. Sometimes I think that maybe it is already too late. I lost the first critical period when I was busy dealing with the essentials of survival and could not spare the time and effort."

Matijia's experience is not unusual in relation to children of the second and 1.5 generation, a concept that describes children who were born abroad but immigrated at a very young age and are growing up in the receiving culture. It illustrates what Portes and Rumbaut (2001) conceptualize as dissonant acculturation, which occurs when children move away from their parents' language of origin and lose links to their parents' cultural heritage, while parents remain steeped in their language and culture. This creates a gap that leads to breakdown of communication and reduced parental authority and control.

Helping her husband with his difficulties placed additional pressure on Matijia. "Not only does he not help me with addressing the children's issues, I also am called to help him with his issues." Her husband, a language teacher by profession, feels very uncomfortable in pursuing a position that requires communication because of his limited mastery of English. Consequently, he works at a manual job and feels hurt because he had to compromise for a position below his educational and earning potential. His family is the victim of his frustration and bitterness, the lion's share of which Matijia exposes herself to in order to protect her children. "I am the mediator, the sponge, the peacemaker, the normalizer. I have seen the same scenario happening in other immigrant families. This is quite a typical script."

Women, according to Matijia, play the central role in their family's adaptation: "We women are more practical." She believes that women bring the calming and balancing voice to the family's life and provide husbands and children with hope and a positive outlook. "Immigrant women work twice as hard as immigrant men. We take more on ourselves. When he comes from work, it is normal for both of them that she will serve him. When she comes from work, she still has to serve everybody. Albeit here it is different, we brought from our culture of origin the expectations that women take care of most family business but are not recognized for all they do for the welfare of their families." This perspective is supported by studies that document the role of women as pillars of their families (e.g., Friedman, 1992).

In her own family, Matijia is the initiator. "All major movements were the result of my pushing. I am the pushing power. The two relocations were a result of my pressure." Her husband stayed in Bosnia when she escaped with the children to Croatia as soon as the war broke out. He eventually was forced to participate in the fighting, was wounded, and experienced traumatic events in his homeland. Consequently, he carries physical and emotional wounds.

This central role takes a heavy toll. "It falls on the women from all directions. I often ask myself why is it always me that needs to find the energy to make sure that everything functions. When I am not around, things just do not operate properly. For example, I had to participate in a retreat at work. When I came home after two days, about three dozen problems were waiting for me to be resolved, the place was a mess, and it took me a couple of hours to restore the functioning of everything."

An additional source of stress is being torn between the commitment to the immediate family and the guilt regarding family members that did not emigrate. "I still have family back in Croatia and Bosnia. A part of you always stays behind in your homeland with those who did not come along. You always feel guilty that you live here an easier life. You send money to help, but it never feels enough. In my case, the sense of having deserted my parents in their old age and deteriorating health breaks my heart. I wish to build a better future for my children here but want to support and be for my parents there. For example, tomorrow my father is undergoing an operation, and I am not there for him. I am here. I can't be in so many places at the same time. Where should I be? Here for my children and husband? There for my parents? The years go by and you feel that you are missing irreversible precious time, but when I go to be with them, I feel the same about my family here. I want to do good for my children and good for my parents, but these two goods conflict and I am torn in the middle." Matijia is describing a conflict that is very common for immigrant women. Pittaway (1999) describes these women as "the upholders of culture and the keepers of hope. They take the responsibility for maintaining family structures and for seeking solutions" (p. 1).

Matijia makes a deliberate effort to maintain her own and her family's bond with the culture of their homeland. The whole family went for a six-week visit to the old country, she insists on speaking Croatian with her children, and she is especially proud that last year her daughter opted to study Croatian in a special weekend program and won a regional prize for her achievements. "If I would not have done it from the start, it would have been very easy to slide into English. I knew that English they will learn at school and growing up in an English-speaking environment, so I wanted to [speak] our language at home. Otherwise, they might have lost it, and that would further rob me of the thread of relationship, which is already threatened by their 'Australianization.'"

With all these difficulties, Matijia struggles to remain optimistic. "I work hard to see the half-full part of the glass. I am the flexible family member, I adjust more easily. Even though we do not have everything the way we would like it to be, we have many successes and we need to learn to be happy with them. I often remember what we went through and what could have happened. We could have lost my husband. This brings a different proportion to problems and contextualizes today's difficulties in a different perspective. We should never forget what could have been." She tries to minimize the problems and emphasize positive results. Her husband has a much harder time adjusting. When the family spent some time in their homeland, he was hospitalized because of stress. "We realized that he was not ready to go back; it was too much for him. It was like going back to the battlefield." Even in all the hardships of immigration she finds a positive side: "Because of my own experiences, I can understand better the problems of our clients and relate to them better."

Matijia's major source of support in her struggle is her sense of her own and her family's accomplishment. "Sometimes I think that OK, I am exhausted, but my children are doing well. They grow up in a safe environment, and I tell myself that my efforts are worth it. If a mother sees that her children are healthy, safe, and successful and that in spite of all the difficulties the family functions well, it justifies it all." Her sister, who was a judge in her homeland, was completing an academic degree in the helping profession at the time of the interview and is an additional example of success for Matijia. "She truly is amazing. She came to Australia with no mastery of English and she is making it. This gives me pride, power, and hope." Her parents' experience of relocation also serves as an empowering model. "They did not move to another country but to another region. This is a less extreme move, but they also had much less resources. The picture of my mother's struggle and success is a source of inspiration for me."

Her sense of responsibility is an additional energizing resource. "I know that if I will not function well, no one in the family will. So, like many immigrant women, I have no choice but to be strong and make it for everybody's sake."

HANG: A SALUTE TO IMMIGRANT MOTHERS

Hang was seven when her family relocated from war-stricken Vietnam to Australia in 1978. The family included her parents and her four siblings, leaving behind a large extended family. To Hang's best knowledge, their migration was the last opportunity for refugees from her homeland to leave in an organized manner. They traveled three nights by boat to Malaysia, where they spent some time in a refugee camp.

Vietnamese refugees first fled Vietnam in 1975 with the fall of Saigon and the Communist takeover of South Vietnam. Estimates of the number of Vietnamese who fled the oppressive government, which usurped private property, range from one to two million people. According to an arrangement known as the Comprehensive Plan of Action, these refugees were screened individually for refugee status before being eligible for resettlement (Loughry and Xuan Nghia, 2000).

Similar to many of the other refugees, Hang's family was forced to live in refugee camps in various parts of southeast Asia while they waited to find another home. The space in the camp was too small for the influx of Vietnamese refugees, and they were removed to a larger camp. Hang remembers that they were given building material with which they had to build their own huts and that many people were sick. "There was one person who knew some basic English. He would take us kids and teach us." From Malaysia they had to move to Indonesia, where they spent several months prior to settling in Australia.

Desperate to escape, some people took severe, life-threatening risks and traveled in dangerous, flimsy, and overcrowded boats, mostly to Darwin in northwestern Australia (the closest point on the Australian continent to Asia). They suffered terrible conditions on the way to set the foundation for the large Vietnamese-speaking community in Australia. By the 1996 Australian census, this community was estimated at around 144,259 people and ranked among the five largest immigrant groups of non-English-speaking background in the country.

Most Vietnamese refugees were unprepared financially and culturally. They typically had skills that did not fit the expectations of a modern culture and had only a modest degree of English competence. Most pressing were high rates of unemployment, language barriers, and, particularly among women and the elderly, social isolation. In addition, as the proportion of Asian immigrants grew, so did the unfriendly atmosphere colored by racism and discrimination, which still exists and affects the daily lives of many Asian immigrants (Hugo, 1995). In spite of these disadvantages, many of the newcomers worked diligently and were successful.

Hang's family was no exception. When they arrived in June 1978, her parents went to work in a factory and studied English and the children went to school. "Everything was strange. Never before did we experience such cold weather. It was odd for us to see children with blond hair and blue eyes. We did not even know that such people existed." They lived in a refugee hotel for about nine months. Later the family bought a restaurant and moved to their own house.

Hang, surrounded by other immigrants and refugees while growing up, was not fully aware of her situation and its significance. "We children knew that we have to work in school as hard as we possibly can and that we must succeed. It did not need to be spelled out, and no overt pressure existed. However, it was made clear to us in many different ways that we came here because my parents wanted their children to have the best educational opportunities, and we had to live up to the highest expectations. It was just made clear. My parents worked very hard in their restaurant, and we raised ourselves, cooked for ourselves, helped each other, and came to help in the restaurant on weekends."

Although she understands that circumstances did not leave her parents much choice, this is not the kind of childhood Hang would want for her own future children. "Children of immigrants grow up too fast, but at the same time they learn early responsibility, sharing with others, and not taking things for granted." Their experience is much more difficult than that of nonimmigrant children. "My parents did not know to help me with homework, could not clarify for me teachers' expectations and how to meet them." This made her even more determined to succeed. "I worked hard to understand what was going on in school, to excel academically, and to understand the Australian middle class."

Hang and her siblings wished to be Australian. "We wanted to be very Australian, more Australian than the Australian, totally immersed and 'Australianized.' Our parents understood what is happening to us and balanced it with stories about Vietnamese history and culture. They maintained for us the part of us that was Vietnamese until we grew up enough to maintain it for ourselves. I see the opposite in my friends whose parents did not make this deliberate effort. They lack this blessed balance that my parents succeeded to bestow on me in all these indirect ways—listening to Vietnamese music, eating Vietnamese food, reading Vietnamese newspapers, and so forth. Our home had a friendly Vietnamese atmosphere, and that was a strong message. We absorbed it without even knowing, and we became to own it as part of who we are."

Hang's mother did not speak proper English until her early death recently of cancer, yet a major part of the family's success was her doing. "She struggled and struggled with no end, never surrendering. There is something about immigrant women, especially immigrant mothers. They are resilient, never give up. My mother, like many immigrant women that I encounter, was always determined to find a way to resolve whatever difficulty she faced. They are the backbone of their families. Many of them believe that emigrating means providing their families, especially their children, and themselves with opportunities that need to be seized, and they capture them with strong arms."

Hang's experience mirrors Matijia's concerns about her children losing the bridge to their cultural heritage. In looking back on the way her mother handled this sensitive issue, Hang commented, "When my mother just arrived, she had to work and make a living and to raise children who were overwhelmed by the relocations. However, like other immigrant mums, she had the big challenge of finding the balance between what she thought right and what her quickly acculturating and assimilating in the dominant culture children believed to be right. It is very difficult to raise children in a strange country and yet give them the best of their own culture of origin."

Hang's parents encouraged their children to take advantage of being bicultural and to adopt what is best from both cultures. "They were always open to listen to what we brought from the Australian culture." Consequently, she learned to weave together her Vietnamese and Australian selves to create a rich embroidery of Vietnamese home-oriented life and Australian society-oriented life. "I and my sisters talk a lot about it. We do many things in the Vietnamese way. We truly feel that it is an integral part of who we are, and we are happy with it, so that we wish to hand it over to the next generation so that our children can enjoy the same broad and rich experience."

Only in her twenties did she start to become aware of her ethnic cultural heritage, to become interested in it, and to foster it. "Only when I came to the university and encountered all these native Australian, I realized suddenly how much about Australian culture I did not know. Only then I realized how different my experience was. I did not know that one could assess one's level of education and sophistication just by the name of the newspaper one reads, which radio stations are 'in.' We were not exposed to the subtleties in the same way that children of Australian-born parents are. At this stage I developed a huge chip on my shoulder." At that point Hang started her journey of realizing how much richer her experience was than that of the average middle-class Australian youth. She started to be active in the local Vietnamese community and the Buddhist community. She learned to read and write Vietnamese fluently. She plans for her future children to have a strong Vietnamese influence, under all circumstances. (Hang is not married and does not currently have children.) Last year she went to Vietnam for the first time since the family's immigration. "I felt as if I always have been Vietnamese. I immediately felt comfortable and at home as much as I feel at home in Australia. It was like a pilgrimage for me. I understood in a deep way how significant my ethnicity is to me and how wonderfully my mother helped me get to that sense of wholeness." At that point, seeing her mother within her culture of origin context and experiencing Vietnam firsthand, Hang could fully grasp and appreciate "what a huge thing immigrant women can do for their children."

Hang finds many ways, both overt and subtle, to send a clear message about being Vietnamese and Australian. For example, in Australia one signs first the given name and then the surname, whereas in Vietnamese the opposite is true. When Hang signs her letters she observes the Australian norm in the typed name but follows the Vietnamese version in her handwritten signature. This reflects Hang's rebellion against social pressure to become exclusively Australian. By the reverse signature ritual, she makes a statement about her dual commitment to Vietnam and to Australia.

Being true to her Vietnamese self granted Hang a lot of power. "We have a lot of familism. One always knows that no matter what happens and how bad things go, the Vietnamese mother always maintains the nest for her 'chicks.' Take me for example—I am thirty and did not leave home until two years ago. This is not unusual, unlike the Australians that send their children the message, 'we raise you until you are eighteen or graduate from the university, and then you are an adult and you should be responsible for yourself.' We, Vietnamese, emphasize family affiliation and belonging throughout life."

Hang summarized her experience of immigrating as a child and growing up with an immigrant mother: "I was lucky to have witnessed my mum's journey through life, how she carried her Vietnameseness and how she handled herself and her family. It made me a better person."

DUNJA: THE PERCUSSIONIST

The original title that Dunja chose for her section was "A history that winds through so many different countries." However, later she asked that it be changed to its current name with the following explanation. "At one stage I thought I would write a book about my life and I would call it *The Percussionist*. I was thrown into playing percussion for our school concert band at the age of fifteen with no music knowledge. It was a very small piece in a much wider picture of what I was achieving around my school and community. I find it is synonymous with how in my life I have played the many various 'instruments' of surviving, moving to a new place and adapting to the native beat of life."

Titling has been used in narrative research and therapy. The assumption is that the title people give their life story is a pretext, which provides the key to understanding the meaning they give to their life story, highlights the text's chief subject, and determines which aspects of lived experience ascribe its meaning (White and Epston, 1990; Kacen, 2002). Percussions are drumming musical instruments with a dominant presence. Music is created by beating the top and is typically forceful. By choosing this musical title, Dunja guides the reader to the theme of actively making her voice heard. In changing the title, she declares her preference to focus on powerfully being there rather than on the experience of wandering.

I first met Dunja at an international conference in Adelaide, a small oceanside town in southern Australia. When this energetic young woman stood up to give the keynote speech to a large crowd of professionals, one could not imagine the fascinating story she was about to share with us in a calm yet vivid voice. When she finished speaking, the room roared with applause. She sounded much more mature than her age, and I asked myself if this is a result of her having moved often and having been exposed to diverse social circumstances and experienced different environments. Dunja graciously agreed to share her story with me. She said, "I have put a lot of my life into perspective through writing this speech, and I hope other people can extract something out of it."

Dunja lives in Auckland, New Zealand, while I spent the semester in Melbourne, Australia. Therefore, geographical distance presented a challenge. Eventually we agreed that Dunja would e-mail me her written comments and we would start a dialogue via the Internet. Thus, this interview was conducted electronically.

At the time of the interview, Dunja had just graduated from high school. Dunja was born in 1983 in Sarajevo, in what was formerly known as Yugoslavia, to a Bosnian Croatian mother and a Bosnian Serb father, who met when both were students of economics. These two cultures are quite different and have recently been in terrible conflict, with war threatening to be reignited as this interview was in progress.

When Dunja was three, the family moved from Sarajevo to Africa and lived in Tanzania for about four years, where her father was overseeing the installation of a power transformer in Mwanza. Dunja remembers the years in Tanzania as "having fun and good experiences." Her fond memories are related mostly to traveling in the country's wilderness. "We went for weekend trips through the Serengeti Plain. We'd see animals in their natural habitat, untouched and free. We'd get stuck in the mud and watch our dad waist deep in mud trying to push out a Landrover driven by a woman five months pregnant. We'd get chased by elephants. We'd be stuck in our car at the bottom of a hill, hotel lights to be seen in the distance, late at night, and wondering how to get up this hill with a steep fifty-degree angle. We'd drive into a village with a broken axle, within minutes we would be surrounded by eager and helpful locals. We'd be driving up to Ngorongoro Crater and have baboons jumping all over the car. My dad had a cup thrown at him by a demanding ape, in captivity, who was drinking Miranda and water together because it had of its own accord decided that the Miranda was too sweet. I had a natural little waterfall and stream run through my school, and I'd have lunch beside it. We ate many coconuts and lots of bananas. We had them and papaya, mangoes, and avocados in our own backyard."

In addition to exploring Tanzania, the family traveled abroad as well as back to Europe for visits. Dunja favorably commented that "Each time we would come back to Europe, we would take a different route and explore different places. So, as a child I got to visit various countries in Europe, Africa, and Middle East. I got to visit the pyramids in Egypt and ride a camel." These memories serve as a refuge for Dunja at difficult times. "All this came at a very receptive stage of my development, and I guess it always gives me somewhere to run away in my head when things didn't go smoothly."

When Dunja was seven, the project on which her father worked finished and the family went back to live in Bosnia. The parents were busy reestablishing the family's life, and Dunja and her brother attended the local school. Two years later the war broke out. "When there were stories on the news how bad things were in Slovenia we started paying more attention to what was happening in our own city." Gradually, diverse signs indicated that the war was coming closer: "I remember coming home and telling mum how at school we'd heard a bomb explode somewhere." They could literally see the war coming "We lived in a suburb next to the airport called Dobrinja. Our building and especially our apartment had a clear view onto the runway, and we could see airplanes of all makes trafficking through. Then at one stage we started to see little diplomat-type planes land and take off in a frenzy. My parents immediately knew that something is the matter."

Several considerations informed the decision by Dunja's parents to leave. There was fighting in Slovenia and Croatia, and it was heading south toward Dunja's homeland. The safety of their children, Dunja and her then five-year-old brother, was a top priority for Dunja's parents. This safety was at risk because they could have been caught in a combat zone. The children of a mixed marriage with parents of the two ethnic groups at war, they would have been trapped in the middle and fit into no ethnic group. Such a situation could have triggered animosity from both sides. In addition, Dunja's father had previously served in the army, and a decision to stay might have meant that he would be called for military service. Her parents felt that the family had no choice but to leave.

The process of leaving was not easy. "My father left one night in early January, and the circumstances were frightening." She vividly remembers the preparation for leaving. Dunja, her mother, and brother left a few weeks later, with very little. "After dad had left, I helped mum get our household items stored into my brother's and my bedroom. I remember the dozens of beautiful glasses I wiped and placed on our study desk. We were going to rent the rest of the apartment out while we were away in England."

The family thought that the stay abroad would be temporary and that they would be back, "But we still felt so much sadness at the airport with all the family around us," she said. "Little did we know that was the last time we would see them in a long time." After spending a night in Serbia, they flew to England, where her father was staying and where friends whom they had met in Tanzania welcomed them. In England she was happy. "I was just a child eager to reunite with her father. I did have an inkling of what was happening. Mum and I had often watched the news, and I'd ask her about the streams of refugees they showed. But what do you tell a nine-year-old? Looking back on it, I was still untouched by it all and in a world of Barbies and Disney."

The trip to England was just the beginning of a saga of relocation that stretched across three continents and nine years. The family stayed in England for a year, but Dunja's father could not find proper employment. The next stop was in the Middle East. Because of a chance of employment in the United Arab Emirates (UAE), he moved there and the family followed him and spent three years there. "I liked it there, but in retrospect I believe that my feelings have to be reflective of the stage of my life I was at." She was mostly sheltered from the external world within her family. Her life included an elite school with children of other foreign experts, family time on the beach, visits to friends, and spending time in the malls and on the tennis and basketball court. "I liked my life in the Emirate, however my parents knew it was not a place where all of us could see happiness in our future. So they decided that it is time to move again. One of my teachers at the school I was attending was from New Zealand. My parents and she became good friends, and she encouraged them to migrate to New Zealand." Saying goodbye again was devastating. "I was terribly upset that I was going to leave my friends and my dog. I felt very accepted and in sync with what was happening and who we were." Her parents tried to offer a bright perspective. "They helped me understand how much we needed a new start and well I kind of got excited by it for a while." What helped her cope with this move was the fact that Dunja was made to feel that she took part in the decisions involved in relocating: "so I wasn't an ignored part of the decision making." Nevertheless, she still remembers the deep sadness of parting. "We were due to leave at midnight for the airport. I remember holding my dog and crying for most of that evening. I was saying goodbye to all that was good about the Emirates through her. It may sound silly, but I knew that I would never be the same again." For the past five years the family has been living and rebuilding their life in New Zealand.

About her immigration experience, Dunja commented, "My life has given me a good definition of what the word 'migration' means to me." Like all immigrants, Dunja expresses a deep sense of loss and grieving: "We've been little molecules moving through the world, just the four of us. We've said goodbye one too many times, and we've parted with ways of life so often. Until recently, my mum hadn't seen her mum or sisters for nine years, and my dad hadn't seen his family for the same length of time."

However, her view of immigration reflects a combination of losses and gains. "In reflecting about it, I realize that migration, though tough at times, has been also nourishment to me and has significantly contributed to the growth of who I am as a person." This perspective that views both detrimental and personal growth in the aftermath of traumatic experiences is in sync with contemporary literature. Recent knowledge on the impact of trauma emphasizes that traumatic events create not only the danger of emotional distress and functional decline but also the opportunity for personal growth (Tedeschi, Park, and Calhoun, 1998).

Dunja learned two major lessons from her immigration experience. She sees her experience as enriching and expanding her horizons. This includes the experience of learning to relocate, leave familiar places and people, and adjust to new landscapes, make new friends, and learn new sets of norms. In addition, the specific nature of each of the different places in which she spent part of her short life contributed its special color to the rainbow and texture to the fabric of her experience. "I've lived in five different countries so far—Bosnia, Tanzania, England, United Arab Emirates, and New Zealand. Each country is different and has brought a wealth of knowledge and self-awareness to me."

From her original country, Bosnia, Dunja believes that she brought a strong sense of family. "Bosnia is a cold place for most of the year, which has led to lifestyles revolving around the cold. As I remembered the place, it is beautiful. It held among its stone buildings, numerous bridges, and ever-white mountains a richness of history dating centuries back. To walk down streets paved in classical times and use door handles touched by royalty hundreds of years ago had a very humbling effect on me. The sense of history contributed to a stronger sense of family within this culture. Family is important and holds very special ties to the person you become. Aunties, grandmothers, and cousins are all part of a caring and loving support network that guides and prepares one for life. It is a reassuring feeling knowing where you come from. It is a spirit I hold within my heart wherever I venture on this globe."

However, Dunja realizes that part of this is nostalgia rather than a realistic perspective. What she carries is more the inner picture of how she remembers Bosnia rather than the way things really were. Such nostalgic transformation of reality is not uncommon among immigrants. Hardly any immigrant, even under the best personal, familial, economic, and social conditions, is ever free of hardships. In light of challenges in the new country, there is a tendency to remember the country of origin in rosy colors. Immigrants that have an opportunity to visit their homeland after they have spent some time in the new culture often develop a more realistic perspective (Mirsky and Prawer, 1992).

This experience was especially distressing for Dunja. In addition to the different perspective she had gained by her experiences away from her country of origin, Dunja left Bosnia as a young child and returned in late adolescence on the verge of becoming a young adult. Furthermore, years of war have also taken their toll of the country and changed it dramatically. Dunja reported what happened to her on a recent visit to her homeland. "Last Christmas I went back to Bosnia, and I experienced a culture shock. Nothing prepared me for what I was to see. The spirit of the people had diminished to a barely visible glow. The war has had terrible effects. It has depressed people, and they have lost trust in one another. I felt a great deal of confusion and sorrow at what I saw. I felt even greater pain at seeing my extended family living in this state of poverty with lack of purpose and direction. Their hearts barely pump with desire to re-create what they once had." The painful sense of loss that she describes is both theirs and hers.

The next stop was Tanzania. Most non-Africans hear about it only when they plan a safari trip, as it is home to one of the largest wild animal populations in the world. This economically poor eastern African country situated on the Indian Ocean, neighboring Kenya on the north and Zambia in the west, is inhabited mostly by native Africans and a handful of Asians, Europeans, and Arabs. "Tanzania I loved. Of my times there I have only the happiest, funniest, and awe-inspiring memories. To me it felt like there was an unseen and almost secret culture of the wild. The magnificence and power that the animal kingdom and the land held put into perspective that we as humans are just one of many living things on this planet, but we are important to its development. The Masai tribes of the plains in the Serengeti live in collaboration with the wilderness that surrounds them. I think it's an inbred respect for the land that keeps them alive."

After this tropical, exotic, third world adventure, England presented a very different experience. Almost any aspect of life is in sharp contrast to the African natural and social climate. "Although it was hard to make friends in England, it was quite lovely. We were in a small village outside of London, where there were a few foreigners. I remember getting a really warm reception in my class. When the teacher came in she said, 'This is Dunja and she can speak two languages.' My English was broken, although I could communicate, but she made it a source of pride rather than something to be embarrassed about. It showed a sense of heart and compassion to a slightly emotionally sidetracked young me." Dunja's teacher illustrated how coming from a different culture can be reframed as resiliency rather than denounced as a shortcoming and a source of problems.

Dunja spent her preadolescent years, between the ages of ten and thirteen, in the United Arab Emirates. This union of seven sheikdoms lies on the coast of the Persian Gulf between Saudi Arabia and Oman. Populated predominantly by Arabs, South Asians, Iranians, and Muslims from other Arabic countries, it became well-known to the world during the 1991 Gulf War. About her experience there, Dunja recounted, "The Emirates was different again. For me it was a harder life because we went to school from eight in the morning to four in the afternoon and then had hills of homework to do. I was in an international school that was very academic. There were exams every week and testing every day. Everything was dependent on me keeping up with the work and being good at it, so a lot of my time was spent studying. However, that didn't mean I didn't have fun. We could never meet up in a mall or at the movies. I think this had something to do with being female in a Muslim-dominated culture. It just wasn't a done thing." Although it might not have been clear to Dunja at the time, the United Arab Emirates is a conservative, male-dominated Muslim society where women are often treated as what another interviewee from a similar country defined as "nonentities." They are perceived as inferior to men and are expected to abide by a strict dress code and conform to traditional norms. Dunja stated that nevertheless, "Most of my weekends were spent with my friends at set parties dancing, laughing, and talking. The friendships and relationships I formed were very real and sober. There were no hints of alcohol or smoking having to play a part in how we were or showed ourselves to be. I really treasured that in friends. I often thought that the sand dunes were a good metaphor of what constant changes we were all going through. Their shapes were always changing."

It is clear that Dunja's life in the United Arab Emirates was very sheltered. When asked about having lived there so close to the Gulf War, she commented, "There is very little I remember being aware of. I do remember the odd comment made by family friends about how they had to board up their windows and how they would freeze when they heard planes in the skies above. However, I don't recall coming to a country where there were obvious aftereffects of a war. People were up and about, functioning unfazed through their daily lives. The general vibes coming from people in general was the same throughout my three years there. My peers and I were enjoying ourselves and working hard. People in the country were enjoying themselves as much as one can in the United Arab Emirates. I just have the safest and content memories."

When Dunja was in her early teens, her parents realized that the conservative and restrictive Muslim environment would not enable her to experience a normal Western adolescence and decided that it was time to move. The new destination was the island of New Zealand. This is a picturesque and relaxed remote land, where people develop a taste for extreme sports such as bungee jumping, skipper gliding, and jet boating that introduce excitement into an otherwise slow-paced life. Dunja reminiscenced about her first period there, "When I came to New Zealand I was coming to what felt like the edge of the world. It was far away from everything familiar to me."

Dunja was also impressed with the absence of ethnic and cultural diversity, except for the native Maori culture, in comparison with neighboring Australia and Western countries such as the United States. "The more I saw of New Zealand, the more it seemed as if it was the same throughout the country. New Zealand is younger than any of the previous countries I had lived in and has not really established a tradition of encompassing other cultures. There are no Chinatowns to explore or markets where you can find food from all over the world." Ethnic enclaves have traditionally offered supportive experience to immigrants by providing familiar language, smells, tastes, and a sense of homeland to the newcomers. Little Vietnam on Victoria Parade in Melbourne; Little Italy, Chinatown, Astoria, and Brighton Beach in New York City; and Little Havana in Miami, Florida—all these are neighborhoods where one can find newspapers, books, and movies in one's language of origin, purchase familiar products and spices, hear familiar sounds, and purchase clothes and household utensils that are familiar. For example, almost every Israeli who went to the United States to work or study was advised by friends to bring along the special cloth used for cleaning the floor because Americans sweep the floor rather than wash it as is the habit in the Middle East. Dunja felt the absence of such escapes. She said, "I mention this because this represents a lack of a place where migrants can come to meet others and identify with the culture of the daily lives they left behind. Once they come to New Zealand they in effect lose a sense of their own culture."

When the family came to New Zealand, they settled in the Bay of Plenty. Located at the northeastern part of the island, this subtropical region is a mix of rain forests, farmlands, and sandy beaches. Dunja was enrolled in what in New Zealand and Australia is called a college school, which is actually a high school. "My school was across town, so I had to catch a bus in the morning."

Making friends in a new environment is a major challenge for all immigrants, especially when they live within a mainstream, dominant-culture neighborhood rather than an ethnic enclave. "Everyone I met lived such a long way from us that it made it difficult to form friendships. I was kind of friendless for a big part of the year."

Immigrants are often excluded and laughed at. This is especially difficult for children in the tender years of adolescence, when a sense of belonging is critical. Dunja was not spared from this experience. "I had quite a few problems. In year nine [the equivalent of the last year of intermediate school or freshman year in high school in the United States], I seemed to be the person everyone picked on and could easily be blamed for all the backstabbing and rumors they spread about each other."

A statement that I heard from almost every immigrant that I interviewed was "at the beginning I cried a lot." Dunja reported the same: "I spent a lot of time crying. I needed to talk." She felt unhelped. "The school counselors did not do anything. They would literally let me sit the whole day in a room crying by myself. No one would come in and try to talk about it. Occasionally someone would offer me tissues and then leave again, but this didn't help much. When I'd go back into class everyone would pretend nothing had happened. I felt quite crazy. I ended up feeling quite depressed about this move. It wasn't new and exciting. It wasn't like the other times we were in a new country. I couldn't pinpoint what made the other experiences more positive, I just knew I wasn't feeling comfortable with myself."

The Bay of Plenty was not the last stop on Dunja's wandering route. A year later she had to cope with yet another relocation, this time within the new country. The family moved west to Auckland, the capital of the country. "My parents said we had to move again, to where my dad was working. I was distraught. I didn't want to go through again what my first year at college had been like. The thought of moving again was daunting. But we had to make the move, so we did. And I started at a new school."

The new school has a very diverse student body. In Dunja's words, it is "a place that is home to students from over fifty-six different cultures." Having learned from previous experience, this time Dunja was very cautious. "In the first few days I was apprehensive of making the mistake of becoming friends with just anyone. I wanted my friends to be nice people this time."

Indeed, this time Dunja found the refuge she was seeking. Given the diversity of the students, she was not alone. "I felt relieved because I didn't feel that I was going to be picked on, and that made the transition so much more happy." She became very active socially. "I auditioned for the school play, and even joined a netball team although I'd never played before it in my life! One of my friends had joined the Anti-Harassment Team which facilitates mediations between students and tries to prevent harassment occurring in the school. At the end of the year I decided I wanted to be part of that team too. I was quite unsure about what to write on my application, but I wrote something and handed it in and was asked to come to an interview. I can't remember exactly what I said my motivation for joining the team was, probably not wanting anyone else to go through what I went through and wanting to make sure there was someone to talk to. I was accepted to the team, and I guess this is when I started to blossom! When I look at photos of myself as a child I can see that I was a friendly little person. I was cuddly and not shy to mix with people. Joining the Anti-Harassment Team made this resurface. I started getting more confident in realizing that I had something to offer other people. I also began working with Kidsline [a telephone support service run for children ages nine to thirteen; it provides counseling and promotes programs to solve bullying problems]. Both in the team and in Kidsline I found places where I could be who I wanted to be, and where I was comfortable with sharing the significant stories of my life."

What has been helping her to cope with constant relocation? What lessons can she teach us about the struggle of adolescents with immigration? Dunja summarized her thoughts: "I think it's really important for people to be able to keep their own cultures intact, or to reclaim their culture where it has been lost. However, we do have to find ways of sharing land. Back home Serbians wanted to keep their culture and they also wanted more land and more control, and this has divided a nation and killed people's spirit. They can have the land, but it means nothing when they haven't got the people with them."

To Dunja, Serbia is still what she refers to as "home." This is a powerful illustration regarding the role of one's culture of origin in shaping one's life and the central part that feeling connected to this culture plays in one's ability to cope with hardships. Dunja spent five years of her life in Serbia (from birth to age three and again from age seven to nine), most of them as an infant and a toddler. The lion's share of her life she spent in other countries, and the number of years she has lived in her current country is equal to the number of years she spent in her birth country. Yet the country in which she was born she perceives as home: "We have hearts that belong to a land far more powerful than we can ever imagine." Dunja's words suggest that this strong sense of belonging to her culture of origin is a source of her power to rejuvenate and blossom in her new environment.

Dunja often uses "we" rather than "I" in discussing her immigration experience, suggesting that a strong family connection also offered a powerful source of help in dealing with hardships of relocation. "We've had some wonderful experiences, but we've also had many losses, and they have their effects. It's sort of a grieving process, but it's also about new beginnings." This supports the commonly accepted view in servicing immigrants that availability of relatives and compatriots with whom to share the experience helps to mitigate the pain of relocation (Harper and Lantz, 1996; Berger, 1996; Chow, 1999).

Furthermore, she feels that not only did the strong family ties improve her abilities to cope with difficulties of relocation, but also closer ties within the family were gained out of the need to constantly migrate. "As a child in my family I was not given a voice too often, until my parents realized that it was only going to be the four of us and that we were going to need to talk with each other in different ways." At the same time, the experience of recurrent uprooting took its toll on family relations. "My mum's history and way of communicating has come down a particular cultural path, whereas mine's broken off and taken a different track. I've learnt new ways of thinking from different places. I respect all walks of life and love learning about the world and people. Trying to combine all this in a family is sometimes really hard."

Dunja borrowed from her experience on the Anti-Harassment Team to explain her strategy of coping with all these challenges: "It's sort of like the mediations we do. One person comes to us with their own story, the way they deal with things and the way they see things. And another person comes with their different ways of thinking which are just as valuable. We have to find ways of respecting more than one way of life." She also kept herself busy. "I guess I have sat on nearly every committee possible at school and a few out in the community." This activity helped her develop her people skills. "For the past four years I have focused more and more on helping other people and developing my communication skills. It kept me from spending too much time doing nothing. I was always on the go with this meeting, or that training, this rehearsal or that shift. Through doing this I realize I have gained some understanding of how to connect with people."

Looking at her experience as a child, adolescent, and young adult immigrant, Dunja feels that she is still struggling to come to terms with it. "I guess my experiences overseas have given me expectations. It's hard to explain. I feel really frustrated and not being able to express exactly what is sitting in my head and heart regarding this. It is difficult to make clear meaning of it."

Relocating from one's culture of origin at a young age may rob a child of a feeling of being rooted and leave a "hole." The absence of culture-dependent idioms and associations that are typically acquired at a very early age may lead to missing the opportunity to fully own one's culture as part of one's identity. "I have never had a culture bestowed upon me. I don't know the basic principles of the Balkan culture. I don't know about traditional dances, songs, history . . . anything really that is learned as part of one's cultural identification. However, I have always loved being part of cultural celebrations, whatever culture I was familiar with. I feel it a very big part of my character, being stimulated by things on a larger scale."

However, Dunja is sure about the valuable contribution of her experiences to her personal growth. "That's one good thing about my background, the whole mix of cultural experiences. I have a history that winds and winds through so many different countries and people. There are friends in so many countries. I guess I have always packed a suitcase full of memories, experiences, and feelings connected to the place where my heart has visited and lived. As I take my journey into adulthood, I won't be alone. All the people who are now part of my history and who support me will be coming too in some way."

PART III:
CONCLUSIONS AND IMPLICATIONS

Chapter 7

Major Themes
in Women's Narratives

The narratives of the women in this study reveal that many of them experienced more than one relocation either within their own country or internationally. Sonia, Genevieve, Klara, Dunja, Tara, Matijia, Natasha—for all of them, the migration from their country of origin included several stops and they lived for long periods in other countries prior to resettling in their current location. Furthermore, some of them envision even more relocations in the future. Teresina, for example, contemplates moving from Israel to Australia in the future. This raises the question of whether we should rethink the traditional view of immigration as a mostly irreversible, single major change and conceptualize it as multiple migrations.

What do the experiences of women in the process of relocation mean for them? What are the effects of these experiences on their life? What are the challenges that they face? How do they struggle with these challenges? What helps them cope? This chapter addresses these and related questions on the basis of the content analysis of the narratives.

The narratives reveal a rainbow of reactions, indicating that the immigration experience for women is not made in one mold. However, in spite of their diversity, some common themes emerged. They are resilience, the experience of duality, and a balance of gains and losses. These themes are discussed and illustrated in the following three sections.

RESILIENCE OF IMMIGRANT WOMEN:
FLEXIBLE STRENGTH

Women do everything, men do the rest.

Russian proverb

Women in this study demonstrate a great deal of resilience and capacity to thrive, despite the hardships of immigration and their heavy burden of responsibilities. Across cultures of origin, circumstances of immigration, personal and family characteristics and backgrounds, and duration of life in the new culture, women show ability to attain considerable personal accomplishments, to grow, and to help their children and families cope. This study, therefore, joins the few voices that started to be heard in recent years recognizing resilience and wellness in immigrants in general and immigrant women in particular. For example, Ferugson (1999) found that "Despite their sense of isolation and dependence, in fact the women revealed extraordinary courage in the way they are coping with resettlement issues" (p. 35). Witmer and Culver (2001), who studied the literature related to Bosnian Muslim refugees, posit that immigration literature is saturated with an overemphasis on pathogenic aspects of immigration and minimizes data that point to resilience and salutogenic factors. Ahearn (1999) emphasizes wellness rather than pathology in the study of psychosocial consequences for refugees. These voices are few, but the current study shows that they are valid. Pittaway (1999) states, "Refugee women are survivors. They come with strengths which many of us will never attain" (p. 18).

The Nature of the Resilience

The voices of women in this study validate previous research regarding gender-specific acculturation. Existing research on immigrants from Mexico, Asia, and other parts of the world to the United States has shown that although acculturation has an emotional cost for women, they tend to adapt better and faster to their new cultural environment than men do (Brock-Utne, 1994). Bystydzienski and Resnik (1994) suggest that because in the majority of contemporary societies, women generally have lower status and are socialized to be more caring and accepting of viewpoints other than their own, they are less likely to feel denigrated upon entering a new cultural milieu and finding themselves "pushed down" financially and socially.

Narratives of women reveal a great deal of pragmatism, flexibility, and effective problem solving. Many of them demonstrate ability to cope with the adversities of immigration, to leave them behind, and to move on. They recognize and acknowledge losses and difficulties of immigration but do not dwell on them and are amazingly quick to pull up their sleeves and rebuild their life within the new context. Their ability to negotiate diverse situations helps them to accommodate the multiple changing circumstances involved in their personal, family, and work life following the immigration.

The flexible strength of immigrant women brings to mind the old Chinese fable about the power of the bamboo tree. There were two trees: an oak tree that stood straight and strong and a bamboo tree that appeared weak and every passing wind could tilt its branches. When a big storm came, the strong and straight oak broke, while the bamboo temporarily bent down and successfully survived the storm.

Resilience of immigrant women is not limited to their own acculturation and to support of their immigrating husbands, relatives, and children. They are often also providers of financial support to their extended family in their native homeland. Maria, Rosa, Sonia, and Matijia send money and goods every month to Cuba, the Philippines, Lebanon, and Croatia, respectively.

The current study shows that women are faster adapters, and they also view themselves as such. Contrary to stereotypes of low self-esteem often associated with immigration, women expressed a positive view of themselves and their accomplishments. One example is Ana, who stated, "Women are more flexible, grow up to be more adaptive, willing to speak the new language even before we have full command of it. In a storm women bend to straighten up later, men refuse to bend and break. Women are like cats—throw them and they jump back on their feet. I see around me men having a harder time than women finding themselves in the new environment and regaining their sense of self-esteem. There is a Russian saying that the man is the head of the family, but the woman is the neck that controls the movement of the head. I knew that I should first support his efforts to acclimatize because I was sure that as hard as it is going to be, I would make it." Svetlana expressed a similar view: "Women are more flexible than men. There [in the Ukraine] men were stronger; here they broke more."

Similar to Ana and Svetlana, many of the women in this study share the belief that women are "the backbone of the family" and the carriers of its cultural heritage. As such, they have the responsibility and the ability to take care of the family's adjustment to stress and crises, which causes them to deal with the hardships of immigration better than men. This finding is similar to the results of a qualitative study of ten Vietnamese refugee women in Australia (Ferugson, 1999). In addition to supporting the notion that women adapt better than men to the hardships of immigration, this offers further credence to research on subjective views of one's experience. Learning from women and identifying factors that contribute to their success can help to inform and develop effective strategies for success for all immigrants.

Positive self-perception in female immigrants seems to be evident more often than is recognized. Similar to the reports by women that I interviewed, Michael (1998), who studied immigrant girls in New York City, found that "girls used generally positive adjectives to describe themselves. In fact, in contrast to assumptions about alienation and depression amongst immigrants, I found amongst the girls a sense of personal strength and generally good self-esteem" (p. 268). Hence, immigrant women appear to be more resilient than often portrayed in literature and to be aware of their resilience.

Sources of Resilience

Women attribute their ability to successfully cope with the challenges of immigration to social, familial, personal, circumstantial, and spiritual factors. Surprisingly, participants minimized the contributions of age and similarity between cultures, which have often been counted in the literature as significantly affecting acculturation and adjustment. Women prefer to attribute their resilience to "internal" factors, such as sense of role, responsibility, inner strength, and knowledge, to use and develop support, rather than to "external" characteristics such as demographics and cultural features.

Social Sources of Resilience

One social source of resilience is the availability of role models. Women frequently mentioned people in their immediate environment who set a precedent and were living inspirations. For Sonia these were her aunts who paved her way by their successful immigration. These two older sisters of her father moved to the United States to study nursing and were viewed by the family as financially independent, professionally accomplished, and socially respectable. "So, since I was a young girl, I knew that there is an option, that that is something that a woman can do," Sonia said. Sabin also had two aunts who had emigrated to England and the United States. "You see," she said, "immigration of women runs in my family." Sarah's brother, who relocated to the United States briefly prior to her, and her sister, who immigrated to New York seventeen years before her, serve as sources of strength.

An additional social source of resilience includes support systems. Identifying, developing, and using supportive networks has three faces. One is reaching out to contacts with representatives from the dominant culture. Participants report making deliberate efforts to seek relationships with natives of the absorbing society, in spite of feelings of awkwardness and discomfort. Sonia reported, "I was building my own little community, and these intense relationships with American young people taught me a lot about the culture and about the ways that people deal with each other." Sarah explained, "Relationships with people, classmates, and friends helped me to find my way. As I opened to the new environment that spoke in difference voices, it became easier." Kasaba (2000) defines this knitting of supportive network as creating a social space for oneself.

The second social source of women's resilience is networking with compatriots, settling close to other immigrants of similar origin, and forming enclaves of familiarity within an alien culture. Ana feels that help from friends was invaluable. "They advised us, offered a place to live until we found an apartment, a loan to pay the initial rent; they really helped us stand on our own feet quickly. Knowing that they are there for us allowed us to cope successfully," she reported. Teresina stated about her Brazilian network, "We talk together, laugh together, eat together . . . so I established my own network; they understand me. They are like a piece of Brazil in Israel."

Finally, socializing with other immigrants, not necessarily of similar backgrounds, is cited by some women as helpful. Parastu felt "more comfortable with other immigrants [than with local people], people who understand me because they share to a certain degree my experiences," while nonimmigrants "are well settled and they fail to understand how difficult it is when one does not have the basics, things that they take for granted."

Familial Sources of Resilience

Families offer a source of resilience in a number of ways. Family history of changes, family legacy, family support, and motherhood were counted as powerful driving forces. A legacy of coping with traumas as they were growing up equipped several women with the skills to cope successfully with the challenges of immigration. Many of the women depicted a family legacy of giving that made them feel uncomfortable with being forced by the circumstances of immigration to become receivers and they worked to regain their status as givers. Ana is a typical illustration of this dynamic. She said, "We never asked for anything. We have always been self-sufficient and providing for others. Here we were forced initially to ask for help every month. This was not a comfortable place for me to be, and I wanted to be my old strong giver as soon as possible."

Tara grew up as an unloved child, facing rejection at home from her domineering grandmother and her young, weak-willed, widowed, and depressed mother who jointly raised her and her brothers after the death of Tara's father. She spent her adolescence as part of the minority Albanian community in a hostile Serbian social environment. "I had to learn to live with these experiences from an early age," she said. "I taught myself how to survive. I developed an iron will and learned never to be a quitter." Sonia also brings skills of coping and thriving from her troubled family of origin, with a father who lost his parents at an early age, grew up in orphanages, and relocated numerous times with his family of origin, as well as with his wife and children.

Women, especially young ones, reported tight family ties as an enormous source of support that helps them thrive. Mare stated, "I had that power, which came from the support of my parents who wish to fulfill their dreams through me and my siblings. Since their circumstances did not allow them to study, they support us to achieve it all and they believe in us." Dunja cited strong family ties as a source of resilience: "My family gave me the power to cope with the difficulties. I knew that they are there for me, they believe in me, and they have expectations of me. This is a strong driving force."

The view of immediate and extended family as a source of support is not limited to young women. Svetlana sees her extended family as the major source of her ability to cope. "We received a lot of morale help. My extended family was very supportive, including some that we never met before, just knew about them; when we came, they all embraced us. We became so close in a way that I never imagined possible. We are one big family with excellent relationships with our relatives; we have this big warm clan." This, she reassured me, made all the difference in her ability to adjust.

For Teresina, support from her in-laws is a source of resilience. "All my husband's family is now my family. They adopted me into their family with open arms. If it was not for her [Teresina's mother-in-law], I do not know how I could have coped with all the hardships," she said.

Some women receive "long-distance" support from their families. Rosa in Australia felt support from her family in the Philippines. "They kept telling me that I am welcome to come back home. They said to me, 'We are not rich, but if it is too difficult for you, we shall share whatever we have. The important thing is that we are all together. This is what counts.' Their reaction gave me the power to endure my difficulties. I knew that I have someone behind me, that I am not alone," she explained.

Although motherhood is a source of stress for immigrant women, it was also cited as a source of power. The wish to give their children the best opportunities is an engine for mothers' resilience. Matijia said, "I made a decision to relocate to give my children a better chance in life and a sense of security, and I have to take the consequences that accompany my decision, including professional difficulties. I have an inner obligation to make it work for them. That fueled my efforts whenever I felt tired and an inner voice that seduced me to let go. Sometimes I think that—'OK, I am exhausted, but my children are doing well. They grow up in a safe environment, and I tell myself that my efforts are worth it.' If a mother sees that her children are healthy, safe, and successful and that in spite of all the difficulties the family functions well, it justifies it all."

Hang concurred, "My mother struggled and struggled with no end, never surrendering. There is something about immigrant women, especially immigrant mothers. They are like lionesses, they are resilient, and they never give up. My mother, like many immigrant women that I encounter, was always determined to find a way to resolve whatever difficulty she faced. They are the backbone of their families. Many of them believe that emigrating means providing their families, especially their children and themselves, with opportunities that need to be seized, and they capture them with strong arms."

Personal Sources of Resilience

Women also name their own personality traits and history of coping with changes as related to their resilience in facing the hardships of immigration. "Gutsiness," "showing them," "determination," "unwillingness to give up" and "hardiness," "optimism, seeing the half full glass," and "seeing the bright side of situations" were commonly reported by women in this study. The drive toward self-sufficiency that has been documented among refugees (Balgopal, 2000) emerges from narratives such as Sarah's. "An inner drive, eagerness and determination to reinvent myself since a very early age in spite of environmental and cultural pressures to the contrary helped me in coping with the challenges of immigration," she said.

These women are fighters who never consider giving up. This endurance comes in various forms. Tara represents the active stand of "I will show them," "I will not let them break me," "I will make it in spite of all difficulties and against all odds." Parastu stated, "I am determined to succeed. I expect of myself a lot and do not let my fears and anxieties stand in my way. I am fearful but go out and perform. I can 'die of fear' but go ahead." Ana expressed a similar view: "I have a strong and positive character. I always see the half-full part of the glass. I am always positive." Mare, who as a young adolescent fought a blind and obnoxious establishment, recalled, "I refused to surrender. I had no support and was told, 'We told you that it would be too hard for you.' I would not listen. I was determined to make it. I fought minute by minute, hour by hour, day by day. And look at me now—a graduate student."

Some women "import" with them resilience from previous life experiences. For instance, in some countries of origin women served as the representatives of the family in the negotiation with educational and medical services (e.g., Remennick, 1999). Narratives of women indicate that this know-how has proven applicable and very helpful in adjusting to immigration.

Circumstantial Sources of Resilience

The possibility to go back to visit their homeland was cited by women in this study as empowering because it offers them the opportunity to test their idealizations against reality. Klara stated, "Only now, when I went back to Israel, I can appreciate what America gave me." Sarah agreed, "A visit to Pakistan four years after immigration offered me some understanding of how life in the United States changed me. The climate was different, the food was different, and neither my children nor I could drink the milk there. I went there with very few expectations, and even those few were not fulfilled. This helped me moderate the nostalgia and feel more comfortable here. I am sure that if I went now, I would have felt much more how much I have changed and get an even clearer perspective on what was and what is."

A pivotal circumstantial source of resilience is the experience of being forced "with their back to the wall." The knowledge that there is no alternative and the feeling of having hit bottom is a driving force. It stimulates women's determination to recruit their power and struggle. Each of the women interviewed could identify a critical "make it or break it" point in their process of acculturation. For Klara, it was a cold and snowy night when she realized that she had nowhere else to go. For Ana, it was the death of her husband. "I knew that I couldn't afford to not succeed," she said.

Some of the women made the decision to emigrate. Others followed the decisions of husbands or parents. For some of the women, being part of making the decision to emigrate was a source of resilience in the sense that they adopted the stand of "I have no choice, I must win." Berry and colleagues (1987) assert that the greater sense of self-determination one has regarding the decision to immigrate, the lower the level of stress one experiences. For Dunja, feeling part of the decision-making process was very important: "I wasn't ignored; I was part of the decision making." Nadra and Maria, who were passive participants in the decision to emigrate, demonstrate a different type of strength in coping with the relocation, the strength that grows out of having no choice, and their power lay in their weakness. Being caught in a powerless position made these women strong.

Whatever the circumstances of the decision to relocate and however they struggled to handle the hardships, none of the women allowed herself to give up, to sink into prolonged depression, to stop fighting. Sarah told me, "It can make you weak or makes you strong. When you reach a pivotal point, there is that inner power that makes you make the inner decision of self-empowering."

Spiritual Sources of Resilience

Two women viewed spirituality as a source for their resilience. According to Rosa, "My strong belief in God and spiritual support from the church gave me the power to fight my battles. We Filipinos, when we are in trouble, go to the priest to confess. At my weakest points, when I felt low and drowning, saying the rosary, praying, attending masses, talking to the priest, and meeting with other people who share my belief gave me the power to struggle with my hardships." Genevieve cited a spiritual contact and sense of belonging to her country of relocation as a major source for her ability to cope with the hardships of immigration. She explained, "My soul did not did not feel good when I was out of Israel, though my body did. My soul feels intact here. This is what gives me the power to survive." Spirituality as a coping strategy in immigration-related situations has also been documented for Puerto Rican women who migrated to the United States (Schmidt, 2000).

THE DOUBLE LIFE OF IMMIGRANT WOMEN: COPING WITH DUALITY

Similar to previous studies, most interviewees reported that reshaping life and creating a home in the new country presented a significant challenge. The challenge of coping with duality stands out as a common motif in the stories of most of the immigrant women in this study.

Natasha is an exception. She denied the existence of duality in her life and believes that immigrants need to let go of their homeland, memories, compatriots, and nostalgia and become one with their new land's compatriots. "I was a foreigner by origin, but I merged into the Australian society. I see myself and am accepted as one of them," she said. However, one needs to remember that Natasha is the oldest among the interviewees and has lived in her adopted country the longest. It is also interesting to notice that in spite of the decisive overt content of her statement, she referred to Australians as "them" rather than "us." This use of language raises a question about the compatibility of what she says and what she feels. Other women, even those who have lived in their new country for fifteen to twenty years, did not share her view.

Danquah (2000) titled her book about immigrants to the United States *Becoming American.* To me, this implies a transformation of oneself from an Israeli, Russian, Cuban, and so forth into an American, Australian, or whatever the absorbing country is. Is this really what immigration demands? Does one shed a previous national skin to become something else? Is it even possible to stop being the original "self" and become another? The stories of most of the other women touch upon these and related questions such as: How much of one's roots, i.e., the previous story of where and who one was, is sacrificed in the struggle to develop the new story, i.e., becoming who one is? What does one call "homeland"? Can one have two homelands? When, if ever, does the country of immigration become home? What does it take? The September 11 terrorist attacks on the World Trade Center, the Pentagon, and in Pennsylvania raised these questions even more intensely for Americans of Arabic origin.

These questions permeate immigrants' daily decisions. How to decorate the house? Should one hang on the wall picture from one's original homeland? How to name children born in the new country?

Five themes related to the experience of duality evolve from the interviews: the nature of the experience, forces that shape the experience, its effects on various aspects of life, its perception and interpretation by women, and ways of coping with it.

The Nature of the Experience

Duality was described by these women as belonging to and having roots and "stake" in two cultures: the culture of origin and the culture of relocation. At the core of this experience is the split between here and there, then and now, the external and internal world, inside the family and out in the world. Teresina summarized it as "It is like I had one life and now I have another life."

This experience may become especially complicated when norms of the culture of origin and the new culture are significantly different or conflicting. Such discrepancy between the two cultures can lead to confusion, disorientation, and a feeling of being at a loss even when the change is from more restrictive toward more liberal and egalitarian norms, which in the Western mind, and often in the immigrant women's own mind, is perceived as an improvement. Sarah's experience is an illustration. "I come from a culture that treats women as inferior to men, familism is highly emphasized, and authority of the elderly is respected [in Pakistan]. Here [in the United States] women's equality, individualism, and youth are leading values. This has been extremely difficult for me to digest," she said.

Even when the dissimilarity is less dramatic, such as in relocating between two Westernized cultures, cultural differences present a challenge. Genevieve, who emigrated from France to Israel, recognizes them: "Our mentality is totally different than the Israelis. They think differently and care for different things."

Some women live with a sense of duality on a daily basis. Others react to a specific event. For Sonia, visits to her homeland, Lebanon, are recurrent wake-up calls. She explained, "I enjoy going back, but upon my return I feel that I am torn between two worlds and experience a culture shock in each of them. I feel like I need to readjust when I go back to Lebanon and also when I come back to the United States. In a way, both places are home and I feel comfortable, and yet both are not exactly and totally home."

For mothers, duality has a special face. Many immigrants relocate to secure a safer life, better education, and improved opportunities for their children and feel that they sacrifice for the sake of their children or future children. To achieve those goals, mothers want their children to acculturate and at the same time fear that they acculturate too much and become strangers to the family's culture of origin. These conflicting expectations have been termed by Lee (2000) "schizophrenic."

Matijia recounted, "Sometimes it saddens me that our children do not respect our origins. They grow up in a different culture than ours. It is good that they feel comfortable in their environment. I wish them to become 'Australianized' to make it here, but it adds to the normal generation gap a culture gap. Their 'Australization' robs me of having a relationship with them and creates estrangement and distance. Sometimes I feel that immigration causes us to lose them, they are sliding between my fingers."

Forces That Shape the Experience

Several social forces contribute to shaping the experience of duality. One is the pressure to assimilate and become one with the new culture ("if you chose to come here, behave like the locals"), as demonstrated by calls for canceling bilingual educational programs.

Its complementary side is the expectation for immigrants to constantly be in the process of acculturation but never really reach it and serve as representatives of their culture of origin whether they chose this role or not. For example, an immigrant from Japan may be addressed as "you, the Japanese," while an immigrant from Israel may be seen as an expert representative of Israeli politics. Or, for instance, a teacher may refer in class to an immigrant child from Peru as "a token Peruvian." It hardly ever occurs to many people that some immigrants find and fulfill themselves in the new culture. Immigrants are automatically assumed to miss their country of origin. People often wonder whether I get homesick, what about Israel I miss most. I often try to explain to people that if I really have the urge to go (it has never happened in the decade that I have been living in the United States), all which separates me from Israel is ten hours and about $700. Even my husband, who has known me for over a dozen years, does not cease to be amazed. "How come you don't miss anything? You grew up and lived there for so many years. How is this possible?" he asks, and almost succeeds in making me feel guilty for feeling at home in the United States while remaining true to my "Israeliness."

A third factor shaping the experience of duality are the attitudes experienced by immigrants that often include suspicion, xenophobia and rejection, and being looked down and made fun of. This experience is sometimes implied and on other occasions is bold and rude, but it is often there. Participants in the study felt that women might be susceptible to such attitudes more often than men as part of the general social oppression of women. Hardly any immigrant woman, young or old, rich or poor, educated or less educated, white or black, did not report some variation of my experience in a neighborhood health club. When I asked a fellow exerciser to move a little so that I could follow my workout in the mirror, she responded, "If you do not like where I stand, you can go back to where you came from."

The immigrants' own attitude toward their homeland also shapes the experience of duality, and this attitude is affected by the situation in their homeland and the opportunity to visit it. As political climate and financial circumstances change, and when immigrants have opportunities to compare nostalgic memories with reality, homesickness is often modified. Some women actually take the trip back. According to Sarah from Pakistan, "When I went back to visit after four years, I realized that all is not as I remembered it. The countryside was not as beautiful, people were not a nice, food was not so tasty; when I came back to New York, I felt much more that this is now home."

Other women opt for avoidance and refrain from visiting their homeland even when this is possible and prefer to cherish the memory of the place that they left rather than meet the current reality. Svetlana does not want to go back. "I know how devastating the situation is, and it breaks my heart to hear what it is like there now," she said. "I do not want to actually see it." Teresina was concerned before a visit to her native land: "I am not sure how it would be for me to go back to the previous life and look at them through my new eyes of the new life, the new me."

Effects of Duality on Women's Lives

Women feel both liberated and intimidated by the restrictions and possibilities related to the aftermath of immigration. The experience of duality affects intrapsychic, family, and social aspects of the women's lives.

Intrapsychic aspects are depicted by Sarah, who related feeling like a daughter of two worlds: "There is the past-me and the present-me." Genevieve, who struggles to cope with the transition from being a successful physician in a prestigious clinic in an affluent town on the French Riviera to working two low-paid positions in the Israeli public health system, concurred, "My body feels good there, but my soul feels intact here." Sonia, Teresina, and most of the other women expressed similar views.

Familial effects of the duality are illustrated by Maria, the immigrant from Cuba who described a split between herself and her Americanized children on one hand, and between herself and her family who remained "there" and for whom she is Americanized on the other hand. "It is like somebody sawed my heart into two. One part remained in Cuba and another part is here. I have my Cuban family and my American family," she said.

Social effects are addressed by Nadra from India, who described herself as "standing on two feet anchored in two separate lands" and offered a picturesque description of duality: "To work I wear business suits and when I come home I change into a sari." Sonia from Lebanon concurred, "I eat a tuna sandwich at work and tabbouleh at home."

Making Meaning of Duality

Although all of the women described duality as a major immigration experience, and for many the question of deliberating between and negotiation of two identities is never fully resolved, their perceptions, assessments, and interpretations of the experience and its meaning vary significantly. Some women view the duality of their existence as a strength and as an enriching opportunity. Mare is a good illustration. "My strength is having in me both Ethiopia and Israel, I am the bridge," she explained. She views having experienced the challenges of immigration as an adolescent daughter of immigrant parents and years later as a helper to new immigrant families, combining the knowledge and memories of Ethiopia with familiarity with the Israeli culture as a major asset. She has two cultural resources on which to build and from which to learn, and she feels that this makes her richer and more complete. Dunja, who has lived in five countries and three continents in her short life, feels that she "is harvesting the best of all worlds and enriched by the multicultural experience."

However, other women see it in a negative light and conceptualize it as a weakness, using expression such as "being torn," "lose-lose situation," "living in no-women-land," "misfit," "foreigner," "being daughters of two worlds, yet not totally of either," and "misplaced" to describe their situation in both cultures. Several immigrant women to the United States pointed to the official concept used for foreign-born permanent residents—alien resident (the official name of the famous "green card")—as an accurate indication of their situation. Tara said, "They call you alien and treat you like one. This makes you feel like one."

Several women described a shattered sense of belonging as a consequence of duality. For example, Nadra, who emigrated from India to the United States, feels that "at this point I became a misfit in both cultures, I am a foreigner in both, an eternal 'other,' that does not belong and do not feel comfortable anywhere." Maria spoke about "not totally belonging to my culture of origin anymore and remaining a stranger to the new culture." The experience of Sarah from Pakistan is identical. "Adopting some of the new culture made me a misfit in my culture of origin. I dress, think, and act differently; I perhaps even look differently. Yet, I do not fit into the new culture. I am nowhere," she described. Sonia from Lebanon concurred, "I am a Lebanese and an American, but not a typical Lebanese anymore, neither a typical American." These feelings echo a recent conversation I had with one of my students, a woman in her early forties, with excellent educational and professional accomplishments, whose two children were born in the United States, to which she emigrated twenty years ago from Africa. " I am a visitor here. It's their country and what they say goes. It's their right," this student said. "I go home [to Africa] every year. A couple of years ago, on my annual trip after my mother died I did soul-searching and asked myself if I really want to live there. I decided that I want to live in the United States. So I am currently looking to buy a home. Until now I always living in rented apartment because it did not make sense to make a huge long-term investment if I am not staying. However, I will forever be the visitor, and no number of years is going to change this for me, and when I die I wish to be buried in the soil of Africa, at home." This description echoed reports in the literature. For example, Cobo (1994), who came from Ecuador to study at a college in Indiana, states, "Part of me is in Ecuador and part of me is in America. When I am in one country or the other, I am always missing people and things from the other country. I often feel that I have a divided life" (p. 73).

Tara, an immigrant from Albania to the United States, perceives the crisis of belonging not only as being unaffiliated but also actively rejected by the dominant culture. She explained, "I face an ongoing experience of exclusion, a lot of joking at my expense. This is an experience of isolation." Even more extreme are women who perceive that the duality made them rejected both in their culture of origin and the culture of relocation. Maria stated, "As Cuban immigrants we are slandered as 'boat people' here and as 'gusanos' [worms] in Cuba, so we get the heat from both sides."

A question that remains to be addressed is what differentiates women who perceive and interpret the duality as a positive and enriching experience from those who view it negatively. What helps women choose the positive rather than the negative route? What does it take?

Coping with Duality

Although the experience of "living in two worlds" is inevitable, a crucial question is how one deals with it. Several approaches of coping with duality have been documented in the literature. For example, in a recent study (Perez, 2000), Latina immigrant women reported that nostalgia helped them to maintain coexistence of the two worlds, selves, and languages set apart through immigration. Contrary to traditional perceptions of nostalgia for the "old home" as regressive and blocking psychological growth, it was shown to have a sustaining and creative function and serves to structure the "new home." Markovic and Manderson (2000), who analyzed adjustment strategies by women from the former Yugoslav republics who settled in Australia during the 1990s, found three adjustment strategies: (1) loss orientation, (2) ambivalence, and (3) future orientation. These findings make one wonder whether deliberating between two identities can ever be fully resolved for first-generation immigrants.

Narratives of women reveal the ability to integrate the two cultures or to successfully oscillate between them. Some women demonstrate creativity and flexibility in coping with the duality by reframing the split as bifocality, integrating components from both worlds and skillfully oscillating between them. Sonia, Sarah, and Parastu are examples of weaving past and present into a delicate fabric with a wide range of cultural hues. They do so by the names they use, the way they decorate their homes, maintaining intensive personal and professional connections, and frequent visits to their homeland. For example, Sonia's one bedroom apartment is furnished with a mixture of American and Middle Eastern accessories. Parastu feels that she succeeds to develop a duality that satisfies both sides of her: "I have the

beauty of Parastu [her Persian name] and the good of Inbal [her Hebrew name]. However, none of them is 'pure' anymore. Parastu includes shades of Inbal, and Inbal has in its tones of Parastu."

Other women prefer to maximize their immersion in the new culture. Natasha stated, "It is imperative for an immigrant to become as
much of the new culture as possible." Genevieve expressed a similar
view: "With immigration, to be accepted and adjust to the new society, we need to change our mentality. A person who opts to emigrate
must be ready to become a new person. We, the new immigrants, join
the ride on the Israeli train, and we need to turn around and go in the
direction that the train goes. We need to get out of who and what we
always were and become somebody else."

A few of the women prefer to cope with the duality embedded in
immigration by maintaining much of their culture of origin. They live
in national/ethnic enclaves and neighborhoods heavily populated by
their compatriots that replicate the culture of origin within the new
country, and they consume books, movies, newspapers, and food
from their homeland. Maria referred to her Cuban homeland as "my
country, my home" and to the United States as America or "this country." Nadra reflected, "I guess I have too much India in me. I prefer to
wear my hair cut Indian style, my dresses are mostly made by an Indian dressmaker who lives in my neighborhood, I eat mostly Indian
food, we observe Indian rituals, and many of my friends are Indian. It
is like I stand on two feet anchored in two separate lands, but the foot
that stands in India is stronger than the one that stands in the United
States."

Unlike I anticipated, women who come from cultures that favor
collective identity, e.g., Hang, Rosa, Nadra, and Mare, do not differ
from women who come from cultures that significantly emphasize
individualistic identity, such as Genevieve and Sabin.

Divided or Multiplied: Can One Person Have More Than One Identity?

Women often pointed to developing a fluid sense of identity or
"multiple identities" as their strategy for success. They value all parts
of themselves rather than making a choice to embrace one part and
disallow other parts of who they are. One's identity reflects one's perception by self and by others as it developed since childhood, shaped

and solidified in adolescence, and transformed throughout the life span. Several women challenged in diverse ways the idea that one should have *an* identity. Sarah, for example, asked, "Where is it written that I have to be one or the other, an American or a Pakistani?" The concept of "transmigrants" coined by Glick-Schiller, Basch, and Blanc-Szanton (1992) to describe migrants who establish themselves in two cultures at the same time, develop loyalty to, and find identification with both fits the experience of these women.

Postmodernism rejected binary views on gender and introduced the concept of fluid gender to address variations of gender identities other than the traditional male-female dyad, such as drag kings, transsexual, and transgender people. It is suggested that in a similar way the idea of binary identity (i.e., that one has and can be one or the other) should be substituted by recognizing the possibility of a fluid identity, i.e., that one can have more than one identity in a functional way.

Bystydzienski and Resnik (1994), in their account about the experiences of women who cross cultures, either by immigration, spending long periods in a foreign cultural milieu, or growing up with immigrant parents, coined the concept "cultural homelessness" to describe being between two cultures without quite fitting into either. Narratives of women I interviewed suggest that this is not always the case and that there is a complementary side to the coin—that of biculturalism with a dual identity. Josefowitz Siegel (1992), in her account of escaping the Nazi occupation from Lithuania to Austria to Switzerland to the United States, states, "I began to feel that I did belong, to some extent, in each and all of the places that I had ever called home, rather than feeling that I did not really belong to any of them" (p. 110).

Women in this study demonstrate their ability to contain and reconcile two identities, feel proud and at home in both, and see both as equally important. One woman said, "What works for me is having developed more than one identity and living in peace with all of my identities." Another commented, "Complementary identities can co-exist—I am both a Russian and an Israeli and feel comfortable with being both." Furthermore, women felt that the coexistence of more than one identity enriches their life and expands their experiences.

My own son once asked me, "So what are we now? Israelis? Americans?" My answer to him and to me is that I do not see a need to decide one or the other; rather, I opt to be both. I found a way to maintain my

Israeli self integrated with my new American self. I do not claim that this is easy, but it is doable. One can have many lives simultaneously.

Immigrant women have been depicted as putting up a show of good adaptation, while remaining torn inside (Bystydzienski and Resnik, 1994). The narratives of these women challenge this stand and suggest that there is a real possibility for feeling affiliated and at home in two cultures. Svetlana reflected on the advantages of multiple identities, "I feel blessed that I can be in both places at once and understanding more than one language. I have developed an outsider's perspective on both cultures. Rather than follow conventional routes, I developed my own independent way through observation and comparison."

The issue of multiple identities has attracted the attention of social scientists in recent years, but it has been applied mostly in the context of sexual orientation and racial affiliation. Discussion of the concept in the context of immigrants has been very limited and recent (e.g., McKay and Wong, 1996; Deaux, 2000; Sakamoto, 2001). These recent works confirm the view of fluidity and flexibility in the adaptation process, which makes room for multiple identities. One way of viewing multiple identities has been suggested by the sociological lens of transnationalism, i.e., the creation of a network across borders which allows immigrants to be "citizens of two worlds" and to continue to play a role in the political, social, and economic fabric of their originating communities, while living and functioning in their receiving communities (Portes, 1998; Levitt, 2000; Salih, 2001). Easier means of electronic communication and mobility between the two cultures, combined with a liberal immigration policy that allows a continuous stream of new recruits from the culture of origin who refresh and replenish the ethnic community, contributes to the creation and maintenance of this double identity. For example, I feel very comfortably rooted in the United States and integrated in its political, social, and cultural life. At the same time, I visit Israel at least once a year, I frequent stores that sell Israeli products, including food, music, books, and videotaped movies, and friends and colleagues who visit from Israel constantly stay with us. One symbolic expression for my double identities is reflected in the fact that I routinely start the day reading *The New York Times* and the Israeli newspaper on the World Wide Web. Narratives reveal that such patterns are not uncommon and foster the expansion of one's identity.

The development of multiple identities can be reflected in many ways. Hang states her commitment to all her identities by the signature that she adopted—signing her name both according to the Vietnamese and the European/Australian way. I attend professional conferences wearing a pin that has combined Israeli and American flags attached to my name tag. Because I live, work, publish, and fill out registration forms in the United States, I am usually formally identified as a representative from my current home, which in my self-perception tells only half the story of who I am. Attaching the two flags is my way to make the nonverbal statement of my dual identity. My experience is that when one feels strongly about the dual identity, it is met with social acceptance.

However, certain situations may challenge the multiple identities and raise dilemmas for immigrants, especially under stress. For example, following the September 11, 2001, terrorist attacks on the World Trade Center, Pentagon, and in Pennsylvania, many immigrants who had come to terms with their combined affiliation with their cultures of origin and of relocation, found themselves again pushed into the debate, "Is there any reason I should not be a proud Arab and an American. When do I become an American? I don't want my children to live the life I've had to lead, always apologizing for who I am. I can either be an American or I can be an Arab, but I can't be both. You know what? I am both" (Scott, 2001, p. 1).

Unlike I anticipated, women do not relate their way of dealing with the duality caused by immigration to factors such as their age at the time of immigration, the circumstances of immigration, and their degree of participation in the decision to immigrate.

Age

Women were at different stages of their life when they experienced immigration. Dunja, Nadra, Mare, Parastu, and Hang were immigrant children. They relocated when they were preadolescents or teenagers. Natasha, Tara, Sonia, Teresina, Sabin, and Rosa immigrated as young adults. Svetlana, Genevieve, Ana, Sarah, Maria, Matijia, and Klara were mothers in their thirties and forties when they relocated with their families. In spite of differences in the timing of immigration in their lives, their struggles with duality are similar, except Natasha's.

Circumstances

The immigration of the women in this study was motivated by a wide array of circumstances. Teresina and Sabin immigrated because of personal reasons. Parastu's family, similar to Tara, escaped the danger of persecution. Sonia, Natasha, Hang, Dunja, and Matijia left war-stricken homelands in search for peaceful life and a brighter future. Klara, Maria, and Sarah relocated mostly because of professional and economic plans their husbands wished to pursue. Rosa followed a dream of personal and financial security and a better life. Genevieve's immigration was ideologically driven. Ana, Svetlana, and Mare's family chose to relocate because of a combination of political, economic, and ideological reasons. Nadra is not even sure what cause her father to decide to relocate. The diversity of circumstances of their migrations does not appear to be associated with the perception of and reactions to the duality caused by immigration.

Degree of Participation in the Decision to Immigrate

The degree to which the women had a say in the decision to emigrate varied for participants of the study. Genevieve, Ana, Svetlana, Natasha, and Klara were active participants in the decision to relocate. For Mare, Hang, Dunja, and Parastu, the decision was made by their parents and they had no control over it. Sonia's immigration was forced by circumstances. Tara, Matijia, Teresina, Rosa, and Sabin made their own decision to relocate. Nadra, Maria, and Sarah were forced to immigrate by their husbands' decision. Narratives do not reflect any effect of the degree of mastery that women had over the decision to immigrate on their perception of and coping with the duality that the move introduced into their lives.

GAINS AND LOSSES

As has been extensively documented, immigration involves multiple losses. However, it also offers gains. All of the women in this study feel that the gains significantly outweigh the losses. Sabin expresses this feeling: "It is true that immigration turns one into an eternal learner of new words, idioms, ideas. While this may be a tiring experience, it also has the potential to be a very gratifying and interesting one. In a sense it gives one the opportunity to live two lives in one."

Gains

The narratives of the women in this study show that much can be gained by immigration. Of particular interest is the fact that women who have opportunities to go back to visit their homeland strongly emphasize the gains. Thus, Klara suggested, "Revisiting one's country of origin helps sobering up from the nostalgia and appreciate the gains of living in a different culture." Sarah echoed, "I revisited my homeland with very few expectations, and even those few were not fulfilled. This helped me moderate the nostalgia."

Distinctive benefits for women from the immigration experience include financial, professional, educational, and social opportunities for themselves and for their children; liberties in diverse aspects of life; acquiring recognition of and appreciation for their abilities; and developing richer and broader perspectives of the world, their environment, and themselves, and personal growth. This finding agrees with work that showed a range of improvements in women's benefits from immigration, including increased control over decision making in the household, greater personal autonomy, and access to resources in the community at large (e.g., Simon and Brettell, 1986; Grasmuck and Pessar, 1991; Foner, 1998).

Opportunities

Immigration opens up new options for women and their children. "Suddenly, I had options, as many options as there were cereal boxes at the supermarkets. I wanted to try them all, try them twice, feeling that I would not be penalized but, rather, rewarded for my spunky spirit" (Lee, 2000, p. 129). For many immigrant women, relocation means the opening of educational, professional, and personal windows that would not have been available for them in their homelands. Mostly, but not exclusively, gaining more opportunities for themselves was reported by women who relocated from cultures in which the dominant discourse limits the lives of women because they are based on power politics that define women as less worthy than men and allows them less access to resources. In spite of glass ceilings, inequality of wages, and discrimination against women, Western cultures offer women many more opportunities than their often conservative and oppressive patriarchal countries of origin in Asia, Africa, the Far East, the Middle East, and even Europe.

Sarah is appreciative of the educational opportunities that immigration offered her. She is convinced that in her Pakistani culture of origin an advanced education and a professional career could not have been achievable. "Immigration to America gave me more opportunities to study a profession in which I am interested and eventually more freedom within my own family with my husband and in-laws," she said.

Mothers often cited that immigration granted their children better chances in various aspects of their life. Genevieve sought for her children freedom from anti-Semitism. Maria wanted to secure her children's educational and vocational opportunities. Ana believes that immigration offered her sons more personal safety. Mare's parents believed that they were taking their children to a longed for "country of milk and honey." Matijia wanted to give her children "a better chance in life and a sense of security." Hang and Dunja's parents wanted to save their children from the horrors of war and give them a quiet and safe life. This wish of mothers reverberates in narratives of immigrant girls. Michael (1998), who interviewed immigrant girls to New York, found that they perceived immigration as increasing their chances for better education compared to their homeland.

Not only does immigration offer opportunities, for many women it represents the introduction of the ability to make choices between options. The mere existence of options is not enough; one has to have the permission to choose between them. In many of the immigrant women's cultures of origin, women are denied the possibility to choose and their role is carved by society's expectations. An immigrant from South Africa who was homesick described leaving America to go back to her homeland as "The foolishness of giving up on the chances of future in the real world, of giving up choice" (Freed, 2000, pp. 63-64).

Liberties

Immigration is recounted by many women as an emancipatory experience. Women in this study named personal and social freedom as major gains of the immigration experience. This freedom has many faces. For some it is personal freedom that Western society offers for women, especially those who come from traditional cultures that practice subordination of women, and they report having gained more liberties and a greater share of power and autonomy. Sonia appreciates the personal freedom that American society offers women as compared to the "controlled freedom" that they experience in her homeland. Although she recognizes its limitations, she also sees in the United States greater equality, which offers women more opportunities for professional promotion according to their abilities rather than their gender.

Their ability to find jobs in domestic work and thus become employed faster than men brings them in close contact with the dominant society and often earns them an improved position in the household (Foner, 1998). Consequently, immigrant women learn the language quickly and are exposed to possibilities other than those to which they were brought up. It "opens their eyes" and makes them aware of the existence of alternative roles for women and gender relationships. It gives them permission to aspire for more for themselves and for their daughters than what is traditional for women in their culture of origins. Parastu stated, "I like the atmosphere here more than in Iran. There I was an exception because of my seeking to be myself, not live according to traditional 'appropriate' ways imposed after the 1979 revolution, which turned the country into a theocracy. I could not do as I pleased. I had to oblige to limiting dress and behavior codes, to wear long and modest attire, convey chastity and purity. I could not do it and stood out like a sore thumb. Here I found myself." Sonia agreed, "I appreciate the freedom to live as I find fit without being concerned of being judged."

Gaining freedom as a result of immigration is not unique to women who relocate from traditional societies to the Western world. Sabin feels that she profits in the sexual freedom gained from emigrating from her Austrian homeland with its strict social norms to the much more tolerant and open Australian culture. "Austria is a conservative and oppressive country, and people who choose a nonconforming route have a very hard time. Here, in Australia, I have the freedom to be who I am and to live openly and in peace with my sexual orientation and share my life with my partner without being a victim to much scrutinizing and criticism," she explained.

Women who immigrate from societies with restrictive political regimes, such as the former Soviet Union, cited greater political freedom and the ability to make choices in their daily life as benefits of immigration.

Higher Self-Esteem

Central for women in this study was gaining more respect for their own abilities and a better view of themselves. They reported learning that they have powers, abilities, resilience, and skills, of which they have not been aware prior to immigration, and recognizing these strengths in themselves, they came to develop a higher appreciation for themselves. Although migration has been documented as often causing men to drop in status, women in this study reported that it elevated their status in society, in their own eyes, and, consequently, often in their families. Their ability to find jobs and share financial responsibilities for the family provides them with a sense of a more equal place and a right to an independent opinion.

Recurrent statements included "I feel good about who I am and what I can do," and "I did not know that I have all these abilities and power." Ana stated, "Had all this not happened to me, I would not have been so strong. I would not have known that I have all these strengths in me." Rosa agreed, "I came out of the ordeal stronger. People tell me I am a survivor. I guess I am, even though I do not always feel so. Sometimes I feel weak and vulnerable. But overall, it gave me more confidence in my abilities to successfully cope with devastating situations."

Sonia echoed the voices in many of the narratives when she stated, "The experience made me meet my own limits, stretched me to the extreme, and made me realize that I am much more powerful than I could have ever imagined. I would have never known that I have in me all these abilities and power if immigration had not forced me to discover and apply them."

Foner (2000) documented higher status and authority within the household and higher self-esteem for women who, following immigration, became—often for the first time—regular wage winners or contributors of a larger share of the family income. What is striking in the current study is that the respect that women develop for themselves is not limited to their ability to become a major force in providing for their families but refers to their ability to cope successfully with the full range of immigration-related issues.

Broadening Horizons

A major gain reported by all women was broadening their horizons, acquiring a wider worldview, and increasing their tolerance for different ways of doing things. Stepping out of their culture of origin was reported by women as helping them to move from a local, provincial outlook to a more comprehensive, multidimensional way of thinking, to develop new ways of looking at the world, a richer perspective, and greater appreciation for other cultures.

Women realize the diversity of various aspects of daily life and are more willing to accept that there is more than one way of doing things. They reported increased tolerance to diverse dress codes and concepts of beauty. For example, the anorexic feminine beauty ideal fostered by the West is hardly compatible with Middle Eastern aesthetic criteria. Women are less judgmental of interpersonal behaviors that differ from their own and more receptive to different cultural habits, such as norms regarding what is acceptable as a present, how to react to a present brought by a guest, and how to greet others. Interviewees reported developing more flexibility to various cultural aspects as central as the pace of life and as minute as table manners, driving styles, and order of serving dishes.

In documenting her story of cultural commuting, Brock-Utne (1994) reflects how moving between cultures made her less adherent to the idea that there is a "right" and "wrong" in taste and manners. Klara expressed the same idea in the current study, saying, "Immigration allows you to develop a more expansive perspectives of people, approaches, perceptions, interpretation, judgment, and reactions to people, events, and experiences. You learn to understand things from many different angles and to gain comprehension of how people from diverse backgrounds see life. It makes you richer internally and more understanding externally." Sarah shared the same view, stating, "Being exposed to the norms of the absorbing culture serves as an eye-opener. One realizes that things are much more complicated, that there are alternatives. I saw that things can be different than when I grew up and was encouraged all my life to believe."

Sabin concurred, "I developed much more understanding of people and more ability to empathize. I learned to appreciate tradition. Back in Austria I experienced tradition as restrictive and customs as binding. Being exposed to the place of tradition in the Aboriginal culture made me realize the vivid, living, and nourishing aspect of tradition. I came to appreciate the beauty of heritage."

My personal experience is very similar. One example was learning about different mourning rituals. When I first came to New York, I was puzzled to never see death announcements on walls in the street. I was amazed when going to my first U.S. funeral that people were sitting in rows in a funeral home with the coffin on a stage and relatives and friends speaking about the deceased. I was used to people being buried in shrouds (nothing should separate the dead from the soil of the Holy Land) and eulogies said at the graveside. It took me a while to understand and learn to respect and accept that there are different ways of mourning.

This finding is supported by previous research on immigrant women. For example, Foner (1998, 2000) documented in Chinese, South American, and Caribbean immigrant women a broadening of social horizons and growing sense of independence that comes with work opportunities which became available to them and with earning a regular wage.

Personal Growth

Personal growth was cited in most narratives. The prospect for posttraumatic growth, i.e., an individual's perceptions of significant positive changes resulting from the struggle with a life crisis, has been documented among survivors of natural disasters, war experiences, violent victimizations, and life-threatening illnesses, as well as among immigrant children (Calhoun and Tedeschi, 1999; Cordova et al., 2001; Weiss, 2002). Narratives of women in the current study suggest that the same is true for immigrant women. Dunja summarized the experience of many women when she stated, "In reflecting about it, I realize that migration, though tough at times, has been also nourishment to me and has significantly contributed to the growth of who I am as a person." Sabin feels that immigration made her a more mature and better person. From the attitudes that she experienced she learned to be more empathic and sensitive. "I learned from this lack of understanding by people of my situation not to judge people until you stand in their place. Not to assume that you know how it is to be there. Not to have the pretension to judge whose suffering is more difficult. I developed a lot of compassion," she said.

Safety and Feeling of Security

Women reported gaining increased political, economic, and social security as benefits of immigration. Specifically, women who relocated from countries such as the Philippines, the former Soviet Union, and other countries with oppressive political systems appreciated the safety offered by their countries of resettlement.

Losses

"I am not even sure if everybody will remember me, especially the little children. It is like my existence may have disappeared from my own family like footsteps in the sand," said Teresina. Reporting the aforementioned gains does not mean that women have not experienced losses and traumas. Although demonstrating considerable success and multiple gains, it would be inaccurate to assume that immigration is a loss-free process for women. In agreement with previous reports, all the women indicated that immigration had significant emotional and social costs. Immigration-related issues reported by women in this study include poverty, unemployment, discrimination, and facing bureaucracy, all of which caused diverse losses. Although material losses of income, assets, and objects have been discussed extensively in the literature as inherent to the immigration experience, women in this study emphasized emotional, cultural, social, and psychological losses most.

Nostalgic memories, idealization of one's homeland, and home-sickness were expressed in various ways. Nina, a teacher who recently relocated from Siberia to New York, sighs deeply, and says, "At home, when I entered the house, the whole place would be smelling of the delicious sweet fragrance of fresh apples. Here, it is like the apples are made of paper, they are synthetic."

Women report losses irrespective to their degree of involvement in the decision to emigrate. Maria did not want to leave Cuba, "But in our country a woman has no choice. She has to go after her husband."

Nadra, Hang, and Dunja had to relocate because of their fathers' decisions. Sonia made her own decision to escape the war in Lebanon, and Rosa sought to better her social and financial opportunities. Matijia was the engine behind relocation of her whole family, and Klara was an active party in the decision making. All of them report similar experiences of loss and agree that immigrant women are often the ones who carry the heaviest load. Matijia said, "The main burden of the family's acculturation and adjustment to the new environment was on me, as it is on all immigrant women. Women are often put at the forefront of the battle for life in the new country."

Emotional Losses

Women reported loss of sense of security regarding their identity and their place in the world. "I did not know anymore who I am" was a recurrent sentence heard in the interviews. Klara explained, "The experience of loss of meaningful objects while you relocate translates in the mind of immigrants into a constant hole, a feeling of emptiness which you constantly strive to fill." Especially painful is the feeling that they do not fit in their culture of origin anymore and fall between the cracks.

Women described the loss of intimate relationships and a social network as extremely disturbing. Many iterated that women are more likely than men to create their "women's group" or circle of close friends with whom they share and consult, and therefore they have a more intense sense of loneliness when this social network is lost because of immigration.

Cultural Losses

Women reported losing familiarity with cultural clues to acceptable behaviors, confusion because of different or conflicting norms between their cultures of origin and of relocation, and a sense of disorientation. Sarah recounted, "Being an immigrant took me away from the familiar social structure which is the compass that supports one to build one's life." Matijia said, "You lose your criteria for what should be done and how. I am not in my natural environment, so things do not just come to me naturally. Everything, even the minutest step, requires an effort, consideration, and calculation. All the time I am scared to make mistakes. I was afraid to ask questions, to look stupid and not know what 'everybody' knows. I felt embarrassed and awkward."

Mothers seem to feel a double loss, that of not understanding themselves and in addition, not understanding the proper norms on behalf of their children. Because often the motive for immigration is to better the chances of the children, this helplessness may create tremendous guilt. Matijia, for example, explained, "Understanding the educational system, the expectations, the mechanisms for decision making, the whole culture of schools and what is going on for your children, the academic plan, it was very difficult to figure out in the beginning and it is one of the first big challenges for immigrant mothers. It takes a lot out of you. You want to make sure that your children get what they deserve, yet nobody tells you the norms, what is good and what is bad, whom to approach how, which channels one has, which options and how to make sense of them for the benefit of your kids. Immigrant mothers are thrown into the roller coaster of these questions in their first week in the new country." Maria concurred, "You brought them there, so you ought to know, and yet you don't. You feel humiliated, guilty, and have a hard time coping with their complains 'so why did we come here?' I felt more than once like throwing my hands in the air in despair and going back."

A particularly important factor in cultural losses in immigration is the loss of language, which all women experienced as detrimental. Immigrant women have been documented to have fewer language skills than immigrant men do, which contributes to their sense of isolation from the wider society (Assar, 1999). Sarah said, "Here I understand the words but not the music, the verbal content but not the cultural codes by which to process the meaning." Parastu explained, "I hated not knowing Hebrew, I felt inferior and ashamed, I was afraid to speak." Her experience was echoed in the words of Natasha, "If you do not have the language, you do not have the people. If you do not learn the language first, you become isolated, your children need to translate for you, and this is humiliating." Matijia explained, "To speak English all day long is fatiguing. It is very, very hard when you have to function all the time in a strange territory."

Comments from Sonia indicate that the experience of loss of language stays with the immigrant for a long time. "One of the main difficulties was the lack of familiarity of the American world of images, associations, and colloquialisms. I knew most of the words but I missed the associations and implications attached to them. I got the pieces but sometimes did not get the full picture and sometimes I still don't even today, after all these years," she related.

Pressures from mainstream society to let go of the previous culture as a statement of loyalty to the new one may amplify cultural losses. Sarah recounted, "A teacher asked me if I am more American or more Pakistani. I said that I am both. She pushed the issue further and asked where I would like to be buried when I die. When I said that I live in America and would be buried here, she concluded that I am more American. But this is not how feel. I feel I am both. I am aware of my past; I cannot just throw it away; these are my roots and this is part of who I am." Sabin shared the reluctance to separate herself from her culture of origin, saying, "I do not apply for Australian citizenship because I will lose my Austrian passport [the two countries do not have an agreement for dual citizenship]. It would be like changing my name, my core of being. Like losing part of who I am. I could not imagine going to my own country as a tourist with an Australian passport. And what if at some point in the future I wish to go back to Austria? Will I have to apply for citizenship in my country of origin? This is inconceivable to me."

Social Losses

Many of the women mourned losing social status. Genevieve has to cope with the change from the high professional status in her homeland to the less prestigious and lower paid status of physicians in Israel. Changing from a giver to a receiver troubles Ana. She said, "We never asked for anything. We have always been self-sufficient and providing for others. Here we were forced initially to ask for help every month. I came to the Jewish Agency [the organization that provides help to new immigrants] and there was that Russian lady sitting, sipping her tea. She did not even offer me a cup of tea. I was deeply hurt. I was treated as nothing, as if I was not a person."

In discussing loss of professional position, women tend to emphasize the social and psychological aspects over the financial aspects of the loss. Genevieve reported the dire financial implications of the immigrant situation but described mostly the pain of career and social status loss.

Some women emphasized the sense of loss particularly during the formal process of changing their status in the new social environment. Sabin recalled her encounters with immigration authorities. "It was a painful, anxiety provoking and totally infantlizing experience. Here I was an independent adult pushed back into dependency. Your whole life is in the hands of other people who do not always mean well and there is nothing that you can do about it. You are totally at the mercy of other people. They can decide to send you away and you have no control. You are helpless and powerless like a leaf in the wind," she described.

Women in this study reported reacting to these losses with sadness and depression, dissociation, loneliness, a feeling of insecurity, constant alert, and confusion. However, for most of them these reactions gradually dissolved and instead developed into a way of coming to terms and in many cases benefiting from the experiences.

Klara described the constant alert caused by insecurity, "You always carry an urge to be equipped beyond the real need, to be prepared for all circumstances." This never-ending alert causes the experience of immigration to be taxing and tiring. Genevieve explained, "All the time we open doors, are disappointed and go on to open another door to be disappointed again and go on for the next door and so on. This is an exhausting process physically and emotionally." Genevieve described her dissociative reaction, which resembles descriptions from trauma survivors: "The following morning I opened my eyes, saw the small, crowded space, felt the heat and asked myself 'what did I do?' I wanted badly to go back, but there was nothing to go back to. I was in a shock. As if all of a sudden I found myself in the midst of a nightmare. I was moving like a robot. I performed routine actions automatically, but I was not there. I was detached. Nothing felt real."

Parastu was very confused and conflicted when she first came to Israel from Iran: "Should I follow the path that my parents taught me? Should I go my own way?" These feelings of social losses stay with immigrant women for many years and may be easily reactivated by later experience of any type of loss. For example, losing money or a job or separating from a partner may throw one back to the experience of the original loss.

SUMMARY: MAIN FINDINGS

The narratives of eighteen women who were interviewed for this study and my own experience reveal several important findings. First, immigrant women, who are often portrayed as being at high risk, also demonstrate a great deal of resilience that has social, familial, personal, circumstantial, and spiritual sources and helps them cope with the hardships of relocation. Second, immigrant women experience duality in their affiliation, loyalty, and identity and find diverse routes to cope with this duality. Most of them find some way to integrate their past and present or to develop "multiple identities." Finally, immigration brings to women a mix of social, economic, personal, and psychological losses, and opportunities for new liberties, educational, professional, and personal growth, and broadens their horizons.

How should these findings inform the development and delivery of services in a way that is designed to minimize the losses and maximize the potential for benefiting from the relocation? Chapter 8 offers guidelines and principles for helpful services designed to enhance the lives of immigrant women.

Chapter 8

Implications for Service Development and Delivery

How can these stories of immigrant women help us develop informed interventions? What should the nature of services be to best build on the strengths of immigrant women and most effectively address their needs? How can the narratives inform service development and delivery? It should be recognized that immigrant women are not a homogenous conglomerate. Their resettlement needs differ, and all of them cannot be treated in the same way. However, some general principles can be generated from the life histories of the women in this study.

ADVANTAGES AND DISADVANTAGES OF SPECIALIZED SERVICES FOR IMMIGRANT WOMEN

Two potentially conflicting findings emerge from the narratives of women in this study. One major finding that emerges from the stories is that immigrant women have specific and unique needs, which have a major impact on the coping of their husbands, children, and extended family. Given this finding, significant investment in services tailored to women are called for because of potential productivity and the need for these services. The failure of general services to effectively address the needs of this population group has been documented. For example, Ferugson (1999) cites gender blindness and monolingual and monocultural services as major barriers to effective service delivery to immigrant women that adversely affect well-being of women and their children. In addition, many immigrants are underserved because of service providers' discomfort in servicing them, and when services are provided, they are often inappropriate

(Healy, 2002). Tailoring services specifically for immigrant women is beneficial in that they target the unique needs of this population and offer culturally acceptable responses to these needs, and therefore have often been recommended (e.g., Cole, Espin, and Rothblum, 1992).

At the same time, the narratives show that women demonstrate resilience, creativity, and resourcefulness in coping with immigration-related issues. Developing specialized services carries a potential risk of solidifying segregation and polarization and maintaining the separation of these women from mainstream society. As the case of "separate and equal" regarding the education of black Americans in the 1960s indicated, such unique services targeting ethnic minorities are at risk of becoming inferior in quality. Furthermore, developing and delivering services from the frame of reference of the service provider imposes on immigrant clients definitions and intervention strategies rooted in the Western, middle-class mind-set. Thus the solution (i.e., the service) becomes part of the problem.

One way to address the tension between the need for specialized services and the potential damage of these same services is to adopt Pittaway's (1999) claim that the overall approach to providing services to immigrant women needs to be changed because, "Sadly, the way in which many services are provided often denies them their power and constrains their ability to use it" (p. 18). She advocates moving from protection to empowerment, i.e., ensuring that the women have opportunities to exert their power, take control of their own lives, and assist themselves and their children. This means moving to partnerships and client-conferencing models of service provision, in which immigrant women are partners rather than service recipients and are consulted on their needs and desires and involved in prioritizing and conceptualizing service development and delivery. Balancing aid and self-help reflects respect for the accomplishments of the women and prevents long-term dependency.

The question remains as to what degree providing services specific to immigrant women represents an act of oppression that undermines immigrant women's independence and contributes to maintaining their status as disenfranchised recipients of services rather than a population that can achieve its own goals. In light of the aforementioned concerns, development of specialized services requires a great deal of caution. The findings suggest that three levels of service should be offered: direct services to individuals and families, community programs, and policy development.

DIRECT SERVICES TO INDIVIDUALS AND FAMILIES

To successfully adjust, a wide range of diverse services specifically designed to address the needs of immigrant women are called for. Services should be offered within diverse contexts, using various modalities, by service providers who are culturally competent, at the right time, and should be promoted in the relevant community.

Types of Services

Many services for newcomers are concrete, often leaving emotional and psychosocial needs unmet. A wide array of services is necessary. They include language, educational, vocational, and professional training, orientation to the labor market, preparation for employment (e.g., help with writing resumes, acquiring skills for self-marketing), psychoeducational assistance, translation, referrals, and individual counseling.

Language

As has been documented extensively and validated by the narratives of women in this study, proficiency in the language of the new culture is a key to successful relocation (Fugita, 1990), facilitates postarrival adjustment, and has considerable psychological and social meaning for immigrants (Hoffman, 1989). Rosa best expressed the importance of literacy in the language of the new social environment in coping with challenging circumstances: "My knowledge of the language and gradual growing understanding of how they [employers, lawyers, judges] think helped me cope with them." Therefore, helping women to learn the language and the culture of the new environment is of utmost importance. Language classes often also create a safe place where women can use the camaraderie that develops as a setting in which to share experiences and heal emotional wounds.

Absence of proficiency in the language of the country of relocation has been associated with greater feelings of depression (Van Boemel and Rozee, 1992). Therefore, teaching immigrant women the language of the new social environment has combined benefits of promoting their prospects of finding jobs and their ability to communicate and be socially integrated, enhancing their sense of accomplishment, and feeling good about themselves and their welfare.

Vocational and Professional Services

Training and employment are important parts of the healing process. Employment is powerful leverage for achieving and experiencing success because it allows women to interact with the social environment. The workplace is an important arena for assisting in the process of establishing relationships within the wider community and offering opportunities to progress in acquiring the language and practicing it, leading to a sense of worth and power. Therefore, development of employment promotion programs that help women to develop work search, job keeping, gaining and retaining employment, and vocational/professional skills are necessary components of services for immigrant women. Working from a strength perspective, it is beneficial to survey immigrant women for the type of talents and abilities that they bring and to develop programs that creatively foster these abilities as income-producing employment.

Part of developing an immigrant-friendly work environment is fostering immigrant-sensitive employee assistance programs (EAPs). Although some organizations (e.g., the EAP division of the California Family Health Council) and some regions, such as the Pacific Southwest, which includes some of the states with the highest rates of immigration such as California and Hawaii, have paid special attention to programs designed to respond to needs of immigrants (e.g., an educational program for Chinese women at risk for breast and cervical cancer), such programs are still an exception rather than the rule.

Part of helping immigrants to find their way professionally in the new environment is to familiarize them with the culture of the world of work. Immigrants come with concepts that may differ significantly from those of the culture of relocation regarding work relationships and norms. For example, when I came as an immigrant from highly unionized Israel, where all professors holding the same rank across universities and disciplines have the same basic salary, I had no clue that in the United States academicians need to negotiate personal contracts and I failed to realize the importance of bargaining.

Exposure to Successful Role Models

Women cited availability of other immigrant women who have been successful and who can serve as powerful role models and inspiration as a significant factor that contributes to their resilience. However, not all immigrant women have access to such role models within their own family or community. Therefore, the development of a program is called for to provide such positive experiences for all immigrant women. Such a community-based outreach program, following principles similar to those of the Big Brother/Big Sister programs, would recruit and match successful immigrant women who "made it" to serve as friends and mentors to newcomers. Such a model is mutually beneficial because it validates and empowers both parties. It helps provide the recipient of the service with understanding, emotional support, and a sense of direction to regain her self-esteem and self-confidence, while instilling new hope for the future, and gives the volunteer an opportunity to review the road that she has walked as a basis for self-validation and enhances her self-confidence and sense of self-worth.

Social Support

Women cited loneliness as a major source of difficulty. Klara's tale about leaving the house at a time of stress, looking for a sympathetic shoulder, and realizing that there was not a soul to whom she could turn, tells the story of social isolation of immigrant women in a very powerful way. Because immigration cuts immigrants off from their natural social support at the time that they need it most, opportunities for social support systems are of utmost importance. This finding is in accord with Lynam's (1985) report about interviews with twelve immigrant women to Canada who identified having a social network to turn to for personal support as a major need.

Developing such a network can be achieved by several ways such as the mentoring cited previously, but potentially the best way is by developing support groups, as is discussed in the section on modalities for intervention.

Counseling

Women in this study indicated the need for and importance of affordable counseling services. However, research and clinical experience indicate that providing counseling to immigrants presents a complicated task. Culture shapes the views of personal-psychological issues and expectations for help in coping with them. Religious traditions and beliefs condition the worldview of many Asian Americans, South Americans, and other groups of immigrants. This impacts on the definition of mental health issues and on culturally acceptable ways of coping with and of treating them (Fugita, 1990; Rodriguez and O'Donell, 1995; Chandras, 1997).

For example, immigrants often come from collectivistic cultures, in which the family rather than the individual is the basic unit of society. A stigma is attached to personal-emotional problems that are perceived as a threat to the entire family. Hence, mental health issues of the individual cast a shadow of shame over the entire family and may compromise their welfare, prospects for marriage, and status within the community. To save the face of the family, such issues are typically kept within the family and the extended family is relied on for handling them. Extrafamilial services are used only after other sources of help such as family and friends have failed (Sandhu, 1997). This leads to underutilization of mental health services by immigrants (Nguyen, 1984).

Some of the immigrants' cultures of origin, such as Latin countries, the former Soviet Union, and East Asian nations maintain a negative stigma of the use of counseling and discourage using mental health and counseling services due to shame, mistrust in authorities, and cultural expectations of concrete services. Narratives of women in this study demonstrate this attitude. For example, Rosa stated, "I was not sure where I could go. I did not know whom to ask. In my culture you do not ask such questions. It makes you look bad."

These communities favor more culturally syntonic traditional healing practices, including rituals, indigenous medicine, meditation, prayer, and mysticism rather than Western mental health practices (Fugita, 1990; Rodriguez and O'Donell, 1995; Chandras, 1997).

Furthermore, many cultures, including the former Soviet Union and Latin America, discourage sharing of intimate and family information with strangers and mistrust traditional talk therapy. Therefore, many immigrants are unfamiliar with Western counseling concepts and prefer to rely on family and traditional healing practices rather than professional help (Nguyen, 1984). These communities also tend to demonstrate underutilization of services (Yamashiro and Matsuolka, 1997; Blair, 2001; Leong and Lau, 2001).

The request of many of the women in this study for available counseling services as well as some of the writer's clinical experience are incompatible with the literature regarding such services for immigrants and raises the need for more clarity about the issue.

Elements of Services

Context

Location of services is challenging, because to be effective and encourage use, they need to be accessible and affordable, flexible, and offered within a nonstigmatized, friendly, and privacy-protecting environment, linguistically relevant, accompanied by child care services on site, and visible. Some of these criteria are potentially conflicting. For example, accessibility and location in the natural environment of the women may compromise privacy protection.

Accessibility and Affordability

Accessibility and affordability are major concerns in providing services to immigrant women (Bemak, Chung, and Bornemann, 1996), and their absence has been identified as contributing to underutilization of services by immigrants (Fugita, 1990). Many immigrant women cannot drive, and in some cultures driving would not be acceptable for women. Many cannot afford a car. Public transportation may be complicated and time consuming to use. Therefore, services that are not easily accessible are likely to be underutilized.

To increase accessibility to services, it is best to locate them in the ethnic/racial community. Flaskerud (1986), who studied use of mental health services by diverse ethnic groups, found that such location increases the chances of clients remaining in therapy. However, it may also make securing clients' privacy more difficult because in many cultures people would be concerned to be seen close to a mental health or social services agency.

Flexibility

Currently many services require that immigrants observe pre-scheduled appointments with professionals. However, it is not uncommon for immigrants to work in multiple, random, and daily jobs. Consequently, they cannot commit to regular appointments with service providers because they cannot predict what their employment situation will be on the designated date. If an opportunity for work presents itself and is in conflict with a scheduled appointment, most likely the immigrants would opt for the opportunity to earn some money. To allow immigrants with such unpredictable and unplanned work schedules to use services, service providers need to develop flexible formats of performance such as walk-in services, unconventional hours (e.g., evenings and weekends), and modes of service (e.g., the immigrant may be serviced by different workers and not necessarily the same worker all the time). This may require agencies to revisit assumptions and principles that traditionally inform their performance, such as the common assumption that developing a long-term trusting relationship between client and service provider is a nonnegotiable condition for the development of productive services.

Nonstigmatized Setting

It is important that services are offered in neutral and non-stigmatized settings as a way for normalizing their use. Many immigrant women come from communities that discourage sharing private information with extrafamilial sources and from cultures in which the concept of mental health is strange. Seeking help may shame the family (Rodriguez and O'Donell, 1995). Consequently, many women lack a cultural context for mental health problems. Therefore, services should be offered within a setting that is acceptable in the women's culture. Services provided within the context of educational institutes and community centers are received better than services associated with mental health facilities, medical schools, or in institutions that are foreign to the populations being served.

Services should also be titled by nonstigmatized labels, because problem-connoting titles may turn people away. For example, in Brighton Beach, a neighborhood heavily populated by immigrants from the former Soviet Union in Brooklyn, New York, acculturation groups for adolescents offered within local schools and defined as discussion groups were much more popular than similar groups labeled as therapy groups which were facilitated by the same professionals in a local mental health clinic.

Friendly Environment

It is crucial to create a friendly environment in which women can feel safe and comfortable with people whom they feel that they can trust. The physical environment of the services needs to be comfortable and convey respect for and acceptance of the immigrants' culture of origin by means of the decor and arrangement, the manners of the staff (e.g., bowing for greeting of Asian clients, appropriate attire), and the context of the service (e.g., in many cultures women would not be allowed to attend mixed-sex cultural activities).

Scheduling of services should take into consideration cultural expectations of women. For example, scheduling activities at times that women are expected to cook, care for children, and be available at home are a prescription for failure. In some cultures, expecting husbands to care for children while the wife goes to learn English or attend a support group is unrealistic, as is the expectation that young unmarried women will be allowed to attend after-dark activities.

Protection of Privacy

To provide services, a sense of trust in the environment and the people needs to be built. The mentality typical to some American communities of openly discussing therapy and receiving psychosocial services is unacceptable to many immigrant communities. For immigrant women from many cultures of origin, securing of total confidentiality is extremely important. This is not always easy to achieve in small cohesive communities, of which workers are also members and when scarcity of workers familiar with the culture is an issue. It may conflict with other principles, such as working with groups of women with similar experiences and locating services within the community, and create ethic and practical dilemmas for service planners and providers.

Linguistically Relevant

Women indicate that availability of services in their language is very important. Teresina, Rosa, Svetlana, and Matijia all cited feeling imprisoned within their limited command of the dominant language. Offering services in their own "mother tongue" allows immigrant women to express themselves more easily and freely and at the same time feel validated. This supports previous research that found that a language match of service provider and clients was strongly associated with whether clients persist or drop out of treatment (Flaskerud, 1986). Lack of fluency in the language of the dominant culture, which is a major stressor (Zapf, 1991), becomes even more so in seeking help with personal issues. Discussing intimate and painful issues is difficult in any language. Struggling to do so in a language that is not one's natural channel of expression amplifies the challenge and deprives women of the ability to convey nuances of their experiences.

Child Care Services

In many immigrant women's cultures of origin, taking care of children is the sole responsibility of mothers, and men are not expected to take part in child care chores. Therefore, one often cannot expect that husbands will watch children while wives are going for services. For many immigrant women, to be able to take advantage of services, child care needs to be provided on site.

Visibility

Development of relevant, affordable services is not enough. Lack of knowledge about available services has been identified as a cause for service underutilization by immigrants (Fugita, 1990). Dissemination of specific information about the nature, location, and conditions is necessary to develop awareness of their availability. Often special efforts are required, especially to women who come from cultures that advocate "cultural fatalism," i.e., a belief that certain negative life events happen regardless of efforts to prevent them (Comas-Diaz and Greene, 1994).

The target population needs to be made aware of the existence of services. Such awareness can be raised by several channels. Most effective is word of mouth among the relevant communities, especially regarding success stories. Reaching out can be done directly by advertisement in ethnic shops and ethnic media, local medical services, and schools that are heavily populated by immigrant children, and indirectly via existing associations, key figures in the communities, and referrals by medical staff, workers in community services, and other service providers.

Modalities and Models for Intervention

Direct services can be provided using individual, family, or group modalities, or a combination of them, and models that are syntonic with the immigrant's culture.

Individual

Given the discourse of mistrust that many immigrant women bring with them, traditional professional relationships between counselor or therapist and client within a hierarchical framework, in which the professional remains neutral and distanced, are not productive. To develop the necessary trust for creating a therapeutic alliance, a more personal approach that involves a certain degree of self-disclosure on the part of the professional is useful. Such self-disclosure sends the immigrant client a message of the social worker's caring and opens the door for a helping relationship.

Brief, solution-focused, and action-oriented models, cognitive and active interventions, and psychoeducational and family system approaches have been found useful with immigrants (Slonim-Nevo, Sharaga, and Mirsky, 1999; Berger, 2001). In light of this lack of trust in strangers, the quest for concrete services, and the heavy emphasis on rational approaches, this population is more receptive to direct and structured strategies for behavior change than to exploration of feeling and traditional therapies.

Although many immigrant women express a wish to have an "expert" who guides and directs them, with some women narrative approaches are useful because they give women an opportunity to tell their story, an experience that is potentially liberating, validating, and empowering by conveying that their experiences and life stories are important. These approaches avoid the power structure typical to traditional models of therapy, in which the worker is in a powerful authority position and the client in a powerless place. Such models tend to reinforce the feelings of dependency that characterize the experience of immigrant women. Instead, narrative models adopt a more egalitarian approach that promotes women's sense of self-worth.

A major challenge for the worker is to tailor the balance between demonstrated expertise ("you are the professional, so you should know what to do and solve my problem") and the empowering personal approach that enables the woman to develop the necessary trust.

Family

Many cultures of origin are familistic societies in which the family has a major role in defining the individual and addressing her or his issues. Accordingly, in many of the narratives women named their family as an important source of their resilience. For example, Dunja, Rosa, Ana, and many other participants asserted that they could not have made it without the support of their families. Many families react to the shared adversities of immigration and subsequent demands of the adjustment process by "closing ranks" and becoming more cohesive and close. In light of these multiple aspects of the importance of the family throughout the process of relocation, working with families is a relevant model of practice for providing services to immigrant women. The *contextual family therapy* model that was developed by Ivan Boszormenyi-Nagy has been advocated to be especially relevant for servicing immigrants because it offers a framework that is respectful of cultural differences and attentive to complexities of trauma (Kuoch, Miller, and Scully, 1992).

Groups

Groups offer an optimal modality to address some of the major issues reported by women and have been recognized as useful in providing services to immigrants (Glassman and Skolnik, 1984; Furnham and Bochner, 1986; Berger, 1996). Because isolation is cited by women as a major source of difficulty in immigration and availability of compatriots as a major source of resilience, a group of women who share the immigration experience and understand the challenges and nuances that are difficult to put into words can help reconstruct women's social networks. For example, in a study of Cambodian participants in groups, improvements in medical and emotional situations and in some aspects of daily functioning were reported (Van Boemel and Rozee, 1992). Furthermore, the same study suggests that for immigrants and refugees who are survivors of torture, as many immigrants are, being confined alone with a representative of the authorities (the therapist) may be too similar to a situation of interrogation and therefore not conducive to help. Groups, on the other hand, provide an empowering social support network.

Several types of groups can be helpful: self-help and support groups, therapy groups, acculturation groups, or a combination of them.

Self-help and support groups. Using groups of other women for mutual support is a natural mechanism for many women. Groups can provide participants with a social network that substitutes for relationships lost to immigration and can reduce social isolation. Nguyen (1984) has termed such groups "network" therapy as a means to reduce feelings of isolation and provide means for reconstruction of social networks that were disrupted by relocation. Many of the women cited social losses as a major part of their experience. Mutual support groups can provide a validating and comforting "emotional cushion." Such groups may enable mourning losses and coping with grief, alleviate loneliness, diminish isolation and the pain of feeling marginalized and discriminated against, and help members realize that many of the difficulties they experience are caused by objective external realities rather than personal failure.

In addition, group members teach one another understanding of the new culture and share information and strategies of coping with the challenges of immigration and adjustment, which they developed through their own personal experience, thus creating a pool of ideas for each individual group member to choose and try. At the same time, the group serves as a laboratory for rehearsing new behaviors and skills essential for living in the new culture. Mastery of such skills helps participants regain a sense of control over their own life and raise their self-confidence.

The aforementioned sharing, mutual validating and teaching, and recovering social networks that occur in the group help empower women to be in contact with their inner strengths and increase the self-esteem and confidence of participating immigrant women.

Such mutual support groups are often created naturally among immigrant women. However, services can help develop them for women who do not have them. Such groups have been developed in various communities. For example, in Ontario, Canada, an area that has become home to a large and growing immigrant population, groups for providing practical skills, education, information, and support are offered to Latina, Caribbean, Punjabi, Somali, Italian, Pakistani, Serbian, Croatian, Bosnian, and Ghanaian women.

These groups can be homogenous and include compatriots or be heterogeneous and include immigrants of various cultures of origin. Mutual help groups of immigrants of diverse origins share with the homogenous model the common experience of relocation but not the specific cultural background. A group that includes women of diverse cultural backgrounds provides a balance of heterogeneity (in culture of origin) and homogeneity (in immigration status). Such a balance has been described as beneficial because it allows group members to lend their strengths to others and receive back resources that meet their needs (Henry, 1992).

Another type of support group is the mixed group of immigrants and nonimmigrants. This offers participants opportunities to gain mutual familiarity, which is a strategy for decreasing xenophobia and animosity. For example, in a workplace where the staff included a similar number of American-born workers and immigrant workers from the former Soviet Union, a weekly discussion/supervision group was facilitated. Initially the atmosphere was of polite cautiousness and politically correct interactions between the "Americans" and the "Russians." As the group process progressed, mutual trust started to develop, and at the end of the year participants reported having learned about their own biases and how they affect their professional performance as well as having acquired broader perspectives of interpersonal relationships and ways of understanding the world.

Mixed groups also help depathologize immigration. Immigration is often blamed for a wide range of psychological and social problems. Although immigration is indeed a major source of stress and issues, it is sometimes "overblamed." As immigrants and nonimmigrants share their experiences, a realization develops that not all ills are immigration related and a more realistic and balanced perception develops.

Therapy groups. In spite of alleged reluctance of immigrant women to disclose in a group personal information because of fear of misuse by fellow immigrants, especially in the context of small and closed émigré communities, practice experience shows that such groups can work and be beneficial for participants. These groups give immigrants an opportunity to be in contact with and develop ways for addressing emotional effects of migration.

Acculturation groups. These groups combine educating immigrants about the effects of life changes with teaching skills to help coping with these changes, such as communication, norms, and cognitive and practical skills necessary for functioning in the new environment. Examples for topics addressed in such groups include understanding the banking system (e.g., it took me quite a while to understand the concept of credit history and how one builds it), acceptable relationships between sexes, and effective methods for interaction with authorities.

The story of Gal and the lock is one small example of difficulties with which immigrants need help. Gal was the adolescent son of two professionals who had relocated to the United States. He was an excellent student and a good athlete, and was quickly well received and felt comfortable with his new classmates. However, Gal continued to face a problem. In spite of many explanations and demonstrations, he could not master the combination lock of his locker. It was not until his father, an engineer by education, asked someone to demonstrate to him in slow motion how to use a lock and he realized that before entering a new numerical code, one needs to erase previous codes, that Gal could use the device. Having taught him the details could have saved a lot of frustration.

Acculturation groups do exactly this—teach immigrants "the everyday secrets" of existence in their new environment and how things are done in their culture of resettlement. Participants in such groups report easier adjustment, develop increased social support networks, improved coping with stressful situations, and gain greater satisfaction with interactions in the new cultures (Edleson and Roskin, 1985).

In a comparative study of the experience of women who participated in different types of groups (Van Boemel and Rozee, 1992), improvement was reported following participation in all groups. This finding suggests that rather than the specific content, the main experience of being and sharing with other women with common experiences is helpful, leading the research to recommend a combined strategy that provides psychological enhancement and skills training as optimal. This finding is similar to my own experience based on supervising groups for adolescent immigrants in the context of the Russian Adolescents Project in Brighton Beach, Brooklyn, New York, groups for immigrant senior citizens, and groups for immigrant parents run by the Jewish Board of Family and Children's Services.

Service Providers

The narratives of women in this study confirm existing clinically and empirically based knowledge regarding the importance of culture-sensitive and culture-competent bilingual service providers. Culture plays a key role in shaping people's perceptions of, reactions to, and coping with immigration. For example, interviews with thirteen social workers and nineteen clients indicate that cultural bridging and culture-sensitive proactive service provision are helpful (Russell and White, 2001).

Service providers who know and understand clients' culture are of utmost importance (Ivry, 1992). The findings of this study concur with previous research that emphasize the importance of ethnic/racial match of therapists and clients because women are more likely to share personal information with women of their own ethnicity (Flaskerud, 1986; Friedman, 1992). The absence of bilingual staff has been found to be associated with underutilization of services (Nguyen, 1984). Rosa's experience illustrates this point. "Here was a person [a worker of a similar origin] who knew where I come from, how things have been for me there and she did not judge or condemn me, she could sympathize with my situation, hear me and help me. Had it been somebody with the best will of another culture, it would not have been the same," she explained.

The challenge is to develop a cadre of workers knowledgeable about the immigrants' language and culture of origin, aware of differences between immigrants from various regions of the home country, willing to reserve judgment, and capable of balancing adherence to the norms in the new country with respect for the old ones. This is not a simple task.

Three main strategies have been used to address this challenge, and each has advantages and problems. One strategy is recruiting clinicians from a similar background to serve immigrants. This is often not feasible because the absence of social work as a profession in many cultures of origin considerably limits availability of such personnel. To address the scarcity, special programs have been developed to train immigrant psychologists, educators, and physicians to become social workers and caseworkers. These professionals are familiar with the immigration experience. They can serve as socialization agents and powerful role models, and a bridge between the immigrants and their new culture. Because of the shared experience of migration, they can also contribute to normalization rather than pathologizing reactions. However, reactions of overidentification and overprotection of clients, assessment of clients' situation through the lens of the worker's experience, and expecting them to adhere to the worker's coping patterns may develop and compromise the effectiveness of interventions.

Another option is using nonimmigrant professionals with the help of immigrant interpreters. This expands the pool of highly trained service providers but may inhibit open discussion of intimate issues and create awkward communication. Furthermore, it potentially causes tension between interpreter and worker by filtering vital information through the perception of the interpreter and strains agency manpower and financial resources (Ivry, 1992).

A third strategy is educating mainstream service providers about the background, culture, and behavior patterns of the immigrants. Raising awareness and sensitizing to culture-related patterns and acquiring knowledge about immigrants' unique characteristics, needs, and issues are helpful in enhancing effective services and minimizing friction. For example, a service provider who is made aware that a client's mistrust is not directed personally and that a "pushy" style of interaction with representatives of the establishment was a survival skill in the culture of origin would tend to be more patient and receptive and not take mistrust by clients personally. However, providing services by nonimmigrants solidifies and maintains the status of immigrant women as dependent on the receiving side.

Timing

Specialized services are often provided immediately following the relocation, assuming that as the acculturation progresses, immigrants will be able to use general services. However, while immediate help is important regarding basic needs, many of the emotional and social needs surface later in the process, requiring help from professionals with expertise in immigration issues. Sluzki (1979) asserts that initially there is a period of overcompensation characterized by denial of emotional aspects of migration and, as practice experience shows, also by some degree of euphoria. This period may last for weeks or even months. Help, which is more readily available during this period, is often underutilized because many immigrants are not receptive to it as its timing does not match their emotional timetable.

When overcompensation changes to a period of decompensation, during which conflicts, symptoms, and difficulties occur and people need and may be open to use help in coping with the ordeal of immigration, often available help has dramatically decreased and eligibility to many services has expired. We do not have knowledge if these phases are associated with gender. To be effective, help needs to be timed to match the phases of the immigration process.

COMMUNITY PROGRAMS

Community programs have three faces: programs for communities of immigrant women, programs for their co-ethnic communities, and those for the general public, all of which are geared toward bridging gaps and promoting the cause of immigrant women. The major vehicles for such programs are community education programs and coalitions for immigrant women's rights.

Community programs for immigrant women focus on education about legal rights, especially, but not exclusively, for those who come from totalitarian and oppressive societies, in which speaking out was dangerous and could have led to vindictive disciplinary actions, and for those who come from traditional societies that oppress women.

Programs for immigrant co-ethnic communities, in which these women live, to enhance receivership of newcomers are most challenging because they require creating efforts to change the way women are viewed and treated within their own communities while respecting the traditional culture of these communities.

Community education programs to increase awareness of issues of immigrants by the general public and to decrease prejudice and discrimination are of utmost importance because they can help reduce prejudice, xenophobia, and racism, lessen the marginalization of immigrants, and open venues for better integration of immigrants into the broader community. Such education needs to take place within the legal system, including judges, lawyers and law guardians, medical personnel, educators, and the general public to help develop a better understanding and consequently greater tolerance toward immigrants' behaviors that are appropriate within their culture of origin or are normal reactions to immigration-related stress and trauma but might be misinterpreted and lead to false conclusions that work against the immigrant. For example, immigrants from the former Soviet Union have earned a bad name among health professionals in Israel. They are often seen as demanding, feeling entitled, and "pushy." These behaviors were necessary and common in dealing with bureaucracies and administrations in their culture of origin, and the newcomers imported with them their familiar sets of customs, which meet with disapproval, anger, and resentment in the new social environment. Programs designed to educate service providers about the background for such undesirable patterns of behavior contribute to the development of more sympathetic and less judgmental lens through which to view the immigrants' modus operandi. Such programs can include mutual activities around issues that are important to the community, e.g., community education programs in schools.

As argued and illustrated throughout this book, much work needs to be done to promote the rights of immigrant women in their communities of resettlement. One channel for enhancing this cause is through the organization of networks and coalitions to coordinate efforts to assert the rights of this population group. A major challenge for such coalitions would be to make services more readily available. It is difficult to move bureaucracies to attend to needs of individuals and families; however, this task becomes even more difficult for people who have always been in the giving role and have a hard time moving into the recipient role, such as Ana, and for those not familiar with the unwritten "secrets," which Matijia described as "the important things that 'everybody knows'; that is, everybody that grew up in the system or has been here for a while" and who do not know how "to work the system."

POLICY DEVELOPMENT

Glazer (1998) points out that in referring to immigrants' issues, we need to talk about "policies" rather than "policy." Although immigration policy (i.e., who is allowed to enter) resides with the federal government, immigrants' policy (i.e., treatment of those who are allowed to relocate) exists on federal, state, and local (municipal and organization) levels. Different policies exist in different states and within the same state/city/organization between different departments/branches.

These policies are reflected in written laws and regulations as well as implied by the way business are conducted, such as provision of medical, educational, and social services in immigrants' mother tongue and messages that reflect expectation for fast assimilation or respect for immigrants' culture of origin and its continuing existence.

Immigrant women are often victims of laws, regulations, and policies that regulate immigration. "Immigration regulations need not be overtly discriminatory to produce sex-specific outcomes. Systematic discrimination can result when migration regulations reinforce gender inequality by accepting stereotypical images of men and women" (Boyd, 1995, p. 84). For example, when admission criteria are based on level of education and type of vocational and professional background, for women who come from countries that bar females from acquiring education and training, a seemingly equal policy is discriminatory because women have fewer chances of being admitted on their own merits.

Consequently, a main principle for allowing entry of women into many countries of relocation is family reunification, because a typical pattern is that men immigrate first to pave the way and the women and children join them later.

These conditions of immigration affect the gender hierarchy and postimmigration power structure in immigrant families. When women gain full immigration status they are better able to negotiate relatively egalitarian family relations, whereas an immigration status that is conditional or temporary and depends on the husbands' status weakens their position in the marital and familial relationships and exacerbates patriarchal relations (Hondagneu-Sotelo, 1994). This creates a basis for domination and abuse under threats and may negatively impact on the prospects for work and eligibility for services.

Rosa's, Teresina's, Maria's, and Sarah's stories are examples of women whose status was dependent on men for their immigration status to be maintained. Although Teresina, Maria, and Sarah were lucky enough to marry men who do not take advantage of the situation, Rosa was helpless against abuse and exploitation by the man on whom her immigration status depended. Teresina, Maria, and Sarah should not need to depend on luck, and Rosa should be protected. One major policy change that needs to be lobbied for is the adoption of more egalitarian policies that allow women to be examined and admitted by their own merits to gain full immigration status.

Funding of programs presents an additional challenge to policymakers. State and local initiatives need to be developed to allow accomplishing many of the goals cited for improving the situation of immigrant women, because many of the aforementioned programs require funding and organizational efforts. Such programs designed to promote policies that enhance their well-being should actively involve immigrant women rather than be developed for them in order to avoid the exclusion from the political, social, and economic life of mainstream society, which is their common experience.

Just as important as language, vocational, and professional training is training women to advocate for themselves and their fellow immigrants. Gaining access to political resources that will enable them to develop the ability to advocate for themselves is empowering. Mostly since the mid-1980s, organizations have been developed and are operating to promote the rights and conditions of immigrant women, e.g., Asian Immigrant Women Advocates (AIWA), Changing Together (Canada), National Asian Pacific American Women's Forum (NAPAWF), and the NOW Legal Defense and Education Fund (please see Resources section for a list of organizations). In addition to direct services, these organizations focus on forging grassroots movements that fight for issues that range from social and economic justice and political empowerment of immigrant women to policy analysis regarding the rights of immigrant women and advocacy for innovative legislation to promote their interests. These organizations are mostly community based and seek to foster empowerment of immigrant women through education, leadership development, network building, and collective action.

These organizations do important and much-needed work. However, a review reveals two interesting points. First, many of them, though not all, target specific groups of immigrant women of certain culture of origin (e.g., Asian, African), a specific geographic area (e.g., Edmonton, San Diego, San Francisco and the Bay area), or focus on a certain issue (e.g., domestic violence, work readiness). Fewer organizations adopt a more inclusionary approach, mostly by targeting immigrant woman with diverse backgrounds or by functioning on regional, national, and international levels. However, many of the latter organizations are inclusive geographically but focus on a specific issue such as violence against women or women's human rights.

In spite of their diversity, immigrant women of various origins share many issues. Therefore, without losing sensitivity to what is unique, unifying efforts across cultures of origins, combining rather than splitting into competing forces, and more united activity may prove powerful (the old "strengths in numbers").

Second, with some exceptions, these organizations often work on behalf of immigrant women under the leadership of representatives of the dominant society, sometimes in collaboration with prominent veteran women of the ethnic group targeted by the organization. Thus, the "strong" advocate for the "weak," sustaining the latter in their weak position, and the immigrant women themselves remain dependent. Narratives reflect the understanding immigrant women have of their needs and their ability to negotiate their environment to generate resources to address these needs. These abilities can be augmented and channeled into an organized advocacy activity by immigrant women for immigrant women.

Achievement of causes for immigrant women requires that they create movements and participate in political activity to voice their needs be taken into consideration in the political agenda. As this book is being written there is a growing recognition among politicians regarding the power of the Latino vote that is leading efforts to cater to the needs of this population. The same should happen specifically regarding the voice of immigrant women and recognition of their unique needs.

A MULTISERVICE CENTER FOR IMMIGRANT WOMEN: A VIABLE SOLUTION

The previous sections described the variety of direct services within an empowering and culture-sensitive environment by culture-competent service providers and community programs, as well as policy development that is needed to address the specific needs of immigrant women. To support the development of such a multifaceted comprehensive approach to addressing the issues of immigrant women, an appropriate structure is necessary.

One such structure that can provide the professional and administrative support is a multiservice center dedicated uniquely to providing a wide range of language, vocational, legal, and therapeutic services to immigrant women, development of community programs, and enhancement of immigrant, women-friendly policies. Such a center which combines a variety of complementary services along a full continuum of care under one roof and is directed by a leadership of immigrant women has several advantages.

First, such a holistic approach creates an umbrella of services that is comprehensive and inclusive. It allows development of a bridging service that provides a space to help women build on their past experience toward their future. Second, it offers women diverse routes for recovery, development, and growth. Women can participate in the activities of the center as clients, members, volunteers, service developers and providers, social activists, lobbyists, and leaders. Third, rather than fragmentation, such a center would create complementarity and integration of services. Combining vocational, professional training, language, and counseling services are complementary and mutually reinforcing. For example, women who do not feel comfortable sharing emotions and private matters and would be reluctant to seek therapy may use a language or vocational training class to indirectly work on psychological issues; gaining better negotiating skills and the ability to compete in the open market help to enhance self-confidence, and working together in a group that prepares a pro-tolerance community campaign has secondary benefits of mutual support and therapeutic effects, such as raising self-confidence and self-esteem. Finally, it offers women opportunities to gradually progress from one role to another as they move along the process of adjustment.

Epilogue

This section describes what happened to me throughout the journey of researching and writing this book and what I take with me from the experience. A qualitative study has been recognized as an interaction that changes all those involved: the informant as well as the researcher. The interaction in collecting the data creates an encounter that exposes the researcher and the informant to each other. Existential philosophers and psychologists such as Martin Buber (1966), Rollo May (1983), and Carl Rogers (1951) posit that from this mutual experience growth and change evolve. Qualitative research methods recognize the researcher-informant encounter as an example of such an interpersonal interaction that potentially changes both participants in the encounter.

To me, this has been a humbling experience. I come out of this voyage with a deep sense of respect for the women who struggle with extremely challenging situations and use them as a springboard for personal growth.

I also left with a much better understanding of myself and who I am and more clarity of my values, of what is important and what is less important to me. I came out with the ability to better endure wounds of loss and separation and learn to live with them in peace and use them as a springboard for my own personal growth. I learned more tolerance and patience toward ways of viewing the world that are different from my own.

I had an opportunity to revisit my own experiences and gain a better insight of what I encountered and how I learned to cope with stresses. Viewing the experiences through the eyes of others, I learned to appreciate the tremendous accomplishments that I achieved in my own journey of immigration. Better understanding of myself, my biases, strengths, and weaknesses are some of the presents I received from the process of writing this book to be cherished for life. I am grateful to all my immigrant sisters who graciously taught me this lesson.

Resources

Asian Immigrant Women Advocates
310 Eighth Street, Suite 301, Oakland, California 94607
Phone: (510) 268-0192
Fax: (510) 268-0194
E-mail: info@aiwa.org
<http://www.aiwa.org>

Changing Together: A Center for Immigrant Women
Edmonton, Alberta, Canada
Phone: (780) 421-0175
<http://www.changingtogether.com>

Massachusetts Immigrant and Refugee Advocacy Coalition (MIRA)
105 Chauncy Street, 9th Floor, Boston, Massachusetts 02111
Phone: (617) 350-5480
Fax: (617) 350-5499
E-mail: mmmovelle@miracoalition.org
<http://www.miracoalition.org>

National Asian Pacific American Women's Forum
PO Box 66124, Washington, DC 20035-6124
E-mail: info@napawf.org
<http://www.napawf.org>

National Network for Immigrant and Refugee Rights
310 Eighth Street, Suite 303, Oakland, California 94607
Phone: (510) 465-1984
Fax: (510) 465-1885
E-mail: nnirr@nnirr.org
<http://www.nnirr.org>

NOW Legal Defense and Education Fund
1522 K St., NW Suite 550, Washington, DC 20005
Phone: (202) 326-0040
Fax: (202) 589-0511
E-mail: iwp@nowldef.org
<http://www.nowldef.org>

Rexdale Women's Centre
8 Taber Road, Second Floor, Etobicoke, Ontario, Canada
Phone: (416) 745-0062
Fax: (416) 745-3995
E-mail: rwc@rexdale.on.ca
<http://rexdale.on.ca/rwc/index.html>

References

Ahearn, F.L. (1999). Psychosocial wellness: Methodological approaches to the study of refugees. In F.L. Ahearn (Ed.), *Psychosocial wellness of refugees: Issues in qualitative and quantitative research* (pp. 3-23). New York: Barghahn Books.

Alexakis, V. (2001). *Talgo*. Tel-Aviv: Yediot Achronot (Hebrew).

Assar, N.N. (1999). Immigration policy, cultural norms, and gender relations among Indian-American motel owners. In G.A. Kelson and D.L. DeLaet (Eds.), *Gender and immigration* (pp. 82-102). New York: New York University Press.

Balgopal, P.R. (Ed.) (2000). *Social work practice with immigrants and refugees.* New York: Columbia University Press.

Baptiste, D.A. (1993). Immigrant families, adolescents and acculturation: Insights for therapists. *Marriage Family Review, 19*(3-4): 341-363.

Beiser, M., Turner, R.J., and Gansean, S. (1989). Catastrophic stress and factors affecting its consequences among Southeast Asian refugees. *Social Science and Medicine, 28:* 183-195.

Bemak, F., Chung, R.C., and Bornemann, T.H. (1996). Counseling and psychotherapy with refugees. In P.B. Pedersen, J.G. Draguns, W.J. Lonner, and J.E. Trimble (Eds.), *Counseling across cultures* (pp. 243-265). Thousand Oaks, CA: Sage.

Ben-Sira, Z. (1997). *Immigration, stress, and readjustment.* Westport, CT: Praeger Publishers.

Berger, R. (1996). Group work with immigrant adolescents. *Journal of Child and Adolescent Group Therapy, 6*(4): 169-179.

Berger, R. (1997). Adolescent immigrants in search of identity: Clingers, eradicators, vacillators, and integrators. *Child and Adolescent Social Work Journal, 14*(4): 263-275.

Berger, R. (2000). Stepfamilies in cultural context. *Journal of Divorce and Remarriage, 33*(1/2): 111-130.

Berger, R. (2001). Immigration and mental health: Principles for successful social work practice. In R.P. Perez-Koenig and B.D. Rock (Eds.), *Social work in the era of devolution: Toward a just practice* (pp. 159-176). New York: Fordham University Press.

Berger, R. and Malkinson, R. (2000). "Therapeutizing" research: The positive impact of research on participants. *Smith College Studies in Social Work, 70*(2): 307-314.

Bernstein, J.H. and Shuval, J.T. (1999). Gender differences in the process of occupational integration of immigrant physicians in Israel. *Sex Roles: A Journal of Research, 40*(1/2): 1-23.

Berry, J.W. (1986). The acculturation process and immigrant behavior. In C.L. Williams and J. Westmeyer (Eds.), *Mental health in resettlement countries* (pp. 25-37). Washington, DC: Hemisphere.

Berry, J.W., Kim, U., Minde, T., and Mok, D. (1987). Comparative studies of acculturative stress. *International Migration Review, 21*(Fall): 491-511.

Bilsborrow, R. (1994). *The migration of women: Methodological issues in the measurement and analysis of internal and international migration.* Santo Domingo, Dominican Republic: United Nations International Research and Training Institute for the Advancement of Women (INSTRAW).

Birman, D. and Tyler, E. (1994). Acculturation and alienation of Soviet Jewish refugees in the United States. *Genetic Social and General Psychology Monographs, 120*(1): 103-115.

Blair, R.G. (2001). Mental health needs among Cambodian refugees in Utah. *International Social Work, 44*(2): 179-196.

Bock, K.P. (1970). *Culture shock, a reader in modern cultural anthropology.* New York: Alfred A. Knopf.

Boyd, M. (1995). Migration regulations and sex selective outcomes in developed countries. In United Nations Department for Economic and Social Information and Policy Analysis Population Division, *International migration policies and the status of female migrants* (pp. 83-98). Proceedings of the United Nations Expert Group Meeting, Italy. New York: United Nations.

Brock-Utne, B. (1994). Reflections of a cultural commuter. In J.M. Bystydzienski and E.P. Resnik (Eds.), *Women in cross-cultural transitions* (pp. 121-132). Bloomington, IN: Phi Delta Kappa Educational Foundation.

Brooks, G.R. (1992). Gender sensitive family therapy in a violent society. *Topics in Family Psychology and Counseling, 1:* 24-36.

Buber, M. (1966). *The knowledge of man: A philosophy of the interhuman.* New York: Harper and Row.

Buijs, G. (1993). Migrant women: Crossing borders and changing identities. In *Cross cultural perspectives on women.* Oxford, Providence: Berg Publishers.

Bystydzienski, J.M. and Resnik, E.P. (1994). Introduction. In J.M. Bystydienski and E.P. Resnik (Eds.), *Women in cross-cultural transitions* (pp. 1-12). Bloomington, IN: Phi Delta Kappa Educational Foundation.

Calhoun, L.G. and Tedeschi, R.G. (1999). *Facilitating posttraumatic growth: A clinician's guide.* Mahwah, NJ: Lawrence Erlbaum Associates.

Carlson, A.W. (1985). One century of foreign immigration to the United States: 1880-1979. *International Migration, 23*(3): 309-334.

Chandras, K.V. (1997). Training multiculturally competent counselors to work with Asian Indian Americans. *Counselor Education and Supervision, 37*(1): 50-59.

Chow, J. (1999). Multiservice centers in Chinese American immigrant communities: Practice principles and challenges. *Social Work, 44*(1): 70-80.

CNN.com (2001). Warship arrives as asylum seekers await transfer. Available at <http://cnn.com/2001/WORLD/europe/09/02/aust.boat.people/>.

Cobo, N. (1994). A divided life: Wanting to be in two cultures at once. In J.M. Bystydienski and E.P. Resnik (Eds.), *Women in cross-cultural transitions* (pp. 69-76). Bloomington, IN: Phi Delta Kappa Educational Foundation.

Cole, E., Espin, O.M., and Rothblum, E.D. (1992). *Refugee women and their mental health: Shattered societies, shattered lives.* Binghamton, NY: The Haworth Press.

Comas-Diaz, L. and Greene, B. (1994). *Women of color: Integrating ethnic and gender identities in psychotherapy.* New York: Guilford Press.

Cordova, M.J., Cunningham, L.C., Carlson, C.R., and Andrykowski, M. (2001). Posttraumatic growth following breast cancer: A controlled comparison study. *Health Psychology, 20:* 176-185.

Damji Budhwani, T. (1999). Acculturative and marital stress: The moderating roles of spousal support, linguistic self-confidence, and self-esteem. Doctoral dissertation in psychology, University of Ottawa, Canada.

Danquah, M.N. (2000). *Becoming American: Personal essays by first generation immigrant women.* Chicago: Little Brown.

Dasgupta, S.D. and Warrier, S. (1996). In the footsteps of "Arundhati": Asian Indian women's experience of domestic violence in the United States. *Violence Against Women, 2:* 238-259.

de Crevecoeur, M.G.J. [J. Hector St. John] (1782). *Letters from an American farmer.* Philadelphia: Methew Carey Press. Cited by A.H. Ahner (Ed.) (1999), *The modern condition: An anthology* (pp. 29-32). Garden City, NY: Adelphi University Press.

Deaux, K. (2000). Surveying the landscape of immigration: Social psychological perspectives. *Journal of Community and Applied Social Psychology, 10*(5): 421-431.

Denzin, N.K. and Lincoln, Y.S. (Eds.) (2000). *Handbook of qualitative research.* Thousand Oaks, CA: Sage.

Donnelly, G. (2000). Coming home. In M.N. Danquah (Ed.), *Becoming American: Personal essays by first generation immigrant women* (pp. 45-54). Chicago: Little Brown.

Drachman, D. and Shen-Ryan, A. (1991). Immigrants and refugees. In A. Gitterman (Ed.), *Social work practice with vulnerable populations* (pp. 618-646). New York: Columbia University Press.

Durrani, T. (1997). *My feudal lord.* London: Corgy Books.

Easteal, P. (1996). Broken promises: Violence against immigrant women in the home. *Alternative Law Journal, 21*(2): 53-57, 63.

Edleson, J.L. and Roskin, M. (1985). Prevention groups: A model for improving immigrant adjustment. *Journal for Specialists in Group Work, 10*(4): 217-224.

Edwards, J.R. (2001). Public Charge Doctrine: A fundamental principle of American immigration policy. Backgrounder, Center for Immigration Studies, available at <http://www.cis.org/cgi/htsearch>.

Eisenstadt, S.N. (1954). *The absorption of immigrants.* London: Routledge and Kegan.

Espin, O.M. (1992). Roots uprooted: The psychological impact of historical/political dislocation. In E. Cole, O.M. Espin, and E.D. Rothblum (Eds.), *Refugee women and their mental health: Shattered societies, shattered lives* (pp. 9-20). Binghamton, NY: The Haworth Press.

European Council on Refugee and Exiles (1997). Position on asylum seeking and refugee women. Available at <http://ecre.org/archive/women.html>.

Ferris, E.G. (1993). *Beyond borders.* Geneva, Switzerland: World Council of Churches.

Ferugson, R.B. (1999). The shadow hanging over you: Refugee trauma and Vietnamese women in Australia. In B. Ferugson and E. Pittaway (Eds.), *Nobody wants to talk about it* (pp. 21-30). Sydney, Australia: Transcultural Mental Health Centre.

Flaherty, J.A., Kohn, R., Levav, I., and Birz, S. (1988). Demoralization in Soviet-Jewish immigrants to the United States and Israel. *Comprehensive Psychiatry, 29:* 588-597.

Flaskerud, J.H. (1986). The effects of culture-compatible intervention on the utilization of mental health services by minority clients. *Community Mental Health Journal, 22*(2): 127-141.

Foner, N. (1998). Benefits and burdens: Immigrant women and work in New York City. *Gender Issues, 16*(4): 5-24.

Foner, N. (1999). Immigrant women and work in New York City, then and now. *Journal of American Ethnic History, 18*(3): 95-113.

Foner, N. (2000). *From Ellis Island to JFK.* New Haven, CT: Yale University Press.

Foner, N., Rumbaut, R.G., and Gold, S.J. (2000). Immigration and immigration research in the United States. In N. Foner, R.G. Rumbaut, and S.J. Gold (Eds.), *Immigration research for a new century* (pp. 1-19). New York: Russell Sage Foundation.

Fonow, M.M. and Cook, J.A. (Eds.) (1991). *Beyond methodology: Feminist scholarship as lived research.* Bloomington, IN: Indiana University Press.

Francis, E.A. (2000). Social work practice with African-descent immigrants. In P.R. Balgopal (Ed.), *Social work practice with immigrants and refugees* (pp. 127-166). New York: Columbia University Press.

Freed, L. (2000). Embracing the alien. In M.N. Danquah (Ed.), *Becoming American: Personal essays by first generation immigrant women* (pp. 55-67). Chicago: Little Brown.

Freidenberg, J., Imperiale, G., and Skouton, M.L. (1988). Migrant careers and well being of women. *International Migration Review, 22:* 208-255.

Friedman, A.R. (1992). Rape and domestic violence: The experience of refugee women. In E. Cole, O.M. Espin, and E.D. Rothblum (Eds.), *Refugee women and their mental health: Shattered societies, shattered lives* (pp. 65-78). Binghamton, NY: The Haworth Press.

Fugita, S.S. (1990). Asian/Pacific American mental health: Some needed research in epidemiology and service utilization. In F.C. Serafica (Ed.), *Mental health of ethnic minorities* (pp. 64-83). New York: Praeger.

Furnham, A. and Bochner, S. (1986). *Culture shock: Psychological reactions to unfamiliar environments.* New York: Methuen.

Gabaccia, D. (Ed.) (1992). *Seeking common ground: Multidisciplinary studies of immigrant women in the United States.* Westport, CT: Greenwood Press.

Gallagher Weisman, A. (2000). Reluctant citizen. In M.N. Danquah (Ed.), *Becoming American: Personal essays by first generation immigrant women* (pp. 187-197). Chicago: Little Brown.

Garza-Guerrero, A.C. (1974). Culture shock: Its mourning and the vicissitudes of identity. *Journal of the American Psychoanalytic Association, 22:* 408-429.

Glaberson, W. (2001). A nation challenged. *The New York Times,* November 30, section B, p. 6.

Glassman, U. and Skolnik, L. (1984). The role of social group work in refugee resettlement. *Social Work with Groups, 7*(1): 45-62.

Glazer, N. (1998). Governmental and nongovernmental roles in the absorption of immigrants in the United States. In P.H. Schuck and R. Munz (Eds.), *Paths to inclusion* (pp. 59-82). New York: Berghahn.

Glick-Schiller, N., Basch, L., and Blanc-Szanton, C. (Eds.) (1992). *Toward a transnational perspective on migration: Race, class, ethnicity and nationalism reconsidered.* New York: Annals of the New York Academy of Sciences.

Grasmuck, S. and Pessar, P. (1991). *Between two islands.* Berkeley: University of California Press.

Grealy, L. (2000). The country of childhood. In M.N. Danquah (Ed.), *Becoming American: Personal essays by first generation immigrant women* (pp. 76-84). Chicago: Little Brown.

Guba, E.G. (1981). Criteria for assessing the trustworthiness of naturalistic inquiries. *Educational Resources Information Center Annual Review Paper, 29:* 75-91.

Guyot, J., Pardun, R., Dauphinet, E., Jospa, Y., Fischli, E., de Mestral, M., Giudici, D., and Scheidecker, C. (1978). *Immigrant women speak.* London: Churches Committee on Immigrant Workers.

Hamilton, D. (1994). Traditions, preferences and postures in applied qualitative research. In N.K. Denzin and Y.S. Lincoln (Eds.), *Handbook of qualitative research* (pp. 60-69). Thousand Oaks, CA: Sage.

Harper, K.V. and Lantz, J. (1996). *Cross-cultural practice: Social work with diverse populations.* Chicago, IL: Lyceum.

Hattar-Pollara, M. and Meleis, A.I. (1995a). Parenting their adolescents: The experiences of Jordanian immigrant women in California. *Health Care for Women International, 16*(3): 195-211.

Hattar-Pollara, M. and Meleis, A.I. (1995b). The stress of immigration and the daily lived experiences of Jordanian immigrant women in the United States. *Western Journal of Nursing Research, 17*(5): 521-539.

Healy, L.M. (2002). Immigration. A paper presented at the Annual Program Meeting of the Council of Social Work Education, Nashville, Tennessee, February 24-27.

Henry, S. (1992). *Group skills in social work.* Pacific Grove, CA: Brooks/Cole.

Hernandez, D.J. and Charney, E. (Eds.), (1998). *From generation to generation.* Washington, DC: National Academy Press.

Higham, J. (2001). *Hanging together: Unity and diversity in American culture.* New Haven, CT: Yale University Press.

Hoffmman, E. (1989). *Lost in translation.* New York: Penguin.

Holtzman, J.D. (2000). Dialing 911 in Nuer: Gender transformation and domestic violence among midwestern Sudanese refugee community. In N. Foner, R.G. Rumbaut, and S.J. Gold (Eds.), *Immigration research for a new century* (pp. 390-408). New York: Russell Sage Foundation.

Hondagneu-Sotelo, P. (1994). *Gendered transitions.* Berkley: University of California Press.

Hua, A. (2000). Travel and displacement: An (ex)refugee and (ex)immigrant women's tale-tell. *Canadian Woman Studies, 19*(4): 110-115.

Hugo, G.J. (1995). Migration of Asian women to Australia. In United Nations Department for Economic and Social Information and Policy Analysis Population Division, *International migration policies and the status of female migrants* (pp. 192-220). Proceedings of the United Nations Expert Group Meeting, Italy. New York: United Nations.

Hulewat, P. (1996). Resettlement: A cultural and psychological crisis. *Social Work, 41*(2): 129-135.

Hunt, J. (1989). *Psychoanalytic aspects of field work.* Newbury Park, CA: Sage.

Iredale, R. (1995). Sponsorship of spouses/fiances to Australia: Domestic violence, rights and polity issues. In D. Lawrence (Ed.), *Future directions: Proceedings of the Queensland Domestic Violence Conference* (pp. 21-36). Rockhampton, Qld: Rural Social and Economic Research Centre, Central Queensland University.

Israel Record (2001). Immigration to Israel. Available at <www.adl.org/ISRAEL/Record/>.

Ivry, J. (1992). Paraprofessionals in refugee resettlement. *Journal of Multicultural Social Work, 2*(1): 99-117.

Jacoby Boxer, M. (1998). *When women ask the questions: Creating women's studies in America.* Baltimore, MD: Johns Hopkins University Press.

Jang, D.L., Marin, L., and Pendleton, G. (Eds.) (1997*). Domestic violence in immigrant and refugee communities: Asserting the rights of battered women.* San Francisco: Family Violence Prevention Fund, the Northern California Coalition for Immigrant Rights, and the National Immigration Project of the National Lawyers Guild.

Jasinskaja-Lahti, I. and Liebkind, K. (1998). Content and predictors of the ethnic identity of Russian-speaking immigrant adolescents in Finland. *Scandinavian Journal of Psychology, 39*(4): 209-219.

Johnson, R.B. (1999). Examining the validity structure of qualitative research. In A.K. Milinki (Ed.), *Cases in qualitative research* (pp. 160-165). Los Angeles, CA: Pyrczak.

Josefowitz Siegel, R. (1992). Fifty years later: Am I still an immigrant? In E. Cole, O.M. Espin, and E.D. Rothblum (Eds.), *Refugee women and their mental health: Shattered societies, shattered lives* (pp. 105-111). Binghamton, NY: The Haworth Press.

Jupp, J. (2001). *The Australian People.* Cambridge, UK: Cambridge University Press.

Kacen, L. (2002). Supercodes reflected in titles battered women accord to their life stories. *International Journal of Qualitative Methods, 1*(1), Article 3. Available at <http://www.ualberta.ca/~ijqm/>.

Kamani, G. (2000). Code switching. In M.N. Danquah (Ed.), *Becoming American: Personal essays by first generation immigrant women* (pp. 95-103). Chicago: Little Brown.

Karger, H.J. and Levine, J. (2000). Social work practice with European immigrants. In P.R. Balgopal (Ed.), *Social work practice with immigrants and refugees* (pp. 167-197). New York: Columbia University Press.

Kasaba, K.F. (2000). Ethnic networks in women's migration: A comparative study of Jewish and Italian women in New York, 1870-1924. In J.S. Knorr and B. Meier (Eds.), *Women and migration: Anthropological perspectives* (pp. 135-150). New York: St. Martin Press.

Kim, H. (2000). Beyond boundaries. In M.N. Danquah (Ed.), *Becoming American: Personal essays by first generation immigrant women* (pp. 113-125). Chicago: Little Brown.

Knorr, J.S. and Meier, B. (Eds.), (2000). *Women and migration: Anthropological perspectives.* New York: St. Martin's Press.

Krefting, L. (1999). Rigor in qualitative research: The assessment of trustworthiness. In A.K. Milinki (Ed.), *Cases in qualitative research: Research reports for discussion and evaluation* (pp. 173-181). Los Angeles: Pyrczak Publishing.

Kunek, S. (1993). Brides, wives and single women: Gender and immigration. *Lilith, 8*(Summer): 82-113.

Kuoch, T., Miller, R.A., and Scully, M.F. (1992). Healing the wounds of the Mahantdori. In E. Cole, O.M. Espin, and E.D. Rothblum (Eds.), *Refugee women and their mental health: Shattered societies, shattered lives* (pp. 191-207) Binghamton, NY: The Haworth Press.

Laksiri, J. and Kee, P. (1999). *The Asianisation of Australia. Some facts about the myths.* Melbourne: Melbourne University Press.

Lalonde, R.N., Taylor, D.M., and Moghaddam, F.M. (1992).The process of social identification for visible immigrant women in a multicultural context. *Journal of Cross-Cultural Psychology, 23*(1): 25-39.

Lamb, C. (1999). Iranian refugee women in Australia: Their experience of marriage, divorce and gender roles. In B. Ferugson and E. Pittaway (Eds.), *Nobody wants to talk about it: Refugee women's mental health* (pp. 74-88). Parramatta, NSW, Australia: Transcultural Mental Health Centre.

Landau-Stanton, J. (1985). Adolescents, families and cultural transition: A treatment model. In A. Mirkin and S. Koman (Eds.), *Handbook of adolescents and family therapy* (pp. 363-381). New York: Gardner Press.

Lee, H. (2000). Disassembling Helie. In M.N. Danquah (Ed.), *Becoming American: Personal essays by first generation immigrant women* (pp. 126-137). Chicago: Little Brown.

Leong, F. and Lau, A. (2001). Barriers to providing effective mental health services to Asian Americans. *Mental Health Services Research, 3*(4): 201-214.

Levitt, P. (2000). Migrants participate across borders: Toward an understanding of forms and consequences. In N. Foner, R.G. Rumbaut, and S.J. Gold (Eds.), *Immigration research for a new century* (pp. 459-479). New York: Russell Sage Foundation.

Liebkind, K. (1992). Ethnic identity: Challenging the boundaries of social psychology. In G.M. Breakwell (Ed.), *Social psychology of identity and the self concept* (pp. 147-185). London: Surrey University Press.

Lim, L.L. (1995). The status of women and international migration. In United Nations Department for Economic and Social Information and Policy Analysis Population Division, *International migration policies and the status of female migrants* (pp. 29-55). Proceedings of the United Nations Expert Group Meeting, Italy. New York: United Nations.

Longres, J.F. and Patterson, D.G. (2000). Social work practice with Latino American immigrants. In P.R. Bolgopal (Ed.), *Social work practice with immigrants and refugees* (pp. 65-126). New York: Columbia University Press.

Loughry, M. and Xuan Nghia, N. (2000). Returnees to Vietnam. In F.L. Ahearn (Ed.), *Psychosocial wellness of refugees: Issues in qualitative and quantitative research* (pp. 153-176). New York: Barghahn Books.

Lynam, M.J. (1985). Support networks developed by immigrant women. *Social Science and Medicine, 21*(3): 327-333.

Mallona, A. (1999). Surfacing the self: Narratives of Central American immigrant women. Doctoral dissertation, Boston College, MA.

Mares, P. (2001). *Borderline: Australia's treatment of refugees and asylum-seekers.* Sydney, Australia: University of New South Wales Press.

Markovic, M. and Manderson, L. (2000). Nowhere is as at home: Adjustment strategies of recent immigrant women from the former Yugoslav Republics in southeast Queensland. *Journal of Sociology, 36*(3): 315-321.

Massey, D. (1995). The new immigration and ethnicity in the United States. *Population and Development Review, 21*(3): 631-652.

May, R. (1983). *The discovery of being: Writings in existential psychology.* New York: Norton.

Mayer, A.E. (1998). Comment on Majid's "The Politics of Feminism in Islam." *Signs, 23*(2): 369-377.

McIntyre, T.M. and Augusto, F. (1999). The martyr adaptation syndrome: Psychological sequelae in the adaptation of Portuguese-speaking immigrant women. *Cultural Diversity and Ethnic Minority Psychology, 5*(4): 387-402.

McKay, S.L. and Wong, S.-L.C. (1996). Multiple discourses, multiple identities: Investment and agency in second-language learning among Chinese adolescent immigrant students. *Harvard Educational Review, 66*(3): 577-608.

Michael, S. (1998). The web of identity: A study of adolescent immigrant girls in New York City. Unpublished doctoral dissertation, The City University of New York.

Mirsky, Y. and Prawer, L. (1992). *To immigrate as an adolescent.* Jerusalem: Van Leer Institute and Elka.

Mittelberg, D. (1988). *Strangers in paradise.* New Brunswick, NJ: Transaction Books.

Morrison, J. (1995). *DSM-IV made easy: The clinicians guide to diagnosis.* New York: Guilford.

National Network on Immigrant and Refugee Rights (2000). Hands that shape the world: A report on the conditions of immigrant women in the US five years after the Beijing conference. Available at <http://nnirr.org/projects/handsthat.htm>.

Nguyen, S.D. (1984). Mental health services for refugees and immigrants. *Psychiatric Journal of the University of Ottawa, 9*(2): 85-91.

O'Leary, V.E., Alday, C.S., and Ickovics, J.R. (1998). Models of life change and posttraumatic growth. In R.G. Tedeschi, C.L. Park, and L.G. Calhoun (Eds.), *Posttraumatic growth: Positive changes in the aftermath of crisis* (pp. 127-151). Mahwah, NJ: Lawrence Erlbaum Associates.

Olsen, V. (1994). Feminism and models of qualitative research. In N.K. Denzin and Y.S. Lincoln (Eds.), *Handbook of qualitative research* (pp. 158-174). Thousand Oaks, CA: Sage.

Paul, F. (1999). English acquisition and mental health for Somali women. In B. Ferugson and E. Pittaway (Eds.), *Nobody wants to talk about it: Refugee women's mental health* (pp. 31-39). Parramatta, NSW, Australia: Transcultural Mental Health Centre.

Perez, M.-J. (2000). Conversations across worlds: The experience of immigration of Latina women who are working as professionals in the United States. Doctoral dissertation, Massachusetts School of Professional Psychology.

Pittaway, I. (1991). *Refugee women: Still at risk in Australia.* Melbourne: Bureau of Immigration Research.

Pittaway, I. (1999). Refugee women—The unsung heroes. In B. Ferugson and E. Pittaway (Eds.), *Nobody wants to talk about it: Refugee women's mental health* (pp. 1-20). Parramatta, NSW, Australia: Transcultural Mental Health Centre.

Portes, A. (1998). Divergent destinies: Immigration, the second generation, and the rise of transnational communities. In P.H. Schuck and R. Munz (Eds.), *Paths to inclusion* (pp. 33-57). New York: Berghahn.

Portes, A. and Rumbaut, R.G. (2001). *Legacies: The story of the immigrant second generation.* Berkeley: University of California Press.

Potocky-Tripodi, M. and Tripodi, T. (2002). Editorial: Research on refugees and immigrants. *Journal of Social Work Research, 2*(2): 123.

Reimers, D.M. (1989). *The immigrant experience.* New York: Chelsea House.

Remennick, L.I. (1999). Gender implications of immigration: The case of Russian speaking women in Israel. In G.A. Kelson and D.L. DeLaet (Eds.), *Gender and immigration* (pp. 163-185). New York: New York University Press.

Richmond, A.H., Kalbach, W.E., and Verma, R.B.P. (1981). Factors in the adjustment of immigrants and their descendents. *Canadian Ethnic Studies, 13*(2): 146-147.

Rodriguez, O. and O'Donell, M. (1995). *Help seeking and use of mental health services by Hispanic elderly.* Westport, CT: Greenwood Press.

Rogers, C.R. (1951). *Client-centered therapy: Its current practice, implications, and theory.* Boston, MA: Houghton Mifflin.

Royal Women's Hospital, Melbourne, Australia (2001). *Working women's health: The journey through: Newly arrived immigrants and refugees.*

Rumbaut, R.G. (1985). Mental health and the refugee experience: A comparative study of Southeast Asian refugees. In *Southeast Asian Mental Health: Treatment, Prevention, Services, Training, and Research.* DHSS Publication No. ADM 85-1399 (pp. 433-485). Washington, DC: U.S. Department of Health and Human Services.

Russell, M.N. and White, B. (2001). Practice with immigrants and refugees: Social worker and client perspectives. *Journal of Ethnic and Cultural Diversity in Social Work, 9*(3-4): 73-92.

Sabatello, E.F. (1979). Patterns of occupational mobility among new immigrants to Israel. *International Migration, 17*(3-4): 267-279.

Sachs, S. (2001). Cracking the door for immigrants. *The New York Times,* July 1, p. 3.

Sakamoto, I. (2001). Negotiating multiple cultural contexts: Flexibility and constraint in the cultural selfways of Japanese academic migrants. Doctoral dissertation, University of Michigan, Ann Arbor.

Salih, R. (2001). Moroccan migrant women: Transnationalism, nation-states and gender. *Journal of Ethnic and Migration Studies, 27*(4): 655-671.

Sandhu, D.S. (1997). Psychocultural profiles of Asian and Pacific Islander Americans: Implications for counseling and psychotherapy. *Journal of Multicultural Counseling and Development, 25*(1): 7-22.

Saunders, E.A. (1995). Resettlement experiences of Russian Jewish immigrants in Vancouver, Canada between 1975 and 1982. *International Migration, 23*(3): 369-380.

Schmidt, B.E. (2000). Religious concepts in the process of migration: Puerto Rican female spirits in the United States. In J.S. Knorr and B. Meier (Eds.), *Women and migration: Anthropological perspectives* (pp. 119-132). New York: St. Martin's Press.

Schmitt, E. (2001). Census data show a sharp increase in living standard. *The New York Times,* August 6, p. A1.

Schuck, P.H. (2001). The treatment of aliens in the United States. In P.H. Schuck and R. Munz (Eds.), *Paths to inclusion* (pp. 203-246). New York: Berghahn.

Schwandt, T.A. (1994). Constructivist, interpretivist approaches to human inquiry. In N.K. Denzin and Y.S. Lincoln (Eds.), *Handbook of qualitative research* (pp. 118-137). Thousand Oaks, CA: Sage.

Schwartz-Seller, M. (1994). *Immigrant women.* Albany: State University of New York Press.

Scott, A. (2001). A nation challenged: The human side. *The New York Times,* November 4, p. A1.

Scott, W.A. and Scott, R. (1989) *Adaptation of immigrants: Individual differences and determinants.* Oxford, UK: Pergamon Press.

Seller, M. (Ed.) (1980). *Immigrant women.* Philadelphia, PA: Temple University Press.

Shin, K.R. and Shin, C. (1999). The lived experience of Korean immigrant women acculturating into the United States. *Health Care for Women International,* 20(6): 603-617.

Simon, R. and Brettell, C. (Eds.) (1986) *International migration: The female experience.* Totown, NJ: Rowman and Allenheld.

Simons, L. (1999). Mail order brides: The legal framework and possibilities for change. In G.A. Kelson and D.L. DeLaet (Eds.), *Gender and immigration* (pp. 127-143). New York: New York University Press.

Singh, J.K. and Siahpush, M. (2001). All-cause and cause-specific mortality of immigrants and native born in the United States. *American Journal of Public Health, 91*(3): 392-399.

Sizoo, E. (Ed.) (1997). *Women's lifeworlds: Women's narratives on shaping their realities.* New York: Routledge.

Slonim-Nevo, V., Sharaga, Y., and Mirsky, Y. (1999). A culturally sensitive approach to therapy with immigrant families: The case of Jewish immigrants from the former Soviet Union. *Family Process, 38*(4): 445-461.

Sluzki, C.E. (1979). Migration and family conflict. *Family Process, 18*(4): 379-390.

Sluzki, C.E. (1983). Process, structure and world view: Towards an integrated view of systemic models in family therapy. *Family Process, 22:* 469-476.

Stewart, E.C.P., (1986). The survival stage of intercultural communication. *International Christian University Bulletin, 1*(1): 109-121.

Szapocznik, J., Scopetta, M.A., and Kurtines, W. (1978). Theory and measurement of acculturation. *Interamerican Journal of Psychology, 12:* 113-120.

Tabora, B.L. and Flaskerud, J.H. (1997). Mental health beliefs, practices, and knowledge of Chinese American immigrant women. *Issues in Mental Health Nursing, 18*(3): 173-189.

Tedeschi, R.G. and Calhoun, L.G. (1995). *Trauma and transformation: Growing in the aftermath of suffering.* Thousand Oaks, CA: Sage.

Tedeschi, R.G., Park, C.L., and Calhoun, L.G. (1998). *Posttraumatic growth: Positive changes in the aftermath of crisis.* Mahwah, NJ: Lawrence Erlbaum Associates.

Tiede, L.B. (2001). Battered immigrant women and immigration remedies: Are the standards too high? *Human Rights, 28*(1): 21-22.

Thompson, G. (2002). Migrants to United States are a major resource for Mexico. *The New York Times,* March 25, p. A3.

United Nations, Department for Economic and Social Information and Policy Analysis Population Division (1995). *International migration policies and the status of female migrants.* Proceedings of the United Nations Expert Group Meeting, Italy. New York: United Nations.

Van Boemel, B. and Rozee, P.D. (1992). Treatment of psychosomatic blindness among Cambodian refugee women. In E. Cole, O.M. Espin, and E.D. Rothblum (Eds.), *Refugee women and their mental health: Shattered societies, shattered lives* (pp. 239-266). Binghamton, NY: The Haworth Press.

Van den Bergh, N. and Cooper, L.B. (Ed.) (1986). *Feminist visions for social work.* Washington, DC: NASW Press.

Weatherford, D. (1986). *Foreign and female: Immigrant women in America, 1840-1930.* New York: Schocken Books.

Weiss, T. (2002). Posttraumatic growth in women with breast cancer and their husbands: An intersubjective validation study. *Journal of Psychosocial Oncology, 20*(2): 65-80.

White, M. and Epston, D. (1990). *Narrative means to therapeutic ends.* New York: W.W. Norton.

Wiesel, E. (1960). *Night.* New York: Avon Books.

Wiesel, E. (1999). The perils of indifference. Available at <http://www.historyplace.com/speeches/wiesel>.

Willis, K. and Yeoh, B. (Eds.) (2000). *Gender and migration.* Northampton, MA: Edward Elgar.

Witmer, T.A. and Culver, S.M. (2001). Trauma and resilience among Bosnian refugee families: A critical review of the literature. *Journal of Social Work Research, 2*(2): 173-187.

Wolfson, M.C. (1999). Narrating the self: Irish women's stories of migration. Doctoral dissertation, Boston Collge, MA.

Wong, O.-N.C. (1999). Silent voices: Help-seeking patterns of recent immigrant Chinese women from Hong Kong to Canada. Doctoral dissertation, University of Toronto, Canada.

Yamashiro, G. and Matsuolka, J.K. (1997). Help-seeking among Asian and Pacific Americans: A multiperspective analysis. *Social Work, 42*(2): 176-186.

Zapf, K.M. (1991). Cross cultural transitions and wellness: Dealing with culture shock. *International Journal for the Advancement of Counseling, 14:* 105-119.

Zimmerman, W. and Fix, M. (1994). After arrival: An overview of federal immigrant policy in the United States. In B. Edmonton and J.S. Passel (Eds.), *Immigration and ethnicity: The integration of America's newest arrivals* (pp. 251-285). Washington, DC: Urban Institute Press.

Index

SPECIAL 25%-OFF DISCOUNT!

Order a copy of this book with this form or online at:

http://www.haworthpress.com/store/product.asp?sku=4988

IMMIGRANT WOMEN TELL THEIR STORIES

_____in hardbound at $37.46 (regularly $49.95) (ISBN: 0-7890-1829-2)

_____in softbound at $18.71 (regularly $24.95) (ISBN:0-7890-1830-6)

Or order online and use special offer code HEC25 in the shopping cart.

COST OF BOOKS_____

OUTSIDE US/CANADA/
MEXICO: ADD 20%_____

POSTAGE & HANDLING_____
*(US: $5.00 for first book & $2.00
for each additional book)*
*(Outside US: $6.00 for first book
& $2.00 for each additional book)*

SUBTOTAL_____

IN CANADA: ADD 7% GST_____

STATE TAX_____
*(NY, OH, MN, CA, IN, & SD residents,
add appropriate local sales tax)*

FINAL TOTAL_____
*(If paying in Canadian funds,
convert using the current
exchange rate, UNESCO
coupons welcome)*

☐ **BILL ME LATER:** ($5 service charge will be added)
(Bill-me option is good on US/Canada/Mexico orders only;
not good to jobbers, wholesalers, or subscription agencies.)

☐ Check here if billing address is different from
shipping address and attach purchase order and
billing address information.

Signature_____

☐ **PAYMENT ENCLOSED: $**_____

☐ **PLEASE CHARGE TO MY CREDIT CARD.**

☐ Visa ☐ MasterCard ☐ AmEx ☐ Discover
☐ Diner's Club ☐ Eurocard ☐ JCB

Account # _____

Exp. Date_____

Signature_____

Prices in US dollars and subject to change without notice.

NAME_____

INSTITUTION_____

ADDRESS_____

CITY_____

STATE/ZIP_____

COUNTRY_____ COUNTY (NY residents only)_____

TEL_____ FAX_____

E-MAIL_____

May we use your e-mail address for confirmations and other types of information? ☐ Yes ☐ No
We appreciate receiving your e-mail address and fax number. Haworth would like to e-mail or fax special
discount offers to you, as a preferred customer. **We will never share, rent, or exchange your e-mail address
or fax number.** We regard such actions as an invasion of your privacy.

Order From Your Local Bookstore or Directly From
The Haworth Press, Inc.
10 Alice Street, Binghamton, New York 13904-1580 • USA
TELEPHONE: 1-800-HAWORTH (1-800-429-6784) / Outside US/Canada: (607) 722-5857
FAX: 1-800-895-0582 / Outside US/Canada: (607) 771-0012
E-mailto: orders@haworthpress.com
PLEASE PHOTOCOPY THIS FORM FOR YOUR PERSONAL USE.
http://www.HaworthPress.com   BOF03